Nos/Otras

SUNY series, Philosophy and Race
_____
Robert Bernasconi and T. Denean Sharpley-Whiting, editors

Nos/Otras

Gloria E. Anzaldúa,
Multiplicitous Agency, and Resistance

ANDREA J. PITTS

SUNY
PRESS

Cover image: "Gold and Leaves," by Manuela Guillén, Philadelphia, PA, 2021

Published by State University of New York Press, Albany

For information, contact State University of New York Press, Albany, NY
www.sunypress.edu

Library of Congress Cataloging-in-Publication Data

Name: Pitts, Andrea J., author.
Title: Nos/otras : Gloria E. Anzaldúa, multiplicitous agency, and
    resistance / Andrea J. Pitts.
Description: Albany : State University of New York Press, [2021] | Series:
    SUNY series, philosophy and race | Includes bibliographical references
    and index.
Identifiers: LCCN 2021016727 (print) | LCCN 2021016728 (ebook) |
    ISBN 9781438484839 (hardcover : alk. paper) | ISBN 9781438484822
    (pbk. : alk. paper) | ISBN 9781438484846 (ebook)
Subjects: LCSH: Anzaldúa, Gloria—Criticism and interpretation. | Agent
    (Philosophy) in literature. | Feminism and literature. | LCGFT: Literary
    criticism.
Classification: LCC PS3551.N95 Z84 2021 (print) | LCC PS3551.N95
    (ebook) | DDC 818/.5409—dc23
LC record available at https://lccn.loc.gov/2021016727
LC ebook record available at https://lccn.loc.gov/2021016728

10 9 8 7 6 5 4 3 2 1

a todas mis relaciones

Contents

Acknowledgments

This book was a collective undertaking and would not exist were it not for the immense networks of support, guidance, and care that I received from others. In this, I would like to extend thanks to some of the people who have made this project possible, and I offer these words as a humble gesture of my love and appreciation for all the time and energy that others have put into helping me get these words to print.

First, I owe tremendous thanks to the close philosophical mentors in my life, José Medina, Adriana Novoa, and Mariana Ortega. In times of frustration, curiosity, and vulnerability, they have created spaces where I could explore and experiment with ideas, including the many reading groups, workshops, panels, conferences, and conversations that we have had over the years. I look forward to many more years of our vibrant intellectual friendships.

Many thanks to Janaka Bowman Lewis, Consuelo Carr Salas, Mariana Ortega, Elisabeth Paquette, and Daniela Recabarren for their participation in the manuscript workshop for this book in January 2019. Their support and insights have helped strengthen both the book and my confidence in my own voice. Also, much gratitude to Shannon Sullivan and Gordon Hull for making that workshop possible through their institutional support.

Thanks also to all the organizers and participants in the writing groups who have supported my research since graduate school, including Brook Ackerly and members of the Vanderbilt Global Feminisms Collaborative, Dace Brown and members of the UNC Charlotte Diversity Writing Group, Vanessa Castañeda and the Charlotte Latin Americanist Writing Group, Consuelo Carr Salas and Elisabeth Paquette with the Coachella Writing Group, and Asia Ferrin for our Summer 2020 writing sessions.

I owe many thanks to the network of people in my life who have offered me advice or have taken the time to work with me through the themes and issues that inform this book. Many of them also created opportunities for me to connect to ideas, scholars, and students in their own communities, which has been tremendously important for the development of this book. To Geoffrey Adelsberg, Mariana Alessandri, Megan Altman, Kathryn Sophia Belle, Talia Mae Bettcher, Alisa Bierria, Jacoby Adeshei Carter, Mel Castañeda, Maria Chaves Daza, Natalie Cisneros, Tommy Curry, PJ DiPietro, Kristie Dotson, Taína Figueroa, Leonard Harris, Robin James, Myka T. Johnson, Tamsin Kimoto, Cat Lemon, Jim Maffie, Jamie Marsicano, Lee Mcbride, Denise Meda Calderon, Eduardo Mendieta, Julie Minich, Charles Mills, Anthony Sean Neale, Cynthia Paccacerqua, Lena Palacios, Goyo Pappas, Gaile Pohlhaus Jr., Omar Rivera, Stephanie Rivera Berruz, Monique Roelofs, Elena Ruíz, Ofelia Schutte, everet smith, Alexander Stehn, Yannik Thiem, Ana Valdez, Emma Velez, Roo George Warren, Christine Wieseler, Ash Williams, and Kelly Zaytoun, I extend my sincerest gratitude for their generosity of spirit and energy.

To my dissertation committee, Linda Martín Alcoff, Lisa Guenther, José Medina, Kelly Oliver, and Lucius T. Outlaw Jr., with whom portions of the research for this project began, I am eternally thankful.

Many thanks to the participants and organizers of the many conferences where I presented research from this book, including the American Philosophical Association, the Caribbean Philosophical Association, the Carlos III University Workshop on Identity, Memory, and Experience, Philosophy Born of Struggle, the Roundtable on Latina/x Feminism, the Society for the Advancement of American Philosophy, the Southeast Roundtable on the Philosophy of the Americas, and the Toward Decolonial Feminisms Conference. Additionally, the support of programs like the UNC Charlotte Junior Faculty Development Program, the UNC Charlotte Faculty Research Grant, and the Woodrow Wilson Career Enhancement Fellowship were invaluable for the completion of this project. Much thanks to the many people, participants, and donors who make those opportunities possible.

To the late María Lugones, I owe so much of my thinking and praxis regarding friendship and scholarly production. For our conversations and exchanges during her time in this world (of many worlds), I am immensely grateful.

Sincere thanks to Carla O. Alvarez at the LLILAS Benson Latin American Studies and Collections at the University of Texas at Austin for their help navigating the Gloria Evangelina Anzaldúa Papers, and much love to Denise Meda Calderon and Goyo Pappas for making my visit to Texas such a wonderful experience.

Mil gracias to Mariana Alessandri, Julie Minich, and Perry Zurn for their comments during my final edits on this project. Their support has been an inspiration and honor.

I also have deep gratitude for the friends in my life who have supported me throughout this project. Whether they know it or not, my academic life has been prefaced on their love and kindness. To Aman Agah, Alejandro Arango, Danielle Boaz, Joshua Burford, Adam Burgos, Rachael Forester, Tamara and Amaya Johnson, Joseph Jordan, David Juarez, Emre Keskin, Erica Lennon, Olivia, Ilan, and Naomi Love-Dembovsky, Alex, Maia, and Adriana Novoa-Levine, Daniela Recabarren, Matt Sparling, and Elizabeth Victor, thank you immensely for the friendship, laughter, and indignation that we have shared over the years.

An early exploration of themes from chapter 3 were previously published on PoliticalPhilosopher.net. Many thanks to Meena Krishnamurthy for that opportunity to discuss my work. Portions of chapter 2 were previously published as "Gloria E. Anzaldúa's *Auto-historia-teoría* as an Epistemology of Self-Knowledge/Ignorance" in *Hypatia: A Journal of Feminist Philosophy* 31 (2): 352–369 and are reproduced here with permission.

Special thanks also to Manuela Guillén for the beautiful cover art, and to the team of editorial and marketing staff at SUNY Press for their time and labor on this project.

Heartfelt thanks to my family for their energy, love, and lessons about the complexity and joys of the world. Much love to Csar for our conversations about theology, queer life, and politics, and sincere thanks to Juan Eduardo for sharing with me the history and memories of our family. I am especially grateful to my father, Jay, for all the storytelling and wordsmithery, and to my mother, Maria, for her unending dedication to friends and family, and for all the times that we laughed ourselves to tears.

Lastly, this book would not have been possible without the love, encouragement, and partnership of Elisabeth Paquette. She has provided both a critical eye and source of strength throughout this project, and I have cherished the reassurance, tough questions, and joyful distractions with our dogs and cats that she has generously shared with me throughout this process. I am forever in gratitude for all that she brings to my life.

Introduction

Anzaldúan Multiplicitous Agency

> It is as if one is chopped into many people and cannot bring one's memory of the chopping and of the turns into a memory of philosophical, theoretical, or activist feminisms. The nondiasporic author, of course, can bring continuity to the turns, but cannot make the continuity live in the collective movement of thought, which is what counts.
>
> —María Lugones, "Reading the Nondiasporic from within Diasporas"

For some, multiplicity poses a challenge. Heterogeneity, for example, has been considered the stuff of frustration for Enlightenment and nation-building projects alike. Philosophers have traversed regions of understanding seeking continuity and scope in the midst of nature's apparent chaos, and artists have frantically and faithfully depicted minute details of skin, hair, and longing to offer clarity across forms of peopled existence.[1] Tomes of information have been scrawled in European languages in attempts to render the entirety of an otherwise ostensibly incongruous world into smooth layers of understanding and classification.[2] In this way, multiplicity has appeared threatening and in need of order. For others, however, multiplicity has been a constant and reassuring glimpse into the promise of the future.[3] The flourishing of life has been prefaced on it, and the hope for human social cooperation wrested on the need for diversification.[4] At times, the maintenance of economic systems and the garnering of profit from otherwise stagnant markets appears to rely on multiplicity, and, conversely, critics of advanced capitalism, white supremacy, and gender violence note that these forces feed on the driving desire to manipulate the pluralities of existence for the sake of power, wealth, and social control.[5]

Yet, in the mundanity of life for many, including myself, multiplicity has been our home. *Los choques*, contradictions, parallel frames of reference, and incommensurabilities are the stuff of the everyday. Ambling through busy streets, the uneven lapping of water on a shoreline or riverbed, or the sonorous presence of differing dialects, languages, and embodied movements become familiar, expected, and comforting. Likewise, for many, negotiating this multiplicity, which may include wading through unpredictable tempers, unsympathetic stares, or hostile words and actions, is commonplace. Sometimes just making it through the day requires an acknowledgment that a lack of continuity is the norm. Other times, however, there can be revelry in multiplicity, such as the chaotic, cacophonous, or incomprehensible movements and sensations that leave us striving, eager to keep up with the pace of a song or the rhythm of a lover's body. In these moments, unification or exclusion for the sake of regularity may feel impossible, or at the very least, highly undesirable.

This book is about the ebb and flow of varying relations of multiplicity, and about possibilities for action and agency within relations of multiplicity. This book is not, however, an historical survey or sociological engagement with forms of difference. While such work is indeed valuable, this book seeks, instead, to question the sense-making, world-making practices of living within multiplicity. Orienting this thematic around the work of Gloria E. Anzaldúa (1942–2004), this book is an attempt to understand what happens when we interpret actions, as she suggests, in "a pluralistic mode" (Anzaldúa 1999, 101). Drawing from an array of Anzaldúa's writings and her readership who have examined the racialized, gendered, and political meanings of multiplicity, this book seeks to understand how context and history combine through action to give rise to new meanings, and how the particularities of a given context are the enabling conditions for action. Specifically, this book develops an account of agency based largely on Anzaldúa's writings and those of her readers called "multiplicitous agency," which is a model for understanding human action prefaced on shared interactions and interdependencies, pluralistic forms of valuation, epistemic and hermeneutical modes of distribution, and patterns of coalition building among historically oppressed social groups. As we explore further in the following chapters, multiplicitous agency focuses on themes of movement, rearrangement, and collective forms of orchestration that allow meaningful actions to emerge.

Yet, as María Lugones reminds us in the epigraph above, efforts to understand the collective conditions for action, those pretexts, prefigurations, and perambulations that make an agent's act intelligible, can be hidden or distorted by what is already known. For example, a number of diverse philosophical practitioners have worked to diagnose and address collective forms of nonknowing, indifference, and misperception found within patterned anti-Black and anti-Latinx racisms, sexual and gender violence, ableism, and colonization.[6] This body of work delves into the high costs of the many attempts to level societal planes of difference and variation. Accordingly, due to such homogenizing practices, multiplicity also makes us vulnerable.

To provide a personal example, having a complicated family migration story and ethnoracial identity are often forms of multiplicity that make one vulnerable to confusion, ambiguity, or misperception. When asked the persistent and nagging question "But where are you *really* from?" or "Are you Latinx?" I often follow up with a brief sentence that rattles off my family's ethnoracial history, including a note about white rural Virginia and three countries in Central America that my interlocutor usually knows little about. Someone once replied to me, for instance, "Panama? Oh, so you must like Van Halen?" Or when mentioning Nicaragua and El Salvador, the birth countries of my grandparents, I have been asked, "Oh, do your grandparents know folk dances?" Rarely do these interlocutors seem curious to know more about the print industry in which my Pápa Juan worked in Central America, or the forms of state censorship that he and his colleagues confronted there. Or that my great-grandmother, Josefa, called the U.S. Marines *los caballos* due to the sounds their boots made as they stomped through her barrio. The leading questions of such curious interlocutors often seem to foreclose the opportunity to tell stories that are important to me, like how my abuela, Tula, was taught to read by Tío Joaquin, a Sandino rebel who fought against the U.S. military in the 1920s. These multiple histories, relations, and experiences are how I know myself, my family, and where I have come from. Such stories are not the stuff of party-rock anthems or annual cultural fairs, and this information rarely makes me appear any more intelligible to the person who is asking where I am from, why I look the way I do, or why I have an Anglo last name.

This seeming discontinuity for peoples who are seeking an easy narrative may be frustrating or uninteresting to those who are asking such questions, which explains why some have reached for familiar songs or tropes of foreignness such as folkloric dance in their replies. For me, such experiences resonate with Lugones's epigraph above wherein she notes that this kind of multiplicity may feel "as if one is chopped into many people" (Lugones 2014, 21). Perhaps a family, a community, or simply one person feels that they are scattered about, torn apart, or in need of a memory or collective movement of thought that renders that movement intelligible.

In a similar fashion, my gender and sexual identities often fit uncomfortably with white-dominant LGBTQ spaces, spaces that sometimes erase or subsume my understanding of myself and my relationships with others. For instance, on a recent trip to a cosmopolitan city in the United States, a young white trans person who I met at a gender-affirming workout space asked where I lived. When I replied that I lived in North Carolina, their reply was a frown and an apology, stating that they were sorry that I had to live there. This person may have meant that they felt sorry about the state repression that has occurred through legislation like HB2, in which trans and gender variant people were targeted for using public facilities, and in which cities in the state were prevented from raising the minimum wage without broader state approval, and through which antidiscrimination employment protections for LGBTQ people were rejected at a statewide level.[7] Or, perhaps my interlocutor was referring to the historical and present-day forms of voter suppression that have been stifling Black and Latinx political participation across the state for well over a century.

These are generous readings of the comment, and unfortunately, my sense was that this person considered North Carolina to be a southern U.S. state that was largely uninhabitable for trans and queer people. My sense is that they did not know the many fierce queer and trans organizers of color who have demanded justice across the region. For example, my interlocutor likely did not know much about Pauli Murray's life as a young person growing up in segregated

Durham and their fight against Jim Crow segregation and sexism in the U.S. South. They also likely do not know queer people of the Catawba Nation, like Roo George-Warren, who continue to fight for Native food sovereignty in the Piedmont, or the Latinx organizers who host annual events commemorating the victims of the 2016 Orlando Pulse Nightclub shooting, and who throw drag balls in clubs and cultural centers to honor Latinx icons. *This* history of the U.S. South is the one that I am familiar with, one that knows and values the contributions of queer and trans people of color, and that recognizes our role in shaping U.S. southern life and culture. This multiplicitous framing—that knows both repression and fear, as well as resistance, beauty, and community building—fits better with my own understandings of my relationships with the queer and trans people in my life, including the family, friends, and mentors who have supported me throughout my life. In this, I consider people such as my uncle Csar, an out ordained priest in Key West, Florida, who lovingly introduced me to the beauty of queer pop culture as a child by sending me 1980s music videos on VHS tape, which were both a delight and opportunity to relish in the sounds and rhythms of queer Florida culture when I was young. *This* is the multiplicity of relations in which I experience and interpret my gender and sexual identities, and perhaps unlike my frowning interlocutor and against the immensely violent homophobic, transphobic, and racist spaces of the U.S. South, these relations and others have helped me understand and appreciate the complexity of the region.

Regarding Anzaldúa's own gender and sexual relations, she reached for terms like "patlache," "jota," "loca," "Chicana dyke," and "una de las otras" (Anzaldúa 2009, 163). Instead, I experimented with the term "tortillera," which I learned from reading Lugones in graduate school. The term, I felt, at the time marked both the word's play on lesbian identities within Latin American contexts and the long lineage of women in my family who made tortillas by hand, women who know the feeling of grit and *masa* between their fingers. This term was a source for me of what Audre Lorde calls the "erotic as power," and affirmed my existence as a desiring and enfleshed being (Lorde 1984). As "erotic" in Lorde's sense, the term provided me with a sense of power in sharing my conception of joy with other people, including the immense power discovered through food, music, and tactile sensation. Today, I settle on "Latinx," and for reasons that I explore in this book, my corporeal and affective relations are, in part, affirmed by the ethnoracial, gendered, and sexual complexity of the functions of the "x" in the term. "Latinx," as an English-language modification of the term "Latina/o" helps me locate myself in my own relations to the swamplands, scrub palmettos, and Latin American–descended populations where my brother, my cousins, and I grew up in what is today Central and South Florida. It also helps me frame my family's history in relation to the moss, sweetgum trees, and racial and settler colonial violence in what is today rural Virginia, and allows me locate myself in relation to others where I currently live today, on Catawba territory, in the foothills of the Appalachian Mountains. "Latinx" names and complicates my existence in these places of the U.S. South, as a person descended from migrants who fled the reign of Anastasio Somoza in Nicaragua, traveling across Central America and eventually finding home in Miami, Florida. "Latinx" may also include whiteness, marking the complexity of the multiple racial configurations that exist within Latin American and Latin American-descended communities. In my case, this whiteness is marked by my light skin and straight hair, shaped by my father's Anglo name and settler colonial lineages of coal miners, school teachers, and middle-class aspirations.

For me, terms like "Latinx" also complicate notions of purity or singularity, as "Latina/o" has never named a unique racial or ethnic category. Instead, as Linda Martín Alcoff has argued (2000), the term refers to a constellation of contextual and historical factors, including relations to various nationalities, races, and cultures. "Social identities," Alcoff states, "whether racial or ethnic, are dynamic" (2000, 28). For example, in the United States, I am often read as white or as "something else," and it is largely other people of color who ask about my Latin American ancestry or note that my pronunciation of Spanish-language words is indicative of a potential ethnoracial identity. Yet, when traveling in Panamá, my mother and I were both hailed and recognized as Panamanian Americans, with seemingly little incongruence for the differences between my mother and I in terms of our skin tones, gender presentations, and relative command of the Spanish language. These latter markers of identity seemed to have little bearing on whether our interlocutors considered us bearing relations to Panamá and Central America. With this, "Latinx" is the means I have for naming my own mixed ethnoracial status and gender identity, and helps me move toward a broader, multiplicitous framing for social identity categories more generally.

Likewise referring to such forms of multiplicity, Latinx feminist authors such as Lugones and Anzaldúa have drawn from a variety of sources to engage in philosophical projects that examine complex forms of heterogeneity. For example, Lugones turns to discourses of "diaspora" when considering questions of belonging and multiplicitous relationality.[8] As figures within British cultural studies such as Paul Gilroy and Stuart Hall have attested, "diaspora" has been used to describe the constant renewal of meaning of place and homeland for peoples who have been displaced throughout the world. According to Hall (1994), among the communities formed through the violence of the transatlantic slave trade, for example, "diaspora" names the multiplicities in which collective Black life has taken shape among peoples that share in figurations of coherence to the many geopolitical spaces, cultures, and histories stemming from the continent of Africa. As Hall notes when discussing the meaning of *diaspora*, diaspora is "not . . . essence or purity, [but] the recognition of a necessary heterogeneity and diversity; . . . a conception of 'identity' which lives with and through, not despite, difference" (Hall 1994, 235). Diaspora thereby names the multiplicitous and heterogeneous configurations of relations to place and history. Moreover, for Hall, diaspora names a process of becoming and a process of transformation: "Diaspora identities are those which are constantly producing and reproducing themselves anew, through transformation and difference" (Hall 1994, 235). Heterogeneity is thus constitutive of diaspora, according to this discourse.

Lugones, then, in her 2014 essay, probes what kinds of collective meaning-making projects would constitute an understanding of diaspora among Latinxs. Regarding nondiasporic positionalities, Lugones harkens to Emma Pérez's analysis of Chicanxs as diasporic subjects, as dispersed peoples with relations to a "mythic homeland [that] is longed for, constructed, and rewritten through collective memories" (Pérez 1999, 78). Pérez argues that Chicanxs, through the " 'imagined community' of Aztlán (which usually refers to the U.S. southwestern territories annexed through the Treaty of Guadalupe Hidalgo), are diasporic subjects, intertwined with processes of creation and re-creation that sustain diasporic positionalities" (described in Lugones 2014, 19). Lugones thus agrees with Pérez's reading

regarding Chicanxs: "The diasporic subject as author is intertwined
with the larger action-thinking-dispersed people. It becomes possible,
and within movements of thought, necessary to see the movement
of their thought and action as not individual" (19). Yet, Lugones
continues, all U.S. Latinxs do not constitute such a group, with
the same shared histories, collective memories, colonial wounds, or
relations to place. Moreover, many people, she argues, "who identify
as Latinas are both racialized through a history of colonization and
are *nondiasporic* subjects" (19, emphasis added). In this vein, she
mentions that while nationally identified groups of Latinxs may spend
time together (e.g., Salvadorans, Argentines, or Colombians), these
groups, from a hermeneutic standpoint within the United States, may
not constitute any shared sets of authorial, political, or normative
commitments. Self-identified Chicanx authors, however, she suggests,
may share in collective relations to place, to Aztlán, to specific social
movements against oppression, or to particular forms of labor that
employ or impact Mexican American communities.

While Lugones appears to run the risk of homogenizing Chicanx communities in her discussion, I do not read her interpretation
of diasporic identities as attempting to diminish the vast differences
among Chicanx communities. Rather, I interpret her as attempting
to note that shared hermeneutical resources may exist to *intertwine*
the agential positionings of Chicanx authors within a broad set of
historical and cultural contexts of dispersed Mexican American peoples. To push the point a bit further, she suggests that such shared
hermeneutical resources may not exist for other Latinx-identified
persons. For instance, despite knowing several other Panamanian
American professional philosophers, I cannot yet say that we participate in a collective revisioning of our relations to "the Isthmus," or
that through my shared indignation with other Central Americans
about the violence of the United States that stigmatizes, criminalizes,
and harms migrants, that I am participating in a *diasporic* Central
American project. In this sense, as a discursive community in academia, our multiplicity does not yet cohere through popular collective narratives, histories, or movements, perhaps considered, more
generically, under the label "Latinx" feminist philosophers. We are
often interpreted as isolated, disunified, or engaged in individualized
or individualizing projects. Lugones writes on this point that the

"nondiasporic subject-author is perceived as an individual and as such as not related to a group, not tied to the movement of thought of a group" (Lugones 2014, 20). We may appear to remain between such worlds of collective sense, meaning, or stability, a point that Mariana Ortega (2016), for example, has noted about identifying as Nicaraguan in the United States.

Yet, while there are differences between the histories of, say, Nicaraguan, Panamanian, and Mexican American feminists, there may also be some shared experiences among Latinxs that potentially unite us, such as feelings of *in-betweenness*, to borrow a phrase from Ortega (2016). Namely, the deep analyses of multiplicity among Chicanxs such as Anzaldúa, Pérez, and others are profound articulations of being between worlds of sense. Senses of belonging or participation within a heterogeneous diasporic movement does not stand in contrast to nondiasporic life. Rather, these shared senses of in-betweenness, as both Lugones and Ortega attest, are the conditions for coalition building. They are not necessarily specific relations to the same places or embodied experiences, but rather, that Latinxs "share a nonlinear, dispersed history of dehumanization and of resistances to dehumanization anchored in our ability to exercise a double or multiplicitous vision" (Lugones 2014, 21). Noting a complex interrelatedness, she writes that "we are all dependent on our inhabitation of interstices, liminal places as offering both revelations and cover as we live oppositionally and creatively" (21). Thus, multiplicity, even with its vulnerabilities, makes us collectively able to thrive against efforts that might seek to flatten, conform, exile, or erase us.

When read in this light, this book asks how, in our varying multiplicities, displacements, and forms of creation, we can sustain collective projects of revaluation and resistance. More specifically, this book is interested in interrogating projects of collective meaning-making that do not reify individualism or the tropes of a homogenizing paradigm that seeks uniformity and smooth congruence. The task is to retain multiplicity—be it of existential, epistemic, or normative pluralities—even when the appearance of unification might seem promising. Accordingly, one site by which such a drive toward individualization and fragmentation occurs is in discussions of agency, including linguistic agency. Vast amounts of responsibility are prefaced on what someone says or on how they behave. However, if we wish to retain life "in a pluralistic mode," following Anzaldúa, how are we to interpret the actions of multiplicitous agents—linguistic or otherwise?

In this vein, Ortega (2016) has begun a rich dialogue on how multiplicity is experienced, and names some of the problems with agential multiplicity. Ortega notes that the manner in which an ontologically plural set of selves can interact remains unclear. She asks this question in response to some of Lugones's work (2003), in which Lugones posits an ontological plurality of selves. Ortega asks, in this vein, if we are composed of pluralities, which "self" is able to remember other selves? Which "self" experiences a contradiction or tension between selves? (Ortega 2016, 91–97). Or, as I ask in this book, how do we hold our selves or other selves accountable for harms or pain that we/they might cause *and* retain our multiplicity in that process? As such, the core question in this book is, how do we interpret actions in a multiplicitous manner? In response to these questions, this book explores how we might retain a form of agential multiplicity, and do so in the service of supporting political projects that aim to dismantle racism, settler colonization, ableism, sexism, and other structural oppressions. To carry out such a project, this book picks up from a number of interpretive threads of Anzaldúa scholarship to explore what such an account of multiplicitous agency entails. Specifically, I propose that Latinx feminist theory has provided a set of rich philosophical resources that offer tools to examine questions of agency. In particular, strands of interpretation of Anzaldúa's work from within existential phenomenology, analyses of her work that explore relational ontology, and readers of her work who develop a coalitional model for political theory, each provide useful framings for my aims here.

More generally, one central reason why Anzaldúa's work has become so important to philosophers seeking to explore the nature of selfhood is precisely because her work and that of other Latina feminist theorists, as Alcoff notes, have taken a "180-degree turn" away from conceptions of unified and individualist conceptions of selfhood (Alcoff 2019, 1). This turn away from individualism and unification, as we explore in chapter 2, provides a critical strand of pluralist framings of identity, selfhood, and agency. Although Anzaldúa's writings present a number of beneficial framings for understanding multiplicitous agency, they are, by no means, without their own problems, and, as such, I hope to explore some of the complexity and transformational potential within her work while retaining the tensions and harms to which her own writings may have contributed. That is, in chapters 4 and 5, I address specific areas of her scholarship on disability, mestizaje, and transness that raise some difficult issues regarding coalitional work. What follows this introduction is a framing of my analysis in the book through three interpretive strands of Anzaldúa's work, each of which allow me to more robustly develop an account of multiplicitous agency. I then conclude chapter 1 by outlining the structure of the book and the contours of my argument.

Chapter 1

Interpretive Threads of Anzaldúa's Work

Existential Phenomenology

One prominent strand of Anzaldúa scholarship takes up resources within existential phenomenology to approach her work. This field has highlighted elements of multiplicity as an important experiential dimension of human life and has drawn from the tradition of phenomenology to frame and interpret the nature of experiences of multiplicity. As a general tradition, existential phenomenology has been characterized in a number of ways. Many researchers outlining the methodological or contentful contours of the field have tended to use a historical lens to trace the tradition's coherence. Beginning with German authors like Edmund Husserl and Franz Brentano, scholars within existential phenomenology demonstrate how commitments to studying themes such as human consciousness, intentionality, and perception have shifted over several generations of thinkers to form a distinct phenomenological tradition.[1] This tradition includes twentieth-century European writers such as Maurice Merleau-Ponty and Martin Heidegger. Other historiographers of this field focus on the "phenomena" or appearance of the world given to experience. In this, the interpretative stance is one toward orientation within the world and the lived experiences one has of the world, which can include racialized, sexual, and gendered forms of being.[2] Within this framework, Latina feminists have long noted the thematic relevance within existential phenomenology for studying how racialization and gender processes shape our experiences of and orientations toward the world.

Jacqueline Martinez (2000) is among the first U.S. Latina authors to explicitly trace how Chicana feminism and existential phenomenology bear deep resonances and shared methodological aims. Martinez's *Phenomenology of Chicana Experience and Identity: Communication and Transformation in Praxis* (2000) is a ground-breaking work that outlines how practices of cultural assimilation, homophobia, racism, and colonialism have shaped Chicana orientations toward the world. Her work examines the shaping of consciousness and embodiment, drawing from resources within Anzaldúa's work. For example, *la conciencia de la mestiza* within Anzaldúa becomes thematized in Martinez's work to express a shifting sensibility toward radical contingency and contradiction (Martinez 2000, 86). Paired with the work of Merleau-Ponty, Martinez argues that Anzaldúa honors phenomenological insights that unearth how embodied and historicized orientations in the world demand grappling with ambiguity and ambivalence, central themes that I address in chapter 3.

Linda Martín Alcoff also deeply engages the relationship between Latina feminism and existential phenomenology. In *Visible Identities: Race, Gender, and the Self* (2006), Alcoff draws from both Merleau-Ponty and Hans-Georg Gadamer to develop her conception of the "interpretive horizon" that is self-understanding (82). Alcoff, like Martinez, by including her own experiences and the writings of Anzaldúa, explores how Latina feminists have provided interpretive lenses that capture the deep incompleteness of philosophical understandings of the self. Alcoff's view supports a conception of selfhood as an ever-unfolding process, which requires hermeneutic resources from a socially and historically embedded environment. Additionally, Alcoff's work addresses mixed racial identities and colonial histories, themes we return to in chapter 5.

However, the philosopher who has perhaps done the most extensive analyses of the relationship between existential phenomenology and Latina feminism is Mariana Ortega, whose work since the 2000s has continued to expand questions regarding the relationship between the two fields. Ortega's work is deeply inspired by both Latinx feminism and European strands of phenomenology, and similar to the ways in which theorists of phenomenology have reframed the question of agency through notions of intersubjectivity, Ortega develops a series of extensive arguments that explore the experiences and theoretical resources within the lives of Latinas.

Specifically, Ortega develops a conception of multiplicitous subject-hood that offers a site for selfhood that is plural and impacted by multiple intersecting norms of identity with varying historical and hermeneutical resonances. Against a Kantian or Cartesian framing of subjecthood, Ortega elaborates the means by which Anzaldúa develops a form of multiplicitous selfhood that resists unified agential modes. Ortega examines whether Anzaldúa's framing of identity would allow agents to simply *choose* their own specific identities (Ortega 2016, 45). Ortega explicitly rejects this position, arguing that the material situatedness of multiplicitous selfhood requires negotiations among differing positionalities, including those of social identity categories such as race, gender, class, ability, nationality, religion, and so on (74–76). Ortega notes that "as a self in process or in the making, the multiplicitous self is continually engaged in these negotiations, which include sometimes having to strategically deploy certain iden-tities in certain worlds" (75).

Building on a productive tension present throughout Anzaldúa's work, Ortega examines the relationship between unification and multiplicity within understandings of the self. Specifically, she pro-poses a kind of existential pluralism "that recognizes the individual and multiplicitous character of the self in terms of the way in which the self fares or is in different worlds" (89).[3] Cleaving a difference between her view and that of another reader of Anzaldúa, Lugones, Ortega seeks to retain the important tensions of lived, experiential forms of heterogeneity, while also rejecting the stronger ontological pluralism that Lugones proposes. Ortega's approach draws from a mode of consciousness whereby the self is multiplicitous in its experiential character, but singular in terms of its ontological status. Ortega's view, then, interprets the functions of remembering oneself in different worlds and how first-person experience is possible under a many-selved view without assuming that a plurality of ontologically distinct selves are acting/existing in the world. To make sense of plural experiences, as Ortega proposes, does not require a plurality of *selves* that move across differing sites of sense and meaning. Rather, experiential differences arise from negotiations with meaning and power across different worlds. On this point, Ortega notes, "There is continuity in myself even when different aspects of myself are highlighted or covered over. . . . Whether I can highlight or cover over a particular characteristic of myself remains tied to normative

structures" (101). Such normative structures, including those that
clash or do not cohere neatly, thereby frame terms, meanings, and
possibilities for understanding oneself across multiple sites, but do not
require a multiplicity of selves that experience or undergo/negotiate
those experiences.

  I take this insight from Ortega's phenomenological strategy
as crucial to this book's framing of multiplicitous agency. While
Ortega notes that Lugones opts to move away from the language of
"agents" and instead relies on notions of "active-subjects," I would
like to honor the interpretive importance of holding the meanings of
actions made by an existentially multiplicitous self and the corporeal
and ontological possibility of a plurality of selves. If we then further
examine the need to negotiate meaning and self-understanding as an
intersubjective process, what are these negotiations? Are there ways
to negotiate our identities that are oppressive and constraining, and
are there ways to strategize our identities that cleave open further
possibilities for marginalized communities to strengthen their own
self-definitions and shared efforts? To address these questions in the
context of this book, understanding multiplicitous agency requires us
to think through the locations and sites of enactment for selfhood that
stem from these phenomenological investigations. Taking my lead from
Ortega's articulation of the multiplicitous self, I contend that agency is
a pluralized site of historicity, material positionality, and meaning. The
conception of social formation outlined in unified and individualized
models of agency appears to presume a consistency among agents and
their interpretive communities and a unified conception of intentional
states that allow agents to uphold their normative, and, thereby, social
commitments to one another. Yet our social lives and histories are
more complex than that. Similarly, the lived experiences and histories
of oppression, and the many resistant forms of mobilization against
oppression, are more multifaceted than a series of shared deontic powers. Existential phenomenological interrogations into Anzaldúa's work
thereby help us address these questions by focusing on issues such
as the functions of intersubjectivity in our experiences of ourselves,
others, and the world. Specifically, unlike phenomenological framings
that place self and world in a seemingly separate or dualistic relation,
for example, that of Heidegger's *Dasein* or José Ortega y Gasset's "yo
soy yo y mi circunstancia" (I am myself and my circumstance) (1961
[1914]), Latina feminist phenomenological framings of selfhood and

world build from the deep multiplicity and interdependency of both seemingly distinct domains of experience, requiring that we take more seriously the plurality and relationality that constitute their stability/instability.[4] Such frameworks also require us to consider the role of our social and historical contexts for understanding how the world appears to us as embodied multiplicitous agents who are capable of acting in the world. Lastly, such existential interpretations honor Anzaldúa's commitment to exploring the depths of first-person experience, and, drawing from Alcoff, how the world appears from within a given embodied interpretive horizon.

Relational Ontology

A second relevant interpretive thread for this book is the shared reading by authors such as AnaLouise Keating (2015, 2008), Kelli Zaytoun (2015), and Robyn Henderson-Espinoza (2016). Delving into questions of intersubjectivity, these readers of Anzaldúa emphasize that within her work is a deeply relational approach within metaphysics. For example, Keating, in a book she edited, describes Anzaldúa as developing a "metaphysics of interconnectedness" that is based on what Keating calls a "constantly changing spirit or force that embodies itself in material and nonmaterial forms" (Anzaldúa 2000, 9). Several authors have described Anzaldúa as following a form of "animism" or "new animism," the latter of which is, according to Keating, "an immanent materialism in which everything that exists is interconnected, conscious, and imbued with/composed of spirit, awareness, mind" (Keating, Zaytoun, and Dahms 2016, 205). Keating contrasts this "new animism" with forms of animism denigrated by anthropologists and philosophers. As part of a colonizing project aimed at primitivizing beliefs regarding consciousness, life, and the place of the human in relation to a given natural order, "animism" has been used to critique and reject the ontologies of colonized peoples across the world. Keating writes that Anzaldúa developed a metaphysics of interconnectedness throughout her work, and that the aim of such a philosophical project was to address deep "social injustices at a root level—to decolonize and, thus, transform the worldview (ontology, epistemology) that, she believed, was foundational to social injustice" (Keating, Zaytoun, and Dahms 2016, 206).

Adding to this interpretation, I would note that Anzaldúa was well aware of the criticisms used within the human sciences to reject relational views of ontology. She states in a 1986 talk at Vermont College that anthropologists like Claude Levi-Strauss and Lucien Lévy-Bruhl who offered depictions of the "primitive mind" of Indigenous peoples have discredited worldviews that value interconnectedness and relationality (Anzaldúa 2009, 105–106). Within such a colonial framing, she notes that rationality is assumed as the pinnacle of a given natural order, and with it, a conception of reality that privileges a kind of epistemological correspondence between rational human subjects and a world of objects. Yet Anzaldúa challenges this view by defending a conception of "spirit" that exceeds or resists such a correspondence view of the world. Such a view assumes that all things can be quantified and understood from an objective point of view. Moreover, as Henderson-Espinoza (2016) has explored, Anzaldúa's view demonstrates deep affinities with a number of theorists in the Western tradition such as Baruch Spinoza, Friedrich Nietzsche, and Henri Bergson whose work likewise rejects conceptions of a pre-given natural order, and who turned to ontological conceptions of becoming (rather than being) to understand the role of the human knower within a broader relational framework.

Moreover, as Keating, Zaytoun, and Henderson-Espinoza point out, such an approach to metaphysics also stemmed from Anzaldúa's affirmation and valuation of Indigenous ontological worldviews and from various forms of mysticism within the Western world. For example, one of her early poems in *Borderlands/La Frontera*, "Holy Relics" (1983), writes of Saint Teresa of Ávila, the Spanish mystic whose body was disinterred and torn apart in order to be used as relics in rituals of veneration for the saint.[5] Additionally, as we explore in chapter 4, Anzaldúa had a keen interest in Mexica/Aztec creation stories and relied on these stories to frame critical aspects of her approach to embodiment and transformation.

Regarding religion, Keating argues that Anzaldúa's conception of spirituality is "highly political, always embodied [and] has nothing in common with conventional forms of religion" (Anzaldúa 2000, 8). Read in this register, her work may tend to connote "New Age" forms of spiritual belief.[6] However, despite "New Age" trends circu-lating in the 1970s, Anzaldúa's work, Keating argues, is less based in the "personal desires and goals" of the predominantly white New

Age movement of this period. Instead, Anzaldúa's investigations into metaphysical questions regarding life itself, matter, and ecological relations stemmed from her lifelong commitments to social transformation. This "relational worldview," Keating suggests through an extensive analysis of Anzaldúa's works across her corpus, including "now let us shift" (2002) and "La Prieta" (1983), is meant to serve as a "holistic worldview to transform one's self and one's world" (2008, 54). Anzaldúa's work aims toward collective and personal forms of transformation that honor the dynamic relations between all forms of existence, including epistemological beliefs, ancestors, artifacts, rocks, soil, water, our bodies, our imaginations, and the materiality of the languages we use to communicate. Accordingly, and as I argue throughout this book, this relational ontology within Anzaldúa's work allows us to frame a conception of multiplicitous agency, a view about action that takes seriously such densely embedded material relationships.[7]

This metaphysical stance, also, as Keating argues, reframes the meaning of "matter" and works within a conception of material dynamism or process metaphysics. Rather than a substance ontology that considers the qualities of matter to inhere within a pregiven substrate, such a relational ontology relies on the continuously transforming relationships that give rise to conceptions of stability and fixity. All matter is constituted via relational movement and multiconstitutive interdependencies. Even objects of traditional philosophical analysis, such as human life, consciousness, rationality, and so on are redefined as relational and interdependent with others and the world, including interconnectedness with the very descriptive claims and questions that emerge about them. So, too, as I argue in this book, language and action are reframed as doings and meaning-making processes, rather than being driven by predetermined intentions made manifest in the world through individual actors.

In this thread, Zaytoun highlights the specific functions of storytelling within Anzaldúa's writings to defend a reading of her work as "post-humanist." Zaytoun writes that "contrary to the self-determined, self-sufficient humanist subject, Anzaldúan subjects are strengthened, not undone, in creative connection to humans and nonhuman matter" (2015, 2). In this, Zaytoun argues, alongside Keating and Henderson-Espinoza, that Anzaldúa should be read as a precursor to contemporary "new materialist" traditions within feminist theory. Often, she notes, Anzaldúa and other women of color authors are "underread and assumed to be focused on strictly identity politics and critiques of white privilege" rather than considered for their extensive work on philosophical projects dedicated to metaphysical and epistemological questions (11). Thus, following this thread, this book delves into Anzaldúa's writings by engaging her on such philosophical terms, and I seek to develop an account of multiplicitous agency, including acts of self-writing, that build within a robust relational ontology.

Coalitional Politics

Lastly, it is important that such a relational approach does not lose grip on relations of power and struggle, and thus the third interpretive strand that I use to analyze her work stems from such a political project. The communities from which Anzaldúa began writing and shaping her theoretical views were deeply engaged in practices of movement building among women of color, for example. Her first coedited collection with Cherríe Moraga, *This Bridge Called My Back: Writings by Radical Women of Color*, demonstrates her early commitments to working with a number of women of color writers engaging in a plurality of struggles. For example, Black feminist scholars such as Toni Cade Bambara, Audre Lorde, and Barbara Smith, as well as Native scholars Barbara Cameron (Lakota), Chrystos (Menominee), and Max Wolf Valerio (Kainai Nation), and Asian scholars Nellie Wong, Merle Woo, and Mitsuye Yamada were all contributors to the landmark collection. Each author presented differing dimensions of struggle for women of color, and showed the immense plurality and range of issues that they face.

On this point, Lisa Tatonetti has highlighted in her work how the contributions from Native writers in *This Bridge Called My Back* demonstrated the specificity of harms to Indigenous communities such as government boarding schools, the reservation system, Native urbanization, as well as the manner in which lesbianism or queerness has become "a barrier" to belonging within some Native communities (Tatonetti 2014, 6, quoting Max Wolf Valerio in Moraga and Anzaldúa 1983, 43–44). Additionally, the Combahee River Collective statement included in the volume attests to the forms of political

mobilization among Black women, tracing nineteenth-century freedom fighters such as Sojourner Truth, Harriet Tubman, and Frances
E. W. Harper alongside feminist contributions to Black liberation
struggles of the 1960s and 1970s (1983, 210–211).[8] Rejecting white
feminist separatism, the Combahee River Collective voiced solidarity
with Black men and their shared struggle against anti-Black racism
and racialized sexism (213). Within this framing, the authors of *This
Bridge Called My Back* navigated a number of important differences
among communities of color and the challenges that they face.

Stemming from these commitments to understanding the
differing forms of struggle among women of color, Anzaldúa left
a career-long legacy in which she was engaging in deep coalitional
projects that sought to find methods for affirmation and resistance
along a plurality of political lines of struggles against racism, sexism,
settler colonization, capitalism, and other patterned oppression. In
a similar vein, Lugones, a careful reader of Anzaldúa, also focuses
on engaging in such a deep coalitional political project. Notably,
Lugones cautions her readers that relations among those seeking to
do coalitional work across what Audre Lorde calls "non-dominant
differences" "can be neither homogenized nor merely wished into
being as relations of solidarity" (Lugones 2003, 84, quoting Lorde
1996). She notes that "logics of domination" are "techniques of producing difference" that "divide and conquer," segregate, fragment, and
instill mistrust between communities in struggle (84). These tensions
then put communities in "oppressing/being oppressed   resisting"
relations, which Lugones argues arise due to the multiplicitous ways
in which we are in differential relations of power (11–12). In this
sense, we must "remap space" by seeking to better negotiate the
ways that we can harm one another even when seeking liberation
or justice. Part of the motivation for Lugones's articulation of the
oppressing/being oppressed   resisting relation stems from the specific relationship between oppression and resistance. Lugones thus
offers a model for interpreting power that does not totalize a given
group or individual's ability to act. As we explore further in chapter
3, Lugones resists the view that being oppressed means that that
person or group is unable to respond, create, or strategize against
oppression. Drawing from Anzaldúa's work, Lugones builds a model
for agential interdependency that suggests ways in which we can
create new hermeneutic tools for understanding the meaningfulness

of our own and each other's actions while engaged in coalitional projects. This will serve as a crucial insight throughout this book.

Another reader of Anzaldúa who has been deeply informed by her coalitional work is Chela Sandoval, whose writings resituated epistemological questions of agency and representation within an antihumanist vein. For example, Sandoval's pivotal work on differential consciousness focuses on a series of theoretical problems regarding resistance and agency. Sandoval lays out a careful argument in *Methodology of the Oppressed* (2000) that proposes that shifts within industrial capitalism, global anticolonial struggles, artistic production, and women of color feminisms have given rise to "whole new expressions of consciousness, politics, and aesthetic production" (5). Sandoval's reliance on "consciousness" through her work stems both from her attentiveness to Anzaldúa's notion of mestiza consciousness and Marxist literary critic Fredric Jameson's framing of postmodernism. Responding to Jameson, she notes that Jameson interpreted globalization and advanced capitalism as leading to the perpetuation of a perspective in the Global North that history and its relations to the present are the result of "sheer heterogeneity, random difference, a co-existence of a host of distinct forces whose effectivity is undecidable" (Jameson 1984, 57, quoted in Sandoval 2000, 17). Sandoval notes, alongside Jameson, that this historiographical shift has drastic consequences within various political, ethical, and aesthetic domains. Specifically, subjectivity, agency, and creativity become "a science-fiction world come to life: its characters trapped inside an unmapped city, drifting inside a transnational space wherein 'the subject loses its capacity to extend its pro-tensions and re-tensions across the temporal manifold' " (Sandoval 2000, 21, quoting Jameson 1984, 71). Sandoval thus connects consciousness to Roland Barthes's conception of *the punctum*—"a zero-degree of meaning, counternarrative, utopia/ no-place, the abyss, *amor en Aztlán*, soul"—wherein historical and situational subjectivity retains an agential hold on the world.[9] That is, rather than accepting the erasure of subjectivity and the demise of creative capacities, Sandoval seeks to preserve a way to respond to the fractured lenses of advanced capitalism and postmodernist framings of history while still retaining agential possibilities that work toward transformation.

Noting the differing modes of struggle among women of color writers including Anzaldúa, differential consciousness is Sandoval's response to this postmodern predicament. Importantly for my project here, differential consciousness is also a form of agential multiplicity and polyphony. Specifically, differential consciousness is a method from which to negotiate complex networks of normative structures. She writes that differential movement "operates as does a technology—a weapon of consciousness that functions like a compass: a pivoting center capable of drawing circles of varying circumference, depending on the setting" (Sandoval 2000, 30). Multiplicitous agency, on this reading, is likewise an account of material relations, like a tool or weapon, and one of pluralistic interpretive possibilities. Reading such transformative hermeneutic relations, she continues that "the effectivity of this cultural mapping depends on its practitioner's continuing and transformative relationship to the social totality" (30). This kind of "cultural mapping" relies on new ways of "reading" one another, new ways of interpreting our intersubjective relations. She states, in this regard, "Reading signs to determine power relations is its principal technique, the readings obtained are the indications that guide all movement. This differential form of oppositional consciousness is a field with no specific content until such readings are produced" (30). In this framing, differential consciousness requires "content" to produce interpretative strategies, novel meanings, and new relationships to "real conditions of existence" (Sandoval 2000, 31, quoting Althusser 1970, 135). Differential consciousness involves, for Sandoval, negotiations between liberal, revolutionary, supremacist, and separatist positions, choosing when necessary to mobilize or operationalize a given strategy. As a rupture between the given terms of stasis and randomness produced within modern and postmodern sensibilities, Sandoval describes differential consciousness as an act of "decolonial love" (Sandoval 2000, chaps. 6–7). Decolonial love is thus an affective desire for liberation and transformation in worlds of oppression and degradation, a view akin to Anzaldúa's commitments to self and collective transformation.

Accordingly, these three interpretive strands of Anzaldúa's writings—on existential phenomenology, relational ontology, and coalitional politics—highlight differing dimensions and stakes of multiplicitous agency. Specifically, existential phenomenology keeps readers attuned to the bodily experience of action and meaning-making, while relational ontology shifts to a larger, more structural focus on the material conditions that shape our relations to one another and the worlds in which we are embedded and upon which we rely. Lastly, a coalitional politics becomes a normative project that guides struggle and accountability to one another within such dense webs of interconnection and experiential description. From each thread, I hope to weave a broader narrative of agency within Anzaldúa's work.

Structure of the Book

Building from these three interpretive threads, this book is an attempt to weave together a conception of multiplicitous agency that considers how to frame action, motivations, and the meaningfulness of individual and collective actions in a plural register. However, as Anzaldúa's work attests, such framings of agency cannot get rid of the inherent ambiguity within the movements and meanings of our actions, and we will explore through her work how to turn "ambivalence into something else" (Anzaldúa 1999, 101). As such, the book is structured to show how Anzaldúa and her readership offer a novel depiction of action and meaning-making for communities of resistance. While I take up sites of criticism of Anzaldúa's work, I also find her work to bear fruitful philosophical insights for feminist theory and critical philosophy of race. Immersed within a deep engagement of struggle across multiple fronts, Anzaldúa's work provides an expansive array of philosophical lessons for theorists interested in exploring how systems of oppression link, how coalitional struggles can be forged against such interlocking systems of oppression, and how we may situate ourselves within such collective endeavors.

The book's overarching claim is that the manner in which Anzaldúa navigates agential themes can be thematized through what she described in her later writings as "nos/otras." This term, I contend, was her way of describing conflicting patterns of group identification and experiential belonging that create deep rifts among differing political projects. By separating the Spanish-language word "nosotras," the feminine pronoun for "we," with a slash, Anzaldúa offered a linguistic gesture toward the contentious divisions between our collective projects and the ways in which, in her words, "we are mutually complicitous" with oppressing one another (Anzaldúa 2015, 79). In this regard, Anzaldúa's discussion of normativity and complicity with structural oppressions are important. Mentioning racial, sexual, and religious distinctions that are fraught with historical and social complexity, she develops an account of responsibility within such "impure" dynamics. Anzaldúa describes the slash, crack, or *la rajadura* between nos/otras as marking the liminal zone between binary oppositions, including self/ other, interiority/exteriority, and inclusion/exclusion. *La nepantlera*, a term adapted from Nahuatl that she uses to describe those persons whose experiences are shaped by liminality, are tasked with the difficulty of confronting the limits of these refigurations of power and positioning. Such relational conceptions of identity and oppression, then, do not leave wholly stable or purified positionalities from which to theorize or act. Rather, action and the possibilities for meaning for action are *between* "nos"/"us"/self/community and "otras"/"them"/ others/distinct communities. They are within the embedded, historical, enfleshed worlds through which historically oppressed communities seek community survival and stability.

Accordingly, the book begins by turning to four key issues that Anzaldúa's writings engaged and that circulate through theories of action and agency. Specifically, in chapter 2, I explore issues of agential insularity, isolationism, individualism, and imperialism and specify how each concept is challenged within Anzaldúa's corpus. These four areas of analysis then culminate through an examination of self-writing, an approach called *autohistoria-teoría*, in Anzaldúa's work. Autohistoria-teoría, I contend, demonstrates the features of shared interaction, collective meaning-making, embodied interdependency, and coalition-building efforts that are hallmarks of Anzaldúan multiplicitous agency.

Chapter 3, building on questions from the previous chapter, then shifts to focus on the question of agential ambivalence, and seeks to demonstrate the conception of becoming that Anzaldúa understood as part of agential ambivalence. Although the "something else" to which Anzaldúa referred is not guaranteed to resolve ambivalence or to end it, we can develop ways in which processes of becoming motivate our continued pursuits for justice in the face of oppression. Toward this end, I turn to the work of two prominent philosophers writing on the nature of insurrectionist acts against systemic oppression to underscore a possible hermeneutic for interpreting the role of ambivalence within Anzaldúa's coalitional project. Specifically, by examining Kristie Dotson's modification of Leonard Harris's insurrectionist ethics, I examine the generative possibilities within notions of ambivalence arising from agential multiplicity. I conclude this chapter by turning to questions of resistant reconstructions of meaning for the motivations of actions, and shift to the work of Lugones, an avid reader of Anzaldúa, to develop a multiplicitous framing of generative agential ambivalence that links back to Anzaldúa's work.

As I underscore in chapters 2 and 3, a critical conception of multiplicitous agency requires historicized and contextualized circumstances through which to theorize and interpret the meanings of actions. In response to this, in the last two chapters of the book, I take up two sites of critique within Anzaldúa's work that may exemplify the kind of agential multiplicity that we glean from her writings. Specifically, in chapter 4, I examine the relevance of Anzaldúa's work for projects working toward disability justice. While Anzaldúa was known to have rejected an identity ascription as "disabled," her work does attend to rich questions of pain, illness, and critical conceptions of embodied and perceptual experience that support disability justice projects. In this chapter, then, I explore how her retelling of the story of Coyolxauhqui, the Mexica/Aztec creation story of the moon, offers a multiplicitous framing of agency that supports contemporary disability justice projects.

Continuing an analysis of embodied multiplicitous agential relations, chapter 5 also highlights how Anzaldúa's conception of multiplicitous agency can shape possibilities for affirming difference through telling divergent historical and contextualist narratives. Specifically, this chapter examines the relationships between conflicting sites of struggle and resistance from within transgender studies and Indigenous studies. The issue addressed in this chapter is Anzaldúa's notion of mestizaje in relation to questions of critical trans politics and critiques of settler colonization. This multidimensional set of problems helps frame the complicated and historized facets of multiplicitous agency, and the chapter concludes by returning to Anzaldúa's notion of nos/otras, as a way to reapproach questions of coalition work.

The conclusion of the book builds from these prior chapters to elaborate how the notion of nos/otras and Anzaldúa's broader conception of multiplicitous agency functions as coalition work. I thereby close the book with a discussion of how generative agential ambivalence helps us continually build coalitions across difference. Such generative ambivalence, stemming from agential multiplicity, I propose, pushes us beyond what Anzaldúa initially proposed in her work, and leads us to new areas of analysis, including what I tentatively describe as "nos/otrxs," a framing beyond binary and dualistic constructions of coalitional struggle. As such, in the pages that follow, I hope to unearth new ways to combine the meanings of our actions with their surrounding hermeneutic landscapes and communities, and to find new ways to share the fruits of our agential labor within pluralistic communities of struggle so that we may flourish collectively.

Chapter 2

Geographies of Multiplicitous Selves

In "Geographies of Selves—Reimagining Identity," Anzaldúa explores complex negotiations within processes of individual and group identity formation. Shifting across a plurality of identity categories including identity formations as transgender, disabled, queer, and being a person of color, Anzaldúa begins to chart a new spatial and material orientation to identity construction. Rather than models of "intersection" for identity categories, Anzaldúa describes the relation between identity categories as a form of "interaction" (Anzaldúa 2015, 66). She also writes of traditional categories of identity as forcing us to be "stuck in binaries, trapped in jaulas (cages) that limit the growth of our individual and collective lives" (66). The chapter then examines what she describes as new "geographies of selves" that allow us to reconfigure our relations to identity categories as embodied and interconnected interactions within the broader ecosystems in which we are located.

This framing of interacting selves points us to several ways in which Anzaldúa's work requires us to rethink how interacting selves engage agentially with one another and the world, including what our reasons for action might mean in light of agential multiplicity. Specifically, I argue in this chapter that Anzaldúa rejected models of agency that relied on *insularity, isolationism, individualism*, and *imperialism*, and opted instead for an agential model of shared interaction, distribution, interdependency, and coalition. Specifically, *insularity* is a conception of privacy or uniqueness that may be considered a feature of epistemic agents, selves, and so on. A contrasting position to insularity would be conceiving of the self/agency as

29

public, shareable, or collectively constructed. *Isolationism* is a view regarding the location or positioning of the mind/self in relation to other minds, the environment, one's body, or the natural world. Against this view, extended conceptions of cognition are common, whereby one's agential capacities are distributed throughout a given body or social environment. *Individualism* is an aspect of a given theoretical configuration that results from distinguishing the mind, the soul, or the self from the social world, or from relying on the individual as the locus of rights or agentic claims. Contrasting positions to individualism include collectivism or views regarding the interdependency between conceptions of self and others. Lastly, *imperialism* is a politicized conception of the self/soul that refers to the aim to dominate or control others, or to make one's own framing of selfhood a primary point of reference. Against such a view, we could utilize coalitional or pluralistic framings of selfhood, truth, and so forth. These four features appear throughout my analysis of agency in this book.[1] In what follows, I explain each of these agential tendencies in more depth and demonstrate how Anzaldúa's work moved beyond these framings of action and agential capacity. These challenges to traditional conceptions of agency, I propose, help shape the agential multiplicity that she develops throughout her corpus, and allow us to turn to questions of agential ambivalence in the following chapter.

Examining Insularity and Isolationism

Readers of Anzaldúa's writings are likely familiar with her deep personal explorations of selfhood and interiority. She describes in many places "inner work" (2015), "delving inward" (2009), "moving inward" (2015), and other rich descriptions of the psychic and imagined lives of phenomenal experience. While such invocations of interiority may suggest a kind of inner self, "spirit," or "soul" that functions independently of the world or body around it, Anzaldúa was also explicit in her rejection of Cartesian dualist positionings between the mind/soul and the body/matter. As we noted in the previous chapter, through secondary scholarship on Anzaldúa and relational ontology, Anzaldúa was engaged in a complex philosophical project *against* substance dualism and separations between embodied, material existence and the workings of the mind or any other "interior" process.

Specifically, I use the term *insularity* to refer to a tendency among theories of agency that frame decision-making, reasons for action, motivations, imaginative possibilities, and so on as inherently private or separated from shared epistemic and hermeneutical resources. Additionally, *isolationism* is the term I use to describe the assumed material and spatial location of framings of agential interiority. For example, some conceptions of agency rely on the brain and its neural networks as a source for decision-making and human cognition, considering the activities of the brain as the *software* of the fleshy *hardware* that is our brain. Against both views, as a number of embodied theorists of mind have proposed, cognition exists not only as an interaction between brains, bodies, and their robust couplings with environments, but cognitive processes themselves change over time and are not static, computational entities.[2] In a similar vein, Anzaldúa's work rejected both insular and isolationist views of cognition and agency, even in her brief forays into discussions of neural activity. Notably, Anzaldúa makes several brief comments in her later work on the brain and its relationship to liminal thinking. For example, she writes in "Geographies of Selves" of a "nepantla brain" that is necessary for "navigating the cracks" between forms of polarity (Anzaldúa 2015, 82). She also mentions that a "nepantla brain" helps one chart subtle perceptual and epistemic biases within one's own phenomenal experience (82). Elsewhere, Anzaldúa writes of a creative process that requires "moving between and among different parts of the brain" (Anzaldúa 2015, 108). Lastly, although a bit unhelpful for critiquing a computationalist paradigm, she describes, in a footnote, the brain as having "the processing power of a hundred billion personal computers joined together" (234, n. 18). While Anzaldúa was writing in the late 1990s and early 2000s, at a time when personal computers were beginning to gain greater availability, she appears to analogize the brain with a computational capacity. In this, we could conclude that Anzaldúa did actually think that the brain was like a supercomputer of some sort, which would bolster an isolationist reading of her view of agency. That is, we could conclude that she believes that our actions, intentions, desires, imaginings, and so on are *merely* or *solely* the result of the firing of our neural networks. Or, as I suggest we do instead, we could turn to her other writings to consider more broadly how she framed conceptions of interiority and epistemic privacy. We can then chart through Anzaldúa's work, for example, how "inner work" is relevantly linked to what she described as "public acts" in one of her later works, "now let us shift" (2015), which brings us into a broader dialogue regarding the assumed singularity or privacy of our cognitive processes.

What I propose is that Anzaldúa suggested throughout her work that the epistemic content of the self is inherently connected to others and not a private or isolated phenomenon. To work through this claim, I propose that we look to her conception of the "geography of selves," as well as some of her earlier writings, as responses to agential insularity and isolationism. First, consider her words from "Geographies of Selves" that "we're composed of information, billions of bits of cultural knowledge superimposing many different categories of experience" (Anzaldúa 2015, 69). From this, we can glean that, by her later writings, Anzaldúa was beginning to reject agential locations as stemming from a purely interiorized source or location. Phenomenal experience, as she suggests here, echoing elements of the European phenomenological tradition, is an interactive and interdependent process. Rather than mere software or a divine interior source, perception, memory, and knowledge is relational. She states, adding to this point, "Identity is relational. Who and what we are depends on those surrounding us, a mix of our interactions with our alrededores/environments, with new and old narratives" (69). "Identity" in the sense she employs it here is an embodied interaction in which "we weave (tejemos), and are woven" (69). Her conception of weaving and being woven provides a depiction of being acted upon and being in a seemingly intentional state of willing or moving oneself. This tension, as an interdependent relation between world and self, is both a temporal and spatial project for Anzaldúa. She analyzes both singular embodied relations between experiential positionings, for example "I" and "you," as well as collective movements and tensions across time. How such tensions interact varies depending on the contextual sites and historical moments in which such agential positionings are located.

Building from this Anzaldúan insight, careful readers of Anzaldúa like Lugones also develop conceptions of intersubjectivity and extended embodiment that challenge insular and isolated conceptions of agential interiority. For example, Lugones argues that "intentions" and "meaning" arise *between* speakers rather than *in* a given subject (Lugones 2003, 208–209). Notably, Lugones constructs a conception of agency that she calls "active subjectivity." Her aims for this conception of agency focus on the challenging and messy forms of collective interaction among social organizers and others seeking strategies for mobilization among historically oppressed groups. Given the multiplicitous social groups that many of us inhabit, Lugones attempts to make space for the variegated ways in which our desires to support and engage one another may sometimes pull us in seemingly opposing directions. Thus, her Anzaldúan conception of active subjectivity stems from the complicated dynamics of acting in coalition with others, rather than through privatized intentions. Lugones's view, she writes, "does not presuppose the individual subject and it does not presuppose collective intentionality of collectivities of the same" (Lugones 2003, 6). Relying on difference as a productive force, active subjectivity, as a form of agency, is, in her words, "adumbrated to consciousness by a moving with people, by the difficulties as well as the concrete possibilities of such movings" (6). Basing her account within an interactive and interdependent framing, Lugones too asks: "How much and what sort of 'agency' do we need to move with others/without falling into a politics of the same, a politics that values or assumes sameness or homogeneity" (6). Lugones worries that some framings of agency will "mythologize place" and her view aims to develop methods for understanding actions that "[attempt] to stand in the cracks and intersections of multiple histories of domination and resistances to dominations" (6). Her words here note the political and social concerns that undergird her conception of agency. Notably, she rejects individualism, as well as a form of collective agency in which all actors must inhibit some similar or shared set of aims. Moreover, she rejects the value of sameness or homogeneity, finding plurality and difference a substantive basis for collective struggle. Lastly, note that her conception of agency described here does not use language regarding interiority and uniqueness. Instead, she remains skeptical of "mythologizing place," which we might also offer as a reason to refuse locating agential cognition in merely one embodied location (e.g., neural activity).

Lugones's point regarding "attempts to stand in the cracks" of multiple spatial and temporal relations to resistant communities thus echoes Anzaldúa's sense of "cracks between worlds" of differing and conflicting agential locations (Anzaldúa 2000, 266). Such liminality operates within what Anzaldúa describes as "mestizaje, the new mestizaje," or living nepantla (Anzaldúa 2015, 71). To track how readers of Anzaldúa like Lugones may have developed threads of agential intersubjectivity, we can more carefully interpret the core theme of mestizaje within Anzaldúa's writings, a thematic that unquestionably shaped Lugones's own theoretical work.[3] More specifically, tropes of mestizaje circulated throughout Anzaldúa's writings, beginning with her groundbreaking chapter of *Borderlands/La Frontera*, "*La conciencia de la mestiza*/Towards a New Consciousness." In that text, she positions herself as "taking off" from twentieth-century Mexican philosopher and politician José Vasconcelos's notion of mestizaje. While mestizaje has traditionally been conceived as a form of cultural and biological mixture within Latin America, Vasconcelos reconceived the idea as one of futurity and divine synthesis in the context of postrevolutionary Mexican nation-building. Notably, while both Vasconcelos and Anzaldúa consider mestizaje a promising method to reject conceptions of purity, Anzaldúa extended and resituated mestizaje as a particularly feminized conception of futurity. She opens her 1987 chapter "*La conciencia de la mestiza*/Towards a New Consciousness" with an epigraph that echoes a famous motto penned by Vasconcelos. That is, she revises Vasconcelos's quotation, "Por mi raza hablará el espíritu"/"Through my race, the spirit will speak" by beginning her essay with the line "Por la mujer de mi raza/hablará el espíritu"/"Through the woman of my race/the spirit will speak" (Anzaldúa 1999, 99). Readers of her work have suggested that this adaptation of Vasconcelos's declaration regarding the future of race in Mexico is a rejection of a previous discourse of mestizaje that had been circulating in Latin America since, at least, the early nineteenth century. Moreover, such critics have read her appropriation of the language of that discourse as a form of feminist and queer distancing from prior masculinist and heterosexist traditions within Chicano and Mexican political and philosophical thought (Arrizón 2006, 8).[4]

While I agree with these interpretations, we can also locate a deep commitment to agential multiplicity from this early conception of mestizaje as well. Anzaldúa notes that when confronted with conflict, for example, "it is not enough to stand on the opposite river bank, shouting questions, challenging patriarchal, white conventions. . . . At some point, on our way to a new consciousness . . . we are on both shores at once. . . . The possibilities are numerous once we decide to act and not react" (Anzaldúa 1999, 100–101). Distinguishing here between action and reaction, we can read her as rejecting a kind of oppositional or confrontational framing for political engagement. However, another possible interpretation leads us to her next point in the chapter, as a kind of "pluralistic mode" in which "nothing is thrust out, the good, the bad, and the ugly, nothing rejected, nothing abandoned" (10). This appears, then, to be an ontologically expansive view that is quite unlike the "aesthetic eugenics" of Vasconcelos, in which the author posits the eventual disappearance of "lower races" within a movement toward the new mixture of human qualities (Vasconcelos 1979, 32).

As her Latinx feminist readers have recognized, Anzaldúa's mestizaje or "mixture" is something else, and she states as much in her later writings, noting that "this new mestizaje eschews the racial hierarchies inherent in older mestizaje" (Anzaldúa 2015, 73). Yet even in her other early writings we see that mestizaje is a response to the deep divides that separate human political goals and desires for belonging. For example, she writes in a 1987 piece, "En Rapport, In Opposition: Cobrando cuentas a las nuestras," of the deep forms of harm that communities of color commit against one another. Instead of focusing on the harms caused by dominant groups, such as the harms that white people inflict on people of color, she focuses on the "internalization" of "neocolonial" attitudes and beliefs whereby communities of color seek to impose ways of being on one another: "Like our exploiters who fixate on the inferiority of the natives, we fixate on the fucked-upness of our sisters. Like them we try to impose our version of 'the ways things should be'; we try to impose one's self on the Other by making her the recipient of one's negative elements, usually the same ones that the Anglo projected on us. Like them, we project our self-hatred on her; we stereotype her; we make her generic" (Anzaldúa 2009, 112). This passage carries resonances of a critique of imperialism, which I further address in the next section. However, for now, we can see that Anzaldúa's framing of mestizaje is not simply one of *any* contingent group mixture. Rather this "new" mestizaje is one that reflects on how pluralism and interconnectedness can be painful. She notes that "identifying . . . with a mestizo identity" is terrifying as it requires "leaving permanent boundaries of a fixed self" (115). Here, again, mestizaje is more than a simple cultural or biological mixture, it is a claim, at an agential and onto-logical level, regarding the *locatedness* and boundaries of self and other, and between identification and othering.

Such a reading of these tensions between differing agential positionings can be found across her corpus, including her later works such as "now let us shift" (2002). In that work, Anzaldúa describes a process of personal and collective transformation through what she calls the path of conocimiento. Conocimiento, more gen-erally a Castilian Spanish term for "knowledge," is given a techni-cal use in Anzaldúa's writings. Although the concept is developed from her earlier work on notions such as mestiza consciousness and la facultad, conocimiento becomes, for Anzaldúa, a resistant form of epistemic practice. In "now let us shift," she states that conocimiento is "skeptical of reason and rationality" and that it is a state of "[questioning] conventional knowledge's current categories, classifications, and contents" (Anzaldúa and Keating 2002, 542). She also describes conocimiento as a "form of spiritual inquiry" that "is reached via creative acts—writing, art-making, dancing, healing, teaching, meditation, and spiritual activism—both mental and somatic (the body, too, is a form as well as a site of creativity)" (542). In this way, Anzaldúa connects human action to an epistemic state of interconnectedness: "Through creative engagements, you embed your experiences in a larger frame of reference, connecting your personal struggles with those of other beings on the planet, with the struggles of the Earth itself" (542). Conocimiento, in this sense, is the term she uses to describe a state of embodied awareness that equips one with a capacity to act and to create by locating the multiplicitous relations in which one is embedded.

The connections in the above passage between spirituality and creativity are tightly intertwined. Amala Levine in "Champion of the Spirit: Anzaldúa's Critique of Rationalist Epistemology," for example, argues that Anzaldúa locates "spirituality physically in the body" (Levine 2008, 174). Akin to Keating's reading discussed in chapter 1, Levine claims that Anzaldúa rejects conceptions of spirituality that position divinity, freedom, and goodness against the corporeal. Levine proposes that Anzaldúa's reclamation of the relationship between creative spontaneity and embodied being resituates the locus of freedom within a materially embedded set of possibilities for meaning and action. Thus, our embeddedness within historical and cultural relations provide the material frames of reference for our meaning-making practices, which guide and shape the possibilities for new forms of self-interpretation and narrative construction. However, such constructions are not constrained by a disembodied form of rationality, spirituality, or intentionality that seeks its fulfillment outside of corporeal forms of human action. Rather, it is our collaborative interactions with others, including their distinct, materially rich histories and enacted practices of meaning-making, that frame and shape our understanding of the boundaries of selves and others. From this, we see that the location of an agential self or others depend inherently on our interconnected "web of identity" (Anzaldúa 2015, 69). As Lugones expands through her readings of Anzaldúa, this conception of multiplicitous agency derives from within those interconnections, between the normative, political, aesthetic, and affective relations that shape our positionings toward one another and the world.

Examining Individualism and Imperialism

From these critical stances away from insularity and isolationism, we shift toward Anzaldúa's interpretive stances that reject individualism and imperial domination. As I mentioned above, her work has been committed to examining the ways in which oppressed communities harm each other, and the modes of othering and exclusion that we place on one another. That is, her commitments to interrelations and dynamism do not mean that criticism and resistance to forces of domination are not permitted. She writes on this point in "En Rapport, In Opposition," "And yes, I have some criticism, some self-criticism. And no; I will not make everything nice. There is shit among us we need to sift through. Who knows, there may be some fertilizer in it" (Anzaldúa 2009, 115). Turning "shit" into "fertilizer" is akin to generating something new from sites of conflict, pain, and trauma. Again, this is not an abandoning or rejection of this pain, nor is it a neoliberal individualized conception of "bootstrapping" oneself away from harm.[5] Rather, her work harkens to a constructive and *collective* form of transformation.

    Individualism, I contend, relies on a notion of agency as singular, and on this view, collectivities are aggregated from such individuals, but they are inherently separate (which likewise relies on notions of insularity and isolationism). Additionally, imperialism, in a broad sense, consists of actions or movements that work toward the domination or control of others, or that make oneself, country, culture, or viewpoint the sole or primary point of reference. Notably, the readers of Anzaldúa's work that I describe in chapter 1 who frame her work in terms of a coalitional politics have picked up on her criticism of such an imperial orientation. For example, Sandoval (2000, 58) and Lugones (2003, 234–235) each consider her work as critical of processes of colonization and normalization. Notably, Sandoval's own stance on imperialism and individualism seems clear given her demand for oppositional strategies to totalizing nationalistic frameworks, her critiques of advanced capitalism, and her desire to underscore the contestatory potential among women of color writers and anticolonial movements. Moreover, she notes that "crises of representation" result from First World academic negotiations with power, which, as David Scott (1999) has noted, may have emerged in response to anticolonial movements and the militant resistant projects of African, Asian, and Latin American social movements worldwide, but are not identical with those movements (Sandoval 2000, 76; Scott 1999). Yet, as both Sandoval and Anzaldúa recognize, there is a need to reframe power and the historical patterns of resistance that surfaced in the academy in the 1970s–1980s and onward. Sandoval, I propose, builds from Anzaldúa's work to offer a theoretical framing of power as multidimensional, a view that challenges both the "sovereign" model of power indicative of modernity/coloniality and the radical contingency/arbitrariness of power among some framings of postmodernism (wherein interrelationality and dynamism may lead to the diminishment of accountability or political/moral responsibility).

In this sense, Sandoval's interpretation of the discursive limits of the academy also puts her in conversation with discourses about interiority, including those that I have outlined in Anzaldúa's work regarding insularism and isolationism. For example, positioning herself in response to Michel Foucault, Sandoval writes that "oppositional and differential consciousness . . . depends on constant rearrangement in relation to a whole paradigm that includes mobile paradigmatic and syntagmatic dimensions, and that requires the perpetual reformatting of consciousness, and practice" (Sandoval 2000, 77). In this way, she notes that traditional framings of subjectivity must be "continually redetermined by the fluctuating influences of those powers that sur-round and traverse us, as well as by the memory of those identities that might have taken, and may still take, 'our' current places" (77). She thus advocates for "new combinatorials" that enact "an ongoing form of semiotic life reading that places the subject differentially inside power" (77). Rather than reifying an ontological commitment to consciousness as a feature of human existence, Sandoval's use of this term, and its subsequent functions as a form of subjectivity, place this notion within relations of power. In this sense, she concedes that there is no outside to power, but only relational negotiations within systems of power. Such a view, which informs the reading I am developing through Anzaldúa's writings and secondary literature, does not mean that resistance and transformation are untenable. Such moves, too, operate within dimensions of power.

To elaborate this point further and to demonstrate how social identities function as relations of social power within Anzaldúa's work, we can explore her engagement with strands of antihumanist Marxist thought, and specifically the work of Louis Althusser. It may come as a surprise to some readers of Anzaldúa that she was engaged with questions regarding Althusserian subject constitution. However, a number of Chicana feminist authors, including Anzaldúa, Sandoval (2000), and Norma Alarcón (1993–94) consistently drew from Althusser's work to develop their own multiplicitous framings of agency, subjecthood, and language. In this vein, we can glean much about the scope of Anzaldúa's work on such issues from her archival materials in which she engaged the French Marxist directly. Notably, we find in her archive that, in the early 1990s, Anzaldúa was reading and writing about Althusser, self-authorship, and sub-ject constitution. For example, in a 1990 draft of a paper on self-representation and autobiography, Anzaldúa writes of the functions of a "post-Althusserian" account of representation. Noting that there is debate regarding the construction of subjectivity, including the account of Althusser, in which the creation of subjectivity is consid-ered merely a part of ideology, she questions this approach through her account of autohistoria-teoría (Anzaldúa 1990, 18). Specifically, Anzaldúa questions the differences between autobiographical writings among authors who occupy racially and ethnically dominant epistemic spaces, notably Anglo-American and European authorial positionings, and the autobiographical positionings of authors whose racial/ethnic communities must write the self from within nondominant epistemic, political, and hermeneutic locations. In this sense, she avers that some of the common tropes of self-writing, as a form of self-aggrandizing creation or fabrication, do not function along the same terms for authors writing from nondominant subject positions. Anzaldúa's focus is often women of color who are writing from conditions of hermeneutical instability in which meaning-making becomes a tool for sustaining oneself rather than a means to glorify the self (25–26). She suggests that women of color write from positions of self-articulation that create different political and normative functions than those in dominant subject positions in that their depiction of the privacy of experience through self-writing creates alternatives to public narratives. Such a form of "prescriptive memory," she states, thereby offers a new function for autobiography as an act of contestation and redescription (31). Rather than assuming that the privacy of experience, when depicted in writing, merely seeks to assert the givenness of experience, the normative functions of autobiography for nondominant subjects require multiplicity, contestation, and ambiguity. Accordingly, the presence of competing lenses of interpretation, including those that may disregard or conflict with the author's telling of an alternative sequence of events, are part of the narrative self-craft of nondominant subjects.

Along similar lines, in her dissertation writings of the early 2000s, Anzaldúa theorizes identity as "a social position" (Anzaldúa 2015, 186). She writes that "identity is about repositioning yourself. It's about willing to be moved from your social position. . . . Identity is always in process, in nepantla (between who we were yesterday and are yet to be tomorrow)" (186). This notion of nepantla is particularly important in Anzaldúa's middle and later writings. While she theorized the "borderlands" in her earlier works, she began shifting her usage of this term in her writings thereafter. She notes in an interview in 1991 that "borderlands" was being used too narrowly as a metaphor so she began shifting to the term "nepantla" (Anzaldúa 2000, 176, quoted in Anzaldúa 2015, xxxiv). Unlike conscious and willful acts or movements, nepantla, she notes, "automatically infuse my writing: I do not have to will myself to deal with these particular points; these nepantlas inhabit me and inevitably surface in whatever I'm writing" (Anzaldúa 2015, xxxiv). As such, "nepantla" is a term that she adapts to refer to potential spaces for movement between differing hermeneutical and normative sites, or a movement *entre mundos* ("between worlds") that are not driven by an individual will or desire. In contrast, "nepantleras" may be interpreted as those forms of agential positioning across and between these differing sites of meaning and normativity. But while self and collective forms of awareness can emerge from such movement, nepantla itself is not self-directed or an intentional way to inhabit such worlds of sense. Rather, Anzaldúa began using terms like "nepantla" and "nos/otras" to describe how the personal experience of shifting and transitioning between differing sites of meaning and normativity takes place in ways that are not necessarily driven by individual will or agential strivings. Such forms of nepantla are also imposed and indicative of the inability to control or change one's own conditions for being. In this manner, writing "from the cracks," in Anzaldúa's words, becomes a way to locate oneself despite the disorientation or displacement that many members of historically oppressed communities face (81).

Anzaldúa's emphasis on writing and thinking "from the cracks" has become important for theorists working within decolonial traditions, such as Emma Pérez (1999), Laura E. Pérez (2019), Chela Sandoval (2000), Elena Ruíz (2011), Catherine Walsh (2018, with Walter Mignolo), Nelson Maldonado-Torres (2006), and Walter Mignolo (2000, 2018 [with Catherine Walsh]). Walsh notes, for example, that one must turn toward interstitial spaces, toward spaces of liminality, and toward sites of struggle between worlds to engage in a decolonial project (Mignolo and Walsh 2018, 250). Quoting Anzaldúa's dissertation writings, Walsh (2018, 250–251) notes that "relational theories and tactics" are invented through dwelling within liminal spaces. Likewise, Mignolo (2012) invokes Anzaldúa's work when articulating notions of "border thinking and "border gnosis," both of which harken to tactics that seek epistemic and hermeneutic resources outside of Eurocentric orders of knowledge production. Mignolo also understood that Anzaldúa shifted the meaning and usage of *nepantla* from its sixteenth-century Nahua origins into a twentieth-century concept (Mignolo and Walsh 2018, 251). That is, as James Maffie (2017), Clara Román-Odio (2013), and others have pointed out, the term "nepantla" first emerges in the Spanish colonial archive in Diego Durán's *Historia de las Indias de Nueva España y Islas de Tierra Firme* in which the Dominican priest describes the words of a Nahua man in the New Spanish colony who is being reprimanded by the priest for appearing careless with money (Román-Ohio 2013, 53). The Nahuatl speaker replies, "Father, do not be astonished; we are still nepantla," and the priest interprets this to mean "to be in the middle" (Maffie 2017; Román-Odio 2013, 53). Another sixteenth-century archival trace of the term, the 1571 *Vocabulario en lengua castellana y mexicana y mexicana y castellana*, also includes "nepantla" where it is considered "an adverb meaning *"en el medio, o en medio, o por medio,"* all variants of something being "in the middle" (Campbell 1985, 212–213). Lastly, Miguel León-Portilla (1970, 1990), who was one of the sources for Anzaldúa's interpretations of Mexica/Aztec worldviews (Anzaldúa 1999, 119), considers "nepantlism," now a noun, as a form of "woundedness" that emerges from the "violent collision of two cultures" (1990, 11). León-Portilla thus considers the devastation wrought on Mexica/Aztec worldviews and ways of life under Spanish colonial conquest as the source for the Nahuatl speaker's use of the term *nepantla* mentioned in Durán's text.

In tension with León-Portilla's interpretation, however, Frances Karttunen (1983) traces the root words of "nepantlah" into "nepan-" and "-tlah," which convey a sense of mutual or reciprocal abundance (Karttunen 1983 16). From this Karttunen concludes that nepantla more likely refers to "a dynamic condition of being abundantly middled, betwixted-and-betweened, and centered" (Maffie 2017). Rather than a colonial woundedness, Maffie and Karttunen, as well as a number of readers of Anzaldúa, consider the Nahuatl speaker's words in Durán's text to refer to something more generative and ontologically significant. As Maffie describes nepantla, "Nepantla-defined processes produce a tertium quid, one that is *neither* fish nor fowl yet *simultaneously both* fish *and* fowl!" (2017, 1). Although we have no evidence that Anzaldúa read this specific interpretation of nepantla from Karttunen, I would like to suggest that Anzaldúa's framing of multiplicitous agency, as a process of transformation, echoes this kind of abundant reciprocity. While not abandoning the León-Portilla framing of the violence of colonial conquest that gives rise to liminality, nepantla, and those who inhabit this mutual relational abundance, nepantleras, I contend, are better understood as dynamic *agential communities* whose work is to create new meanings and material possibilities within webs of interconnection.

This framing of mutual and reciprocal abundance also gives new meaning to Anzaldúa's usage of the term "nepantla brain" (Anzaldúa 2015, 82). As something akin to an embodied and enactivist view of cognition, we might consider the "nepantla brain" as an articulation of the generative relationality between neural activity and embodied movement, including conceptions of cognition that consider the brain's relationship to environmental factors and social life.[6] One contemporary approach to cognition studies that might allow us to better interpret what Anzaldúa meant by the "nepantla brain" is Victoria Pitts-Taylor's *The Brain's Body: Neuroscience and Corporeal Politics* (2016), wherein the author works through a series of literatures on mirror neurons and neural plasticity to offer readings of their impact on studies of racism, including the surveillance and police killings of Black Americans. Against a dichotomy between biology and politics, Pitts-Taylor studies the "social brain" as a phenomenon through which to examine the politics of neurobiological research, including how structural oppressions take shape and root within these fields of science. From this register, the nepantla brain, working "in the cracks" of structural oppressions, human material embodiment, and the discursive terrain of the natural and human sciences, may be better read as a description of such a "social brain."

Lastly, regarding the sources for anti-imperialism and anti-individualism functioning within Anzaldúan nepantlism, we can see that her work sheds light on more than a decolonial turn away from Eurocentrism and the search for "post-Occidental reason," although it certainly includes this as well. As Elena Ruíz (2011) and Ortega (2017) each analyze, unlike decolonial theorists like Mignolo (2000, 2012) and Aníbal Quijano (2000), Anzaldúa and other Chicana decolonial theorists were engaged in forms of grassroots political activism, and the interstitial possibilities described by these writers stem from negotiating how their bodies, languages, and desires were navigating racism and sexism within those social movements As Ruíz describes it: "Chicana writers' positionality in multiple cultural and social realities enabled them to shift perspectives more easily and to ground their methodologies on destabilizing practices" (Ruíz 2011, 352). Thus, for Anzaldúa, nepantla and the generative possibilities therein emerge from her interstitial relations to her own agential communities, which included, among other experiences, the patterned homophobia she experienced from members of her family in the Río Grande Valley, the sexism she endured within the Chicano rights movement, and the racism and forms of cultural erasure within the lesbian, feminist, and academic communities that she traversed. Her framing of nepantla includes both the sense of "woundedness" from the León-Portilla reading and a sense of novelty or "tertium quiddities" that arises from being *no one* particular identity positionality alone, but rather *simultaneously all* or *more than* any one specific racialized and gendered/sexualized positionality. Against insularity, isolationism, individualism, and imperialism, this interpretation harkens to an ontological reframing of Anzaldúa's work that normatively hails us to locate ourselves and others within the abundance of relations or webs of interconnection in which we are all embedded.

In this light, nepantla and Anzaldúa's notion of autohistoria-teoría, as I elaborate below, are ways in which Anzaldúa attempted to bring her readers to the collective and resistant coalitional possibilities for agency. Rather than singular acts from individual sources, resistance and transformation, both personal and collective, occur through interconnection and ecological shifts. To demonstrate this, we turn in the final section of this chapter to her conception of autohistoria-teoría as a site of such collective agential movement.

Learning from Nepantleras

Numerous works in Anzaldúa's oeuvre foreground the act of self-writing; however, for my purposes here, we can examine how Anzaldúa's writings develop, via first-personal articulations of the experiences of the author, key insights through the notion of autohistoria-teoría. Autohistoria-teoría is characterized by several important features: it is collaborative, sensuously embodied, and productive of critical self-reflection, which can be both harmful and enabling. These features illustrate deep relational facets of Anzaldúa's approach to self-writing, as well as offer a way to avoid the reification of an insular, individualist, and isolationist positioning.

Although Anzaldúa never offered a systematic definition of the concept of autohistoria-teoría, she did utilize the notion throughout her writings, interviews, lectures, and teaching (Keating 2008, 5–6). A brief discussion of the concept appears in a footnote in her 2002 essay "now let us shift . . . the path of conocimiento . . . inner works . . . public acts": "Autohistoria is a term I use to describe the genre of writing about one's personal and collective history using fictive elements, a sort of fictionalized autobiography or memoir; and autohistoria-teoría is a personal essay that theorizes" (Anzaldúa 2009, 578). From this brief articulation, Anzaldúa appears to point to the manner in which the act of giving meaning to oneself provides a platform for collaborative forms of meaning-making.

To elaborate, we can find a parallel claim articulated negatively in Alcoff's essay "The Problem of Speaking for Others." She writes that we cannot "retreat into one's discrete location and make claims entirely and singularly within that location that do not range over others" ((Alcoff 1991–92, 20). She thereby denies that there are "neutral place[s] to stand free and clear in which one's words do not prescriptively affect or mediate the experience of others, nor is there a way to demarcate decisively a boundary between one's location and all others" (20). Alcoff here rejects the view that speaking merely for oneself can prevent making normative claims about others. Such a view, as both Anzaldúa and Alcoff propose, is not possible. Thus, put positively, Anzaldúa proposes autohistoria-teoría as a way to refer to the explicit task of developing theoretical resources out of descriptions of oneself and one's experiences. In this sense, speaking for oneself can extend toward others in ways that can be positive and conducive of further actions and forms of meaning-making.

Anzaldúa does not fully articulate the theoretical scope of the concept of autohistoria-teoría, but the practice of autohistoria-teoría is performatively demonstrated throughout her writings. As such, through analytic engagement with her earlier work, we can glean the collaborative, embodied, and productive features of what she names "autohistoria-teoría." For instance, in her 1987 essay, "*Tlilli, Tlapalli/* The Path of the Red and Black Ink," Anzaldúa states: "I write the myths in me, the myths I am, the myths I want to become. . . . Con imagenes domo mi miedo, cruzo los abismos que tengo por dentro" (Anzaldúa 1999, 93). In this statement, Anzaldúa notes the importance of creating stories that narrate one's life. Although other philosophers have examined narrative notions of identity, including, for example, Alasdair MacIntyre (1984) and Charles Taylor (1989), Anzaldúa provides an account of how to theorize collaboratively with others via one's articulation of the embodied experiences of one's own life. Because readers interpret their own embodied experiences and vulnerabilities through the narrator's descriptions, this serves as a collective form of meaning-making. In this sense, autohistoria-teoría enacts one of the lessons from Alcoff's essay, that is, that there "is no neutral place to stand free and clear in which one's words do not prescriptively affect or mediate the experience of others" (Alcoff 1991–92, 20). This idea, embraced by Anzaldúa as well, is used to develop epistemological resources for understanding how acts of self-writing are productive sites for communication with others.

Anzaldúa also describes what she would later refer to as auto-historia-teoría in her 1990 piece "To(o) Queer the Writer—Loca, escritura y chicana." She argues that the reader's interpretation within processes of reading and writing plays a central role in the production of knowledge and meaning: "More and more today the reader is becoming as important if not more important than the author. Making meaning is a collaborative affair. . . . This interaction comes with the realization that writing is a collaborative, communal activity not done in a room of one's own. It is an act informed and supported by the books the author reads, the people s/he interacts with, and the centuries of cultural history that seethe under her skin" (Anzaldúa 2009, 168). This account of the centrality of audience uptake presents a rich hermeneutical position on the distributive nature of knowledge-production and meaning-making practices. The epistemic and affective content of written and spoken works is considered "a collaborative affair" that develops in situ. Moreover, by referring to "the centuries of cultural history that seethe under [an author's] skin," Anzaldúa describes an interpretive and materially embedded horizon of meaning that constitutes the possibilities of meaning for a given text, performance, speech act, or action in general. Ruíz has called such maneuvers the "interpretive labors involved in being multiply situated" (Ruíz 2016, 429). Such labors are the polyphonic normative shifts that are enacted through the interpretive actions of multiplicitous agents.

As a demonstration of autohistoria-teoría, we also see in "To(o) Queer the Writer" that Anzaldúa's medium for theoretical articulation is a story about her own situated bodily experiences. For example, her comments about her readership are set in an essay that describes a first-personal account of delivering readings in the San Francisco Bay area. She describes different responses from her audiences and the manner in which differing constellations of identities among her audience members also position her own authorial self as a writer. Some audiences passively received her words, often, as she describes, expecting her words to fulfill certain expectations for them about a "Chicana" or "lesbian" author, but other audiences opened discursive and hermeneutical space in novel ways. She writes of specific audiences " 'reading' her readings," that is, maintaining a self-reflective awareness of her positioning as a queer woman of color invited to present her written work to them. She states: "Their faces were not blank nor passive. They saw me as vulnerable, a flesh-and-blood person and not as a symbol of representation, not as a 'Chicana writer.' They saw me as I wanted to be seen then—as an embodied symbol" (Anzaldúa 2009, 169). She remarks that although the majority of the audience were "white and colored hippies, straight beats and non-literary people," their mutual class backgrounds brought them together as reader-and-audience more than she had experienced with queer audiences and Chicana/o audiences in other readings in San Francisco (168). This is significant because it indicates that epistemic situatedness is not simply a cognitive feature of knowers. Against the isolationist patterns noted earlier, Anzaldúa's depiction of knowledge practices, including self-knowledge practices, are dependent on how we exist in the world as concretely embodied beings in relation to others.

In "To(o) Queer the Writer," Anzaldúa comments that "identity formation is a component in reading and writing whether through empathy and identification or through disidentification" (171). On this latter aspect of reading/writing, she writes, "Even if one notices things that are very different from oneself, that difference is used to form identity by negation—'I'm not that, I'm different from the character. This is me, that's you' " (171). Anzaldúa's description of reading and writing as processes of identity formation requires that we take into account the situated and embodied locations of audiences and readers. In her essay, this means that the class, sexual, and racial identities of her audiences affect whether and how they will understand and interpret her work. This is not a simple reduction to identity politics or a claim about a determinacy of reader reception. Rather, she argues that certain "sensibilities" allow readers to "fill in gaps" in her work. These gaps are hermeneutical possibilities made through "doors and windows" that a writer creates in her texts (171). This spatial metaphor, in addition to presenting writing as a sensuously embodied act, also supports an embodied account of reading, that is, a view that works against the image of a solitary reader who attempts to encounter a text abstractly. Prominent theorists of Spanish-language Latin American literature defend such a view of reading. For example, both Sylvia Molloy and Doris Sommer have argued in their respective works that cultural and historical trajectories that bring a reader to a text will shape how a reader encounters the possibilities for meanings in a text (Molloy 1991; Sommer 1999).[7] Whether a reader is invited in or kept at a distance through a text will vary depending on the social and historical location of the reader.

Adding to this point, we can draw from other readers of Anzaldúa to further interpret Anzaldúa's conception of self-writing as a kind of orientation. For example, readers of Anzaldúa such as Stephanie Rivera Berruz (2014, 27–28) have described how linguistic communication ought to be understood as "an orienting practice." By this, Rivera Berruz refers to the embodied practices and habits involved in speech communication, not simply the mouth, throat, and tongue, but also the use of arms and legs as modes of "expression and orientation" within spoken linguistic communicative practices (27–28). Such embodied movements depend on and engage social space, and she states that "we garner ways of being in social spaces by how our bodies are allowed to extend and interact with space" (27–28). Language as an orientation is thus a series of movements that extend across socio-materially rich spaces, interacting with others and offering normative terms by which others can orient themselves in response.

Rivera Berruz's insight echoes that of disability theorists who have critiqued the assumed centrality of spoken language, thereby neglecting or diminishing the significance of nonphonemic forms of communication. Regarding such embodied modes of communication, for example, Deaf studies scholars and artists such as Jolanta Lapiak and H-Dirksen L. Bauman have noted that phonocentrism and the primacy of audible speech over other forms of communication have contributed to the oppression of deaf communities worldwide (Lapiak 2010, 2007; Bauman 2004).[8] They argue that audism, "the discrimination against individuals based on hearing ability," signals the impermanence of meaning and the nonlinearity of nonphonemic forms of communication (Bauman 2004, 240). Thus, against views of lack or pathology that frame deafness, Bauman proposes that signed languages serve to "critique Western constructions of language and human identity" (244–245).

While we return to discussions of disability within the context of Anzaldúa's writings in chapter 4, for now we can note how Rivera Berruz's reading of language draws out significant embodied features of linguistic acts that resonate well with how Anzaldúa described linguistic communication. In reference to Anzaldúa's work to frame such interpretations of the politicized role of language and embodied orientation, other readers of Anzaldúa such as Monique Roelofs (2016) consider such orientations "addresses," and locate a rich series of insights within Anzaldúa (and Lugones) to support a theoretical framing of address. "Modes of address" are understood within Roelofs's work (2014, 2016, 2020), for example, as "multisensory forms of signification that we direct at human and non-human beings, objects, and places, and that these entities direct at us" (Roelofs 2016, 371). In this sense, Roelofs interprets Anzaldúa's interactions with "persons, objects, and places" as modes of address within her writings.

With these accounts of language shaping our interpretation of Anzaldúa, the account of multiplicitous agency developed in this book treats linguistic action as only one variation among the many materially embedded forms of normative and hermeneutic address possible. However, to avoid a stark dualism between language and embodied actions, we can thus interpret language via Anzaldúa as a sensually embodied series of acts that *address* or *orient* linguistic agents within their worlds of sense and meaning. Additionally, given functions of address from objects and places, this conception of linguistic orientation situates Anzaldúa's work within a broader relational ontology that fits well with the models of relational ontology developed by Anzaldúa scholars such as Keating, Zaytoun, and Henderson-Espinoza, as discussed in chapter 1. That is, like the "new animism" mentioned in Keating's interpretations of Anzaldúa (Keating, Zaytoun, and Dahms 2016), linguistic orientation is one mode of address, but objects similarly address language users as well. For example, focusing on Anzaldúa's modes of embodied orientation toward objects as a child, Roelofs notes that Anzaldúa's modes of address toward books, in particular, mark her as different from the relational modes of other girls and women in her life at the time

(2016, 372). Rather than ironing her brother's shirts or cleaning the kitchen cupboards, Anzaldúa constructs an orientation during childhood toward written words and reading that are derived from books and the sensuous materiality of language (372).

Building on Rivera Berruz's and Roelofs's work, we can glean that against a more abstract view regarding the aesthetic experience of written language, Anzaldúa's own orientation toward written language involved the addresses or orientations that the material media of written language direct toward readers as well. Namely, in "*Tlilli, Tlapalli*/The Path of the Red and Black Ink" from *Borderlands/La Frontera* (1987), Anzaldúa plays with Mexica/Aztec conceptions of storytelling, music, dance, and poetry to described her orientation toward the written word. She describes the storyteller as a "nahual"/"nagual," a shapeshifter or trickster figure who is the manifestation of processes of creative artistic expression (Anzaldúa 1999, 88). As Zaytoun notes, Anzaldúa referred to the *nahual* or "nagual/a" throughout her writings, including in her later works such as "now let us shift" (2002) and "Putting Coyolxauhqui Together: A Creative Process" (1999), as well as in a number of unpublished short stories (Zaytoun 2015, 2–3). In this same manner, from "*Tlilli/Tlapalli*: The Path of the Red and Black Ink," there are strong resonances with a Mexica/Aztec cosmology, including how creative practices in music making, storytelling, and dance are understood from within this worldview. That is, following Maffie's work, Nahua ontology, which is a broader term for a collection of Mesoamerican Indigenous groups that includes the Mexica/Aztec, is a monistic ontology that is based in *teotl* (Maffie 2008). Teotl, according to Maffie, is "a single, vivifying, eternally self-generating-and-self-conceiving as well as self-regenerating-and-self-reconceiving, sacred energy, power, or force" (98). Maffie proposes that, in English, we should consider teotl a verb, "as ever-flowing and ever-changing energy-in-motion rather than as a static entity or being" (98). Regarding this process, teotl is also an "artistic-creative process" and "the cosmos and its contents are teotl's ongoing work of performance" (102). Nahual, as the term for shapeshifter or *bruja*, is the disguise or shifted form of teotl. The appearance of the "thingness" of objects in the world as static entities is such a process of disguise or shifting form (102). Similarly, Maffie notes that teotl's mask or disguise, in this way, is an epistemological notion rather than an ontological one. The "illusion" of reality is not a metaphysical categorization (as it was for Plato, Maffie notes), but rather one regarding human perception and judgment, wherein we mistake the appearance of the staticness of things or of contradictions such as life/death, rather than the underlying dynamic process of teotl (103).

Connecting Anzaldúa's work to this worldview, she states in her account of writing in "*Tlilli/Tlapalli*: The Path of the Red and Black Ink" that she believes "in an ordered, structured universe where all phenomena are interrelated and imbued with spirit" (Anzaldúa 1999, 88). She follows this point by noting that her written work is a "dance" that has "a mind of its own . . . for me, it is alive, infused with spirit. I talk to it; it talks to me" (88–89). Bringing together Roelofs's framing of address and elements of Nahua metaphysics then creates an opening to interpret Anzaldúa's characterization of written acts as part of a creative process of becoming, whereby the author is addressed and oriented toward the material enactments of language.[9] Such enactments include, as she notes, "the smooth touch of the paper" and words as "blades of grass pushing past obstacles, sprouting on the page" (93). She describes writing as her "Aztecan blood sacrifices" and gestures made "in open-air places around the *xochicuahuitl, el Arból Florido*, Tree-in-Flower," which harkens to the name for Nahua poetry and artistic expression, "flower and song" (*xochitl* and *cuicatl*) (Anzaldúa 1999, 88; Maffie 2008, 112; Karttunen 1983, 329). As such, poetry as "in *xochitl*, in *cuicatl*" is an expression for the human understanding of teotl (Maffie 2008, 112). Additionally, "sacrifice" within such a worldview is a nonhierarchical ordering or rearrangement (Maffie 2014, 99–100). This allows us to reinterpret her conception of the "ordered, structured universe . . . imbued with spirit" (Anzaldúa 1999, 88). Anzaldúa appears to be referring to a notion akin to the human creative process of written expression as a material offering, "a blood sacrifice," in her words, that reorders and rearranges the material world to share in the unfolding nature of teotl (97). As we see echoed through readers such as Rivera Berruz and Roelofs, Anzaldúa conceives of writing as a collective process of material movement and interconnection, rather than an individualizing process of singular artistic genius.

Elsewhere, Anzaldúa refers specifically to self-writing through the notion of autohistoria-teoría, although self-writing too shares such notions of interconnection and movement. That is, with respect to the productive nature of autohistoria-teoría, in reference to public readings she conducted in San Francisco, the phrase "embodied symbol" appears to be an early articulation of what Anzaldúa calls in her later work "the Coyolxauhqui imperative." While we delve into this concept in further depth in chapter 4, put briefly, the Coyolxauhqui imperative is, for Anzaldúa, a call to "re-member" a self through narration. Drawing from a Mexica/Aztec creation story, she weaves images of the figure of Coyolxauhqui into her own self-narrations. The story of Coyolxauhqui tells of her body being torn apart by her brother, Huitzilopochtli, and being scattered down Coatepec, the sacred mountain temple. Lastly, her head was tossed into the sky to become the moon. I propose that we read the Coyolxauhqui imperative, one of the stages of conocimiento and illustrated through practices of autohistoria, as a desire for new personal and collective forms of self-knowledge. As mentioned above, in a rich demonstration of self-writing, "now let us shift" outlines the stages of conocimiento and this outward movement via a reflection on the author's personal experiences. The essay includes her reflections on the Loma Prieta earthquake that struck Northern California in 1989, on receiving a diagnosis of type I diabetes in 1992, and on the hysterectomy that she underwent in 1980 (among other events in her life). Throughout the essay, Anzaldúa writes of a process of dismembering and re-membering herself. She states of this desire for self-remembering, "As the modern-day Coyolxauhqui, you search for an account that encapsulates your life, and find no ready-made story, you trust her light in the darkness to help you bring forth (from remnants of the old personal/collective autohistoria) a new personal myth" (Anzaldúa 2009, 559–560). Harkening here to acts of myth-making, Anzaldúa emphasizes the terrifying process of re-membering one's personal and collective stories. She describes this "nueva historia" as resembling Mary "Shelley's Frankenstein monster" at first—"mismatched parts pieced together artificially" (561). However, such a figuration of oneself or others also "inspires" and prompts the narrator to engage "both inner and outer resources to make changes on multiple fronts: inner/spiritual/personal, social/collective/material" (561). Part of this transformational process requires confronting what she calls one's "shadow self," which includes one's own forms of ignorance and potential agential complicity with values and material processes that other interpretive aspects of oneself might not endorse. This confrontation, she states, offers a seeming paradox: "the knowledge that exposes your fears can also remove them" (Anzaldúa 2009, 553). In these senses, the Coyolxauhqui imperative marks both the creative and the painful side of autohistoria-teoría, both themes that we return to in chapter 4.

The kind of confrontation with one's own forms of ignorance and ways of self-knowing that Anzaldúa describes is an important point of convergence with what José Medina (2012) calls epistemic resistance. Epistemic resistance, in Medina's work, echoes Anzaldúa's distinction between "inner works" and "public acts," and her distinction between the "inner/spiritual/personal" and the "social/collective/material" (Anzaldúa 2009, 561). Medina argues that epistemic resistance appears in two forms, "internal" and "external," with two potential valences: positive and negative. Internal epistemic resistance comes from one's own cognitive resources. This appears to support a kind of isolationist locating of one's cognitive contents. Internal epistemic resources, in this sense, can be positive "insofar as it is critical, unmasks prejudices and biases, reacts to bodies of [one's own] ignorance, and so on" (Medina 2012, 50). Additionally, internal resistance may have a negative valence, wherein one's own "inner work" "involves a reluctance to learn or a refusal to believe" (50). External epistemic resistance is enacted from "outside" one's own cognitive and affective resources. In its positive valence, Medina calls epistemic resistance "beneficial epistemic friction," which is a form of resistance that forces one "to be self-critical to compare and contrast one's beliefs, to meet justificatory demands, to recognize cognitive gaps, and so on" (50). Beneficial friction would then be epistemic motivations that lead individuals and groups to reassess their own positions or views, to consider viewpoints that they do not hold, to attempt to defend or explain their own position in a way that others would understand better, or to recognize their own epistemic limitations and patterns of ignorance. Detrimental friction, however, can also be negative insofar as it "[censors, silences or inhibits] the formation of beliefs, the articulations of doubts, the formulation of questions and lines of inquiry, and so on" (50).

To connect Medina's theoretical resources to Anzaldúa, we can look at a series of examples of productive tensions illustrated in her autohistorias. For example, internal epistemic resistance in its positive valence echoes what Anzaldúa describes as the motivations that she attributes to herself in order to write. She states in "*Tlilli, Tlapalli*" that "to write, to be a writer, I have to trust and believe in myself as a speaker, as a voice for the images. I have to believe that I can communicate with images and words and that I can do it well" (Anzaldúa 1999, 95). This form of motivation or force acts as a self-critical assessment of one's own capacities as an author. As a form of "inner work," this requires confidence in one's own creative capacities as a writer, which are forms of self-confidence that are often discouraged for women of color. Consider on this point as well Patricia Hill Collins's description of Black women's forms of epistemic resistance: "Unlike the controlling images developed for middle-class White women, the controlling images applied to Black women are so uniformly negative that they almost necessitate resistance. For U.S. Black women, constructed knowledge of self emerges from the struggle to replace controlling images with self-defined knowledge deemed personally important, usually knowledge essential to Black women's survival" (Collins 2000, 100). Thus, positive internal epistemic friction is constituted by self-affirming forms of critical self-reflection, which, for many women of color, allow them to retain a self-attributed sense of epistemic stability and confidence. However, note, too, that against a dominant agential paradigm, such views of "internal" friction are not conducted in isolation from others. Rather, the generative sources of critical self-reflection are enacted through material engagements within a social and material world. These relations are the source of frictions and material interactions between self-descriptions and perceptual experiences. Anzaldúa's autohistoria-teoría emerges, then, from the processual interactions between self and world, rather than generating from one or the other source.

Furthermore, because many women of color are often denied the authority to determine the meanings of their own identities, epistemic friction can also be detrimental. For example, in "To(o) Queer the Writer," Anzaldúa discusses the way others understand her as an author. She discusses being labeled a "Chicana writer" and "a lesbian writer," and her own understanding of her identity as a writer, which rejects these two identity ascriptions (Anzaldúa 2009, 164). She defends her own authority to describe herself as a "Chicana, tejana, working-class, dyke-feminist poet, writer-theorist," but she rejects the normative impact of being labeled a "Chicana writer" or "lesbian writer" by others. She states that such labels "mark down" her identity. That is, she cannot be a writer, but must be marked as a nonstandard or "inferior" writer via gender and racial stereotypes and stigmas. In some cases, especially for persons who are members of historically oppressed groups, epistemic resistance from others can lead to self-doubt, shame, or political inaction.

In Anzaldúa's other writings, these themes of detrimental epistemic friction emerge from her discussions of the borderlands, the Coatlicue state, and nepantla. For example, nepantla can sometimes identify a "transitional temporal, spatial, psychic and/or intellectual point of crisis," often signaling moving from self-doubt to conviction and conocimiento (Anzaldúa 2009, 322). Also present in her earlier and later writings, the Coatlicue state refers to "a prelude to crossing" from mictlan—the Aztec underworld—to new forms of consciousness (Anzaldúa 1999, 70). The "descent into mictlan" is brought about by "[our] resistance, [our] refusal to know some truth about [ourselves that] brings on that paralysis, depression, brings on the Coatlicue state" (70). She writes that once in this state of inaction and despair, "every increment of consciousness, every step forward is a travesía, a crossing. . . . Knowledge makes me more aware, it makes me more conscious. 'Knowing' is painful because after 'it' happens I can't stay in the same place and be comfortable. I am no longer the same person I was before" (70). These descriptions of the movement into the Coatlicue state, the descent into mictlan, and the path toward new forms of consciousness can be used as theoretical bridges to both her later notion of conocimiento in the early 2000s and to the task of theorizing through the notion of autohistoria-teoría. The path to conocimiento expands the travesía that she begins to theorize in *Borderlands/La Frontera*, and provides an account that converges with her later claims of theorizing via acts of self-narration. That is, the descent into mictlan, the first stage, is brought about by a "refusal to know some truth about [oneself]" (70). In this vein, the source for the self-doubt and the epistemic withdrawal will determine the location of the feeling of resistance. Moreover, the pain that she describes with every step highlights forms of resistance that allow or disallow one from learning about oneself or from learning from others.

Finally, in such painful confrontations with one's own ignorance, we can also locate her position on shared forms of epistemic responsibility, a theme that emerges in various forms in feminist philosophy (for example, Young 2006, 2011; Medina 2012). For example, in "Let Us Be the Healing of the Wound: The Coyolxauhqui Imperative—la sombra y el sueno," the last piece published by Anzaldúa during her lifetime, the author writes of the attack on the World Trade Center in New York City on September 11, 2001: "The day the towers fell, me sentí como Coyolxauhqui, la luna. Algo me agarro y me sacudio, frightening la sombra (soul) out of my body. . . . Wounded, I fell into shock, cold and clammy . . . suspended in limbo in that in-between space, nepantla, I wandered through my days on autopilot, feeling disconnected from the events of my life" (Anzaldúa 2009, 303). Here, she harkens back to her descriptions in 1987 of "[un] susto [when] the soul [is] frightened out of the body," and such an event is what she describes as leading to the descent to mictlan (Anzaldúa 1999, 70). Interestingly, following from this form of external, detrimental epistemic friction, we see her defend a notion of shared epistemic responsibility. She writes of her desire to speak out to condemn the United States' "act of war" and to situate herself against the United States. Yet she also writes that "sadly we are all accomplices . . . As an artist I feel compelled to expose this shadow side which the mainstream media and government denies. In order to understand our complicity and responsibility we must look at the shadow" (Anzaldúa 2009, 304). Here, readers can note that Anzaldúa does not excuse herself from responsibility for the United States' military actions, a point we return to in chapter 3 through a discussion of ambiguity. Rather, in this piece, her last and perhaps most explicitly engaged piece of writing on transnational politics, she proposes a distributed form of epistemic responsibility that demonstrates beneficial epistemic friction for her readers. The events of 9/11 led her to interrogate and to express her own relationship to the actions of the United States government. Such events are indicative for her of "our collective shadow" (311). "Our collective shadow" symbolizes the historical violence and fragmentation that, she claims, we are all now called to confront and to re-member. The Coyolxauhqui imperative is both her symbol for a necessary process of "dismemberment and fragmentation" and for "reconstruction and reframing" (312). However, as she states, "there is never any resolution, just the process of healing" (312). The process of healing that is called forth through practices of autohistoria involves creating new personal and collective narratives that can render one's experiences meaningful and transformational. Developing new forms of autohistoria is presented as a difficult task, and one that involves critically interrogating one's own social position within embedded frameworks of meaning and knowledge production. Perhaps more important, as she asserts in "To(o) Queer the Writer," it also includes searching for communities and hermeneutical resources to make sense of one's own experiences and responsibilities. The practice of "putting Coyolxauhqui together," she states, "represents the search for new metaphors to tell you what you need to know, how to connect and use the information gained, and, with intelligence, imagination, and grace, solve your problems and create intercultural communities" (Anzaldúa 2009, 563). These practices emerge via the forms of autohistoria that she describes, and require an interpretive community that can collaboratively render such experiences and forms of knowledge meaningful.

Autohistoria-teoría thus highlights several important features of epistemic agency regarding self-knowledge/ignorance. It foregrounds the fundamental interdependency between authors/speakers and readers/audiences that is necessary for any form of self-knowledge/ignorance to emerge. For feminist epistemologists like Medina and Lorraine Code (1991), for example, this might be interpreted as a description of the kind of nurturing environment that is necessary for an individual to develop a notion of selfhood. As we considered earlier with respect to the "nepantla brain," Code (1991, 82) claims that moral and epistemic agency relies on a "communal basis of moral and mental activity." This does not mean merely an abstract reference to others as objects of moral or epistemic analysis. Rather, it means that agency itself, that is, the very enabling conditions of our actions and judgments, must be based on the relationships that we have with others.

In addition, forms of cognitive, affective, and embodied transformation, including attempts to re-member one's own story and self, require taking epistemic risks. This means that knowers/readers should be able to face that they may be mistaken about their beliefs about themselves and about others. Or, as Anzaldúa states, they must be able to confront their desconocimiento and shadow sides. Accordingly, as many women of color theorists have argued, given different relations of power under conditions of structural injustice, some persons will find themselves confronted with self-doubt and detrimental epistemic friction quite often, while other, more privileged groups and individuals may be afforded ample forms of epistemic security and confidence. An awareness of how a self or others might be vulnerable to structural harms can bear on how a particular re-membering of self may be interpreted.

Anzaldúa suggests that the process of writing, including writing collective stories through autohistoria, effectively hails an audience and potentially dismisses others. Autohistoria-teoría makes this claim explicit via the proposal that writing about oneself provides the theoretical tools for others to critically interrogate their positions and the world. This would also then include the orienting or disorienting hails that might compel a reader to critically assess her/his/their own epistemic positionality and responsibility. However, as Sara Ahmed and others have pointed out, disorientation work "is not always radical . . . the forms of politics that proceed from disorientation can be conservative, depending on the 'aims' of their gestures, depending on how they seek to (re)ground themselves" (Ahmed 2006, 158). Thus, the forms of epistemic responsibility and action made possible through Anzaldúa's writings should not be considered a determinate grounding for normative action or without their ambivalences, a theme I address in the following chapter. Rather, autohistoria-teoría is a critical call to interrogate ourselves via the normative resistance that her views create. What follows from her account and from my elaboration of her views is that judgments of self-credibility, self-orientation, and self-worth are always subject to resistance and criticism from others. This is because, as Code notes, even our capacities to carry out such activities are premised on the social character of knowledge that makes these practices meaningful.

Accordingly, this means that our judgments of others, including credibility assessments, judgments of merit, and so on, require that we self-reflectively mirror back to ourselves our own situatedness as judges, that is, we must read ourselves as readers, to extend Anzaldúa's phrase. This requires that self-knowledge, like all forms of knowledge, is subject to political and social forms of critique. Privilege, subjugation, and resistance function with respect to our abilities to know ourselves and others. Although such an epistemic position cannot normatively map out the ways in which we ought to act in a given situation, it does prescriptively call us to remain attentive to the groups of *nos*/us and *otras*/others in which we find our own self-understandings made available. In the next chapter, we thus confront what such forms of ambivalence entail.

Chapter 3

Turning Ambivalence into Something Else

Stemming from our previous discussion of Anzaldúa's collective, distributed, and interdependent conception of living and acting "in a pluralistic mode," I begin to unpack in this chapter what Anzaldúa means by developing "a tolerance for ambiguity" (Anzaldúa 1999, 101). In *Borderlands/La Frontera*, for example, the author explicitly notes that "rigidity means death" and that shifting from positions of ambivalence is crucial for the forms of collective and personal transformation that she associates with mestiza consciousness (101). She writes in this text, however, that she is "not sure exactly how" the new mestiza "can be jarred out of ambivalence" (101). Yet she notes that this may occur via "an intense, and often painful, emotional event which inverts or resolves the ambivalence" (101). To understand this process of transformation and the potential "inversion" or "resolution" of ambivalence, we turn more directly to this process in this chapter. Additionally, given that Anzaldúa's work appears to prioritize analysis of forms of collective meaning-making and explorations into how divisive norms/practices may cleave apart struggles against oppression, this chapter also turns to questions of how the meanings of actions—or the reasons we attribute to individual and collective agents—may be interpreted through an Anzaldúan multiplicitous lens. Specifically, I begin to work out questions regarding *reasons for action* or the *meaningfulness* of action within a broader coalitional dialogue within strands of Black feminism and critical philosophy of race. To underscore the stakes of coalition building across "nondominant differences," as I mentioned in the introduction,

I turn to two theorists whose work has addressed why agential motivations are of particular concern to theorists and practitioners interested in dismantling structural oppressions. More specifically, I take up an argument proposed in 2002 by Leonard Harris regarding what he describes as *insurrectionist ethics*, and I ask how Anzaldúan multiplicitous agency can be read as a coalitional praxis of such insurrectionism. To tighten the connections with Harris's work in critical philosophy of race, I also examine an augmented version of insurrectionist ethics provided by Black feminist philosopher Kristie Dotson that demonstrates how Dotson's work illuminates a method for understanding the generative potential within ambivalence, a theme that we find throughout Anzaldúa's corpus.

To clarify these claims, in this chapter I first outline Harris's account of insurrectionist ethics. Then I underscore Dotson's modification of a new condition of an insurrectionist ethics in an effort to begin to link Dotson's and Harris's work to a Latinx feminist conception of multiplicitous agency. To make these connections, I propose that we do not directly turn to Anzaldúa at first, but rather to María Lugones, a careful reader of her work. In this, we find a common discourse among Harris, Dotson, and Lugones that focuses on the construction of judgments that explain reasons for action. Thus, to conclude, I then place Lugones's central claims back in conversation with Anzaldúa's political writings to show how Anzaldúa's work bolsters important connections between Black and Latinx framings of resistance and solidarity.

Insurrectionist Ethics and Agency

To begin to frame the generative potential of ambivalence, we can turn to a debate within critical philosophy of race regarding normative framings of insurrectionist acts. Notably, Leonard Harris's pivotal essay "Insurrectionist Ethics: Advocacy, Moral Psychology, and Pragmatism" (2002) provides a set of standards addressed to U.S. philosophers that seek to develop novel frameworks that uphold a normative demand that resistance to slavery is morally meritorious. Harris's argument traces acts of rebellion among African American abolitionists in the antebellum South, as well as acts of opposition to slavery by white abolitionists during that same period. As we see below, one relevant facet of Harris's account with respect to its connections to Anzaldúan multiplicitous agency involves the functions of what he calls "representative heuristics." That is, Harris proposes that insurrectionist acts often involve the utilization of identity categories by insurrectionist agents that the agents themselves may seek to overturn. For example, Maria W. Stewart and David Walker, both born free people of color, developed narrative voices that identified their respective goals with the overturning of U.S. racial slavery. These goals entailed the elimination of categories such as "slave," "slaveholder," and all other administrative and legal apparatuses that supported the institution of slavery. Specifically, Harris notes that they each harnessed "a sense of identity" or collective "we" in their respective writings that directed their normative demands within a group dynamic that called for the transvaluation and transformation of the extant racial categories that existed during their lifetimes.

Regarding representative heuristics more directly, Harris appears to develop the term, in part, from the work of another important African American philosopher, Alain Locke (1885–1954), including, most notably, Locke's 1916 lectures at Howard University. Locke played an large influential role on Harris's work more generally, as Harris is an avid reader of Locke's work and was largely responsible for reintroducing Locke within Anglophone academic philosophy in the United States (Harris 1989, 1997, 1999; Harris and Molesworth 2008; Carter and Harris 2010). This history within African American philosophy is relevant in that we can find detailed dialogue among philosophers of color in the United States focusing on practices of community survival and valuation, including discussions of how identity-related claims play a role within practices of resistance. With respect to representative heuristics, in particular, we can find resonances of Harris's view with that of Locke's through Locke's analysis of "civilization types." Specifically, regarding the 1916 Howard lectures, Harris writes with Charles Molesworth (2008) that Locke considered racial groups and their values as "best understood as represented by a 'civilization type'" (Harris and Molesworth 2008, 122). This term, drawing from the works of Georg Simmel and Alexander Crummell, refers to a kind of ideal that arises from the cultural exchanges among differing races or social groups (Stewart 1992, xxxi). Within this ideal, races and social groups maintain their identifications and cultural specificity, as Locke rejected the assimilation of nondominant groups under a dominant model (Stewart 1992, xxxi). "Representative classes" or "representative types" would thereby provide a way to preserve the distinctiveness of groups in the face of potential erasure under assimilation. Harris and Molesworth write in this regard, "Locke believed that group identity was inevitable, and the only way to manage it was to make it possible to have groups offer reciprocal tolerance to each other and for each to encapsulate its values into a representative type" (2008, 125). This form of representative type seems to play a pivotal role in Harris's framing of the importance of representative heuristics. An insurrectionist ethics appears to reframe the focus of Locke's critical insight regarding group solidarity, and Harris continues to explore the need for aesthetic and conceptual representatives of social groups that are necessary for the preservation of group cohesion, valuation, and meaning.

This is relevant for our purposes here in that understanding group solidarity requires a closer examination of how and under what terms members of differing racial, class, sexual, and gender groups can seek to understand one another in their efforts to collectively resist forms of oppression. In particular, Harris's views on telos, history, and social agency are relevant in this regard. He states in "The Horror of Tradition or How to Burn Babylon and Build Benin While Reading *A Preface to a Twenty-Volume Suicide Note*" (1992–93) that his own view "resonate[s] with the politicized side of [an] invention approach to the history of traditions; it holds, in general, that traditions are historical constructions" (Harris 1992–93, 98). Within this approach, Harris includes the work of contemporary philosopher V. Y. Mudimbe, a Congolese theorist whose work Harris contrasts with that of the nineteenth-century writings by Edward W. Blyden on the role of an underlying telos or structure of history. Notably, Harris writes that "Blyden's *Christianity, Islam, and the Negro Race* [1887] has an appeal that V. Y. Mudimbe's *The Invention of Africa* [1988] does not" (106). That is, Blyden's work renders sacrificial actions for future generations as "primordial and providential," while "the nexus Mudimbe provides is accidental, contrived, alien, and the consequence of adaptations to force" (106). In this sense, Harris notes the tremendous appeal that a providential or historicist view, like that of Blyden, provides. Yet he locates his own position within that of Mudimbe's (and arguably Locke's) whereby "living persons in a multiplicity of associations and networks participate in the shaping and reshaping their being, individual and social. . . . Persons share in a common nature as transvaluing social agents bonding through fluid forms of social identity" (106). Elsewhere, in another essay examining the role of telos in history through an analysis of Blyden, Harris echoes the point above, stating that "there is no Blyden-type intrinsic logic of history, one that assures regeneration, redemption, vindication, and self-realization as a function of unchanging natures or an imagined destiny" (Harris 2014, 65). Thus, Harris's writings support a view of history as committed to the struggles and solidarity of African and Afrodiasporic peoples, but he also asserts that these ends occur through the social agency, pluralism, and creative capacities of diverse groups that do not share an underlying "logic," "nature," or "destiny."

This point, then, reframes Harris's commitments to what he describes as representative heuristics in "Insurrectionist Ethics: Advocacy, Moral Psychology, and Pragmatism" (2002). In that essay (as Dotson highlights in her response to his essay), "there are no revolutions or insurrections without representative heuristics, that is, without women who see themselves as representing 'women' as an objective category; without persons who see themselves as representing the interests of the poor; without workers who see themselves as the embodiment of meritorious traits; without environmentalists who see themselves as pressing for the best interests of all sentient beings by pressing for the interests of environmentalists" (Harris 2002, 202). Here, Harris draws from a strand of naturalized epistemology to argue that acting on behalf of some cause involves a form of "representing" that cause. Yet what is meant by "representing" in this case is unclear, and Harris poses such a challenge to his contemporaries. Namely, he appears to be seeking support for the commitment that giving meaning and "cause to a willingness to sacrifice for future generations and defend African peoples" is morally justified, but it does not require an underlying essence or intrinsic quality of any sort. That is, "representative heuristics" appears as a proposal for philosophers in the twenty-first century to develop framings of agency, institutional organization, historiography, and so on that honor the commitments that oppressed peoples have to eradicating the terms and sometimes peoples who are oppressing them. Yet, against figures like Blyden, who argue that such "representatives [are] living vessels, and sacrificial vassals for a future as conceived by the dead or living imaginations," Harris turns to Lockean notions of instrumentalism, pluralism, and contingency among resistant struggles.

Under such an account, Locke's conception of "civilization types," as a form of "consciousness of kind" or "a sense of kind belonging" whereby individuals consider themselves as members of social groups, appears relevant (Harris 1997, 244). Locke, as Harris explains in a 1997 essay, believed that such inclinations for "kind-belonging" or community identity were "healthy, natural, normal, and an instinct that may go astray" (224). That is, while identifying with one's race, nation, or class may arise from an inclination, such inclinations are not "intrinsic to a given group" (245). They are, rather, contingent social constructions that arise through cultural exchanges (245). As Harris puts it, "The relationship between a social group and a kind consciousness is thus asymmetrical; the first is contingent on the second but the second is neither contingent nor causal of the first" (245.). In this framing, when consciousness of kind or forms of identification are viewed as "permanent and invariable" this is when such inclinations may, in Harris's words, "go astray" (244).

Thus, representative heuristics, when read through this Lockean lens, entail that what is "represented" by insurrectionist agents when acting on behalf of a given social group is not the reification of some naturalized ontology. Social identities are not images or depictions of underlying permanent features or shared characteristics. Rather, as Harris writes in "Insurrectionist Ethics," "representative heuristics is replete with inferential problems. . . . Some of the classical ways that representative heuristics is used in relation to racial and ethnic stereotyping include metonymic displacement, metaphysical condensation, fetishistic categorizing, and dehistoricizing allegories that strip the racial or ethnic category from being understood as a historically changing group. Representative heuristics is often a way of reifying the subject" (Harris 2002, 197). Here, similar to his discussion of the "going astray" of Lockean consciousness of kind, Harris directs our attention to epistemological views regarding group- and individual-identification that can also go astray. However, such forms of thinking are, nonetheless, helpful and thereby "inform [us of] what sorts of categories we live through and how those categories inform our lived experience" (198). This view, then, in the 2002 essay on insurrectionist ethics, includes Locke's own quest to end "limiting and provincial identities of segregated communities" that would eventually open up to a "broader identity of humanity; a broader identity that would be mediated by local identities with much less meaning and stability than existed in human history" (198). Such a view in Harris, as we see in the final section of this chapter and elsewhere in the book, appears to be quite congruent with the questioning of identity categories that Anzaldúa offered throughout her writings. That is, a concept like nos/otras notes the relevance of forms of identification, but also the provisional status of identification terms and their significance within our struggles against systemic injustices.

Digging deeper into the implications of Harris's commitments to such a nonessentialist form of resistance, Dotson (2013) further examines the functions of representative heuristics in Harris's account, and she asks how interpreters of insurrectionist acts can re-create the patterns of resistance of insurrectionist agents. Drawing on resistant acts that produce ambivalence regarding the social categories and precise conditions that demand transvaluation and transformation, Dotson adds an additional criterion to Harris's account. She augments his approach by adding a new condition to an insurrectionist ethics: "the ability to provoke when necessary the epistemic demand to situate oppression so as to better approximate the bonds of oppression and the range of oppressors that one faces" (2013, 89). Dotson's addition to Harris's account is meant to provide a framework that addresses the contextually complex ways in which people and groups confront multiple forms of oppression. As we will see below, Dotson's added criterion brings to light important features of Harris's views about insurrection and normativity: that both oppression and resistance are the result of multiplicitous forms of agency, a view that links us directly to those of Latinx feminists like Lugones and Anzaldúa.

From her reading of Harris's work, Dotson distills four main criteria for an insurrectionist ethics:

1. The ability to render insurrectionist acts as moral duties (193–194).

2. The ability to render acts of representing, defending, or promoting just causes meritorious (192).

3. The ability to demonstrate the moral importance of the exercise of broad instrumental reasoning (202–203).

4. The ability to detect the importance of social, self-
identity that is representative and, often, transvalued
for moral motivation (198). (Dotson 2013, 76)

Dotson points out that for a theory to meet conditions 2–4 most
likely entails that that theory meets condition 1, and renders insurrectionist acts moral duties. For the purposes of this chapter, it is
important to highlight just a few salient points regarding an analysis
of multiplicitous agency. Namely, an Anzaldúan approach to multiplicitous agency already endorses criteria 1–2 as part of a coalitional
project with nondominant groups in struggle against oppression. In
fact, despite Anzaldúa's critiques of representationalism mentioned
in chapter 2 (found in her unpublished writings on Althusser, for
example), the precise points through which her readers can develop
her account of agency are often through acts of "representing,
defending, or promoting" just causes. This requires, namely, that
we connect Harris's notion of "representative heuristics" within our
broader commitments in the book to multiplicitous agency without
reifying isolationism, insularity, and individualism.

To expand these points, consider Dotson's elaborations of criteria
3–4, which bring out important features of an insurrectionist ethics
that will help support an account of multiplicitous agency. Namely,
Dotson states that insurrectionist ethics demonstrate the moral importance of broad instrumental reasoning. Dotson distinguishes broad
instrumental reasoning from narrow instrumental reasoning in order
to accommodate one of the requirements of Harris's proposal for an
insurrectionist ethics. Harris states the following from which Dotson
draws her distinction: "The unpredictability of outcomes does not
stand as a sufficient reason to defeat the justification that oppressed
individuals or groups can offer for pursuing instrumentally useful
paths. There is no human progress without the discord of social
conflict, insurrections, and revolutions. These are instrumental social
actions. The outcomes are uncertain" (Harris 2002, 203). For Harris, the criteria for an insurrectionist act are not its success, either in
the short term or long term. Thus, it cannot be a criterion to have
predictable outcomes and effectiveness in order for an act to serve as
a morally justified act. Narrow instrumental reasoning, Dotson states,
is a common feature of moral theories, wherein a moral agent acts
according to predictable outcomes and to the likely effectiveness of

one's actions. However, this is insufficient to justify insurrectionist acts for which, for example, the abolition of slavery did not occur, or for which the destruction of one's oppressor was not successful. In such cases, both Harris's position and Dotson's reiteration of this criterion want to take into account the meritorious features of acts of insurrection that were seemingly futile, ineffective, and, yet, nonetheless morally justified and praiseworthy.

Dotson's means for accounting for such acts is to restate the form of reasoning used in insurrectionist acts as "broad instrumental reasoning": "Broad instrumental reasoning does not provide a decision-making procedure based upon a specific problem, with a presumably specific solution or set of solutions whose outcomes will be predictably effective. Rather, broad instrumentalism takes into consideration historical observations of change. . . . If human progress is contingent upon social conflict, then the goal of insurrectionist acts, as acts of social conflict, is human progress whether that end is immediately achieved or not" (Dotson 2013, 78). Dotson's claim is that instrumental reasoning need not limit one to the efficaciousness possible within the parameters of one action or even within one's own lifetime. Rather, "historical observations of change" shift the scope of an individual or group's relevant considerations for means-ends reasoning (78). This is important, because as I discuss below, if we propose that Anzaldúa's conception of multiplicitous agency counts as upholding relevant forms of meritorious insurrectionist acts, such acts need not have narrow instrumental efficacy as a criterion for being morally justified and praiseworthy.

I would also like to highlight criterion 4, in which Dotson goes to great lengths to elaborate and explain its insufficiency for understanding what she describes as *internally generated* forms of ambivalence within insurrectionist acts. Recall that criterion 4 states the following for an insurrectionist ethics: it must offer "the ability to detect the importance of social, self-identity that is representative and, often, transvalued for moral motivation" (Harris 2002, 198). For Harris, this means that a moral agent must use representative heuristics as a means by which the agent makes a claim or commits an act in the service of some representative group (e.g., an act for enslaved Black peoples) or against some other representative group (e.g., against slaveholders). While Harris duly notes that it is often the case that representative heuristics can serve as a means to oppress peoples (e.g., stereotyping and profiling), for an insurrectionist ethics, this form of heuristics is important, as representative heuristics also preserves group identification and forms of solidarity. This can be through self-identification and other-identification within some description, or this can mean identification with a broader humanity that demands justice of the sort sought by the insurrectionist agent. Moreover, representative heuristics can also mean identification with a group that the agent may wish to destroy, for example, self-identification as an enslaved person. This kind of representative heuristic includes a condition for transvaluing the category of which one is a member—that is, seeking to transform and revalue a given category. Harris states on this matter that insurrectionists often reject "block universals, absolutes, and arid abstractions" and often work to prevent "treating abstract social entities as stable categories" (198). On this reading, Harris argues that self-identity becomes a form of both transvaluation and being "representative of a kind—if the category that one understands oneself to be representing is a category that one is seeking to destroy" (198). Drawing from Jacoby Adeshei Carter's work (2012) on the notion of transvaluation also developed through the work of Locke, Dotson states that "the transvaluation of representative identities, then, allows for the ability to accept, at one time, a specific social identity, while simultaneously accepting the importance of the dissolution of that very identity" (79).

This notion of identity is relevantly linked to what is described within Latina feminist philosophers as a multiplicitous self. In Anzaldúa's writings, for example, this form of heuristic transvaluation is described through the notion of *nepantla* whereby the act of crossing conceptual and material terrain becomes a crucial site of transformation. That is, as we discussed through her elaboration of autohistoria-teoría in the previous chapter, even self-descriptions are multiplicitous invitations to others that seek collaboration and critical engagement. For our purposes here, we can extend this idea of transformation to the transvaluation of "representative" identities. Namely, there are some acts that both show that the agent and her/his/their community are attempting to transform prior forms of meaning and reference for identity terms and categories and offering new modes of engagement for others to take up these terms. For example, the use of terms like "Latinx," "Latin@," and "Latines," which have been used to modify gendered terms like "Latino" or "Latina" and to describe persons of Latin American descent in the United States, are ways of seeking to provide novel modes of engagement and identification. That is, given the gendered language of the masculine *Latino* and the feminine *Latina*, the term "Latinx" has circulated over the last decade or so to mark a nonbinary or gender-neutral term for persons of Latin American descent living in the United States. The term is also attempting to provide a linguistic act that can normatively include transgender and gender variant persons of Latin American descent who reject a gender binary. Latinx as a term for nonbinary persons who identify as people of Latin American descent becomes a way to note the normative aim to decenter binary gender references for persons descended from Latin American communities, a point to which I return in the closing chapter.[1]

As I also discuss in the closing chapter of the book, within Anzaldúa's writings the author was consistently urging her readers of the insufficiency of given identity terms, which itself expresses the provisional status and desire for transvaluation of identity categories in Anzaldúa's work. In "The New Mestiza Nation," Anzaldúa describes the *nagual* as "a shapeshifter . . . we shift around to do the work we have to do, to create identities we need to live up to our potential" (Anzaldúa 2009, 211). She states that she uses this term to "refer to a person who is changing identity" (211). However, the possibility for such transformations in the service of eradicating oppressions requires that, theoretically, philosophers of agency must find tools to reinterpret the insurrectionist potential within our actions and those of others in struggle. To clarify these matters, we can look further at Dotson's analysis of insurrectionist ethics.

One of the significant amendments to Harris's argument that Dotson offers is a distinction that helps sharpen our analytic focus on his Standard 4. The distinction is between *externally* generated ambivalence and *internally* generated ambivalence. Dotson offers this distinction to address the ability to detect social identities that are "representative" of a group or, at times, in the name of a common humanity. She raises this distinction because the process of linking insurrectionist acts with social identities is important for determining the morally meritorious features of an act. Namely, acts of violent resistance, for example, require more than an understanding of the motivation of causing harm (i.e., for the sake of harm alone). Such acts also require what Dotson calls "a logic of violent resis-

tance . . . to adjudicate, often predictable, responses of ambivalence"
(Dotson 2013, 80). Here, the locus of the ambivalence becomes
significant. In an example provided by Dotson, non-slaveholding
whites may be killed during an insurrectionist uprising held by
enslaved people seeking to end the bonds of their oppression. In
the case of externally generated ambivalence, there are contingent
social factors that give rise to an ambivalence about an insurrectionist
act. As Dotson states, there is "a clash between particular lifestyle
choices, i.e. non-slaveowning, white people, and the broader social
context, where all white people are potential slaveowners" (80–81).
Individual "lifestyle choices" do not change the broader existing
social contexts in which oppression exists (80). She notes that while
specific "lifestyle choices can . . . invoke ambivalence to violent
acts . . . this ambivalence is external to such logics of resistance"
(81). This description means that the locus of ambivalence is a society
that permits the social oppression of one group over another. Thus,
whether a potential oppressor engages in an oppressive act or not is
a contingent feature of factors external to the possible meaningful
motivations of the insurrectionist agent. Dotson writes on this point:
"The motivation for such acts lies largely in the social identities of
the oppressed population resisting and the social identities of the
oppressor population who are a threat to the liberation of the relevant oppressed population" (79). Here, the social identity of the
oppressors and oppressed groups is crucial for meeting the standards
of insurrectionist ethics. In this case, "representative" heuristics that
locate oppressing groups and oppressed groups is one way to attempt
to locate the site of externally generated ambivalence.

Internally generated ambivalence, however, does require an
instability of meaning regarding the motivations within a given logic
of resistance, and the heuristics of the insurrectionist agent engaged
in struggle require some further analytic attention. The example that
Dotson analyzes in relation to Harris's account of insurrectionist
ethics is the 1856 case of Margaret Garner and the representative
heuristics involved in Garner's killing of her infant daughter. While
seeking passage on the Underground Railroad, and upon being sur-
rounded by an armed white mob in a house outside of Cincinnati,
Ohio, Garner kills her youngest daughter rather than allow her to
be returned to slavery. A trial ensued upon the capture of Garner,

and she was eventually remanded back to slavery. Garner's case is discussed at length in Dotson's piece and the essay offers a study of the conditions of Garner's life during this period and the legal trial that followed her capture in Ohio. Dotson argues that Harris must add a fifth criterion to an insurrectionist moral theory to interpret the complexity of this historical event and Garner's action. The main concern highlighted by Garner's act for Dotson is that killing one's child points to what she calls an "internally generated ambivalence":

> The ambivalence that characterizes infanticide is far more difficult to reconcile given [that Garner's] resistance could have taken a number of forms, which some will judge preferable to infanticide, presumably, *according to her very self-identification*, e.g. according to a mother's duty to protect the lives of her innocent children or a parent's obligation. I call this form of ambivalence "internally generated ambivalence." Internally generated ambivalence refers to negative affective responses to deep inconsistencies in real or imagined causal links between one's actions and one's motives for acting, i.e. one's logic of violent resistance. That is to say, the sense of being torn in one's judgments of infanticide follows from the inconsistent ways one can cast the motives for killing one's children that renders such motives, at best, spurious, and, at worse, exceedingly thoughtless. (Dotson 2013, 87)

The concern here is that the representative heuristics of Garner as an enslaved Black mother make it difficult to judge that her act was aimed solely at the destruction of her oppressor or the bonds of her oppressor. If we interpret Garner as an enslaved Black person, this act could be aimed at the overthrow of the bonds of oppression of slaveholders, and the destruction of slaveholding conditions. Dotson states, however, that this is not the only characterization of Garner that we could offer. She writes against this narrow interpretation: "Garner is more than a black slave. She is also a mother and a woman. Garner is [a] slave mother. And though I can certainly conceive of her hoping for the end of the category 'slave,' 'slave mother,' and, quite possibly, 'black,' I wonder if it is reasonable to impute upon

her the hope for the end of the categories 'woman' or 'mother'"
(86). Thus, this kind of ambivalence creates a limitation for Harris's
initial articulation. Dotson thereby adds a fifth criterion that is
interchangeable with the fourth, that "any moral theory that does
not include an epistemic demand to identify the situated oppression
to which insurrectionist acts are likely responding will not have an
adequate conception of the range of morally relevant insurrectionists
acts" (88). She thus proposes that an insurrectionist ethics must
also have "Standard 5: The ability to provoke when necessary the
epistemic demand to situate oppression so as to better approximate
the bonds of oppression and the range of oppressors one faces"
(89). Understanding Garner's decision to kill her infant daughter
tracks the violence done to enslaved women who were forced to rear
children that they knew would be vulnerable to sexual assault and
exploitation, resentment and violence from white women and men,
and the eventual requirement to birth and rear children who would
be subject to the same cycles of racial violence and degradation. In
this sense, without a multiplicitous interpretation of oppression and
the "range of oppressors" that one faces, Harris's framing of an
insurrectionist ethics cannot easily accommodate acts that generate
such forms of "internal" ambivalence.

With respect to Dotson's augmentation of Harris's work, this also
means that representative heuristics, on its own, is not sufficient to
determine whether one's act is done for reactionary or self-interested
reasons, or rather is done in the name of long-term goals through
which one hopes to effect change. Often, the motives for one's
acts are ambiguous, unable to be made intelligible, and, at times,
an agent may be reduced by others as merely seeking self-interested
or seemingly unreasonable ends rather than furthering the goals of
a group that is calling for justice. However, understanding the normative facets of action actually helps shed light on *how* agents may
seek the "destruction of one's oppressor and the bonds of one's
oppressor" by examining the further methods by which ambivalence
shapes our material lives and public space. In this, we turn in the
following section to reconstructions of the motivations of agents
that seek to honor the multiplicity and potentiality for broad forms
of instrumental reasoning that might help locate an agent's actions
within a morally meritorious history of resistance.

Resistant Reconstructions and Ambivalence

From the reading above, Dotson's distinction between internal/ external ambivalence need not track individualistic, isolationist, insular, or imperialist tropes. That is, Dotson appears to be describing the means used to construct *moral* claims, rather than *ontological* claims regarding the existence of differing individual intentions or structural mechanizations. Dotson points to differing sites whereby questions regarding the reasons for actions or the interpretive possibilities we might create for actions arise. It may be that Dotson, like Anzaldúa, uses representationalist language in her descriptions of "interiority" and "exteriority"; however, we need not retain this reading to support how such interpretive lenses operate in relation to the account of multiplicitous agency we are developing here. To support such a reading, I suggest that we turn to a careful reader of Anzaldúa to discern how such an account of multiplicitous reconstructions of moral reasoning might develop. Namely, Lugones's descriptions of "liberatory syllogisms" offer such an approach to practices that seek multiplicitous reconstructions for understanding moral agency. This focus on Lugones's writings allows us, then, to connect Harris's and Dotson's analysis of insurrectionist acts to Anzaldúa's approach to multiplicitous agency, connections that will be further clarified in the final section of this chapter.

Regarding the moral dimensions of Lugones's work, as early as her 1978 doctoral thesis, "Morality and Personal Relationships," we find concerted attention to metaethical debates regarding agency that appear relevantly linked to the author's later discussions of coalition building across sites of ambivalence and difference. For example, her discussion of liberatory syllogisms and the nontotalizing nature of oppression found in her early publications "Have We Got a Theory for You! Feminist Theory, Cultural Imperialism, and the Demand for the 'Woman's Voice'" (1983, with Elizabeth Spelman) and "Structure/Anti-Structure and Agency under Oppression" (1990) are helpful pieces to consider in this regard. In her dissertation, however, written as an explicit project in moral philosophy, Lugones examines the specificity of friendship within forms of practical reasoning. Seemingly against some of the philosophical tendencies of her dissertation chair, Marcus Singer, whose work focuses on principles of generalization and universalization within ethical theory, Lugones argues that friendship entails special, caring relationships toward other people. In such cases, unlike in cases wherein one is only institutionally or formally familiar with another, and thereby bound under more duty-bound or simply more generalizable norms, friendship entails particular, individuated senses of knowing another person. Under such conditions, one need not rely on moral principles that are generalizable, because the ethically relevant considerations at hand are unique to that person, your relationship, and the context that you are in. In addition to an argument about the ethics of personal relationships such as friendships, Lugones also develops a careful argument against the role of moral generalization within reasons for action. Here, similar to what Harris provides through his framing of an insurrectionist ethics, we see Lugones offer an analysis within philosophy of action regarding the epistemological layers of moral reasoning (i.e., what do I know about another and why is it morally salient?), and how constructing practical syllogisms can play a role in understanding reasons for action.

These latter concerns end up playing a central role in some of Lugones's works that were published throughout the 1980s and early 1990s, texts in which Lugones clearly begins incorporating work by Anzaldúa and other Latinx authors. Namely, in "Have We Got a Theory for You!" Lugones coauthors a text that focuses specifically on questions of solidarity within feminist theory. While the dissertation was not itself directed to feminist audiences, and this early work—seemingly Lugones's first published work following the dissertation—addresses questions specifically within feminist theory rather than moral philosophy more generally, we can see some overlapping themes. For example, in chapter 5 of the dissertation, Lugones explains the difference between considering someone as an individuated moral subject (i.e., "an individual") and considering someone by virtue of their membership in some given identity category. She notes that considering someone from the position of their social category requires that one has a "different 'Gestalt' than in seeing him [sic] as an individual" (Lugones 1978, 98). She notes that from a categorical perspective "one can usually shift from one to the other, but when one does this, or when this happens to one, a perceptual shift occurs" (98). She then provides the example of viewing someone through an ethnoracial category: "For example, if one sees Pedro as a Chicano one pays attention to those properties he has in virtue of his being a Chicano, and ignores those properties he has that are unrelated to his belonging to that category. If one sees him as an individual one sees him as someone who is among other things a Chicano" (Lugones 1978, 98). The emphasis on individuation here for Lugones is that from within this moral stance one obtains a sense for the other, not merely as a member of distinct category configurations, but as a unique and particularly situated material being embedded within a set of concrete circumstances and agential framings. From this positionality, she argues, we are able to understand the actions that that particular moral agent undertakes, and we can better frame practical syllogisms that do not require generalizable moral duties but rather an intimate care for the other person's welfare.[2] As such, Dotson's account of internally generated ambivalence appears to stem from a similar kind of particularity clause. Considering an agent as situated in multiple ways, perhaps in innumerable normative and interdependent relations with others, requires us to perpetually continue to seek out further ways in which that person is embedded in differing oppressive/enabling structures. Note here the resonances with Dotson's added criterion to an insurrectionist ethics. Dotson requires that we seek to better understand the range of oppressors that one faces when we are confronted with ambivalence regarding the identity categories under consideration for transvaluation. On Lugones's reading, moral theorizing too requires this epistemic demand to resist generalizing under category configurations that might obfuscate or ignore the range of interpretations for actions that would allow us to place another person within their own multiplicitous webs of normative and material positionalities.

In this early work, Lugones appears to be beginning to frame the tense relationship between being considered a member of an ethnoracial or gender category—which is also included in the dissertation (1978, 100)—and being a fully complex person in relation with multiple others, including members of one's own ethnoracial or gender categories. In this same direction, by 1983, in "Have We Got a Theory for You!," Lugones's use of what she calls her "Hispana voice" articulates a call for her Anglo feminist readers to understand the discrepancies between themselves and the women of color with whom they seek relations of solidarity. More concretely, Lugones begins to trace the problems that surface five years later in

her article on world-traveling wherein women of color are forced to
venture into the intimate meaning-making spaces of white women for
support and affirmation along gendered lines. Yet, through this form
of mobility and vulnerability, white women mistakenly assume that the
relationships achieved are capable of a symmetrical form of support
and fulfilment. She offers, in her own voice in the 1983 essay, "In
the intimacy of a personal relationship we (Hispanas) appear to you
(Anglas) many times to be wholly there, to have broken through to
have dissipated the barriers that separates us because you are Anglo
and we are raza. . . . we appear to ourselves equally whole in your
presence but our intimacy is thoroughly incomplete. When we are
in your world we ourselves feel the discomfort of having our own
being Hispanas disfigured or not understood" (Lugones and Spelman
1983, 576). Lugones and Spelman then draw on this asymmetry,
and the incomplete framings of agency that appear to derive from
generalizations about the relationships between differing identity
categories (one's ethnoracial identity and one's gender identity), to
outline suggestions for nonimperialistic, nonethnocentric forms of
feminist theory.

In 1991, we also see Lugones's first articulation of the light
side/dark side distinction that characterizes her decolonial approach,
a view that she develops more fully later in a 2007 article "Heterosexualism and the Colonial/Modern Gender System." She writes in
a 1991 book chapter for an anthology on feminist ethics: "I wrote
this paper from a dark place; a place where I see white/anglo women
as 'on the other side,' on 'the light side.' From a dark place where
I see myself dark but do not focus on or dwell inside the darkness
but rather focus on 'the other side'" (Lugones 1991, 35). "The
other side" where light and dark are highlighted is a different positionality than that of white women. In this essay, also republished in
Pilgrimages/Peregrinajes in 2003, Lugones attends to the asymmetry
between white women and women of color, and marks how the
category of "women" is insufficient to trace such differences. In this
case, she examines the multiplicity of white women. In particular,
she analyzes how white women appear in the eyes of women of
color, as blocking identification with monoculturalism, as erasing
whiteness and Anglo cultural norms, and as assuming responsibility
for the well-being of women. In this sense, this emphasis on a feminist sense of responsibility is keenly connected to the ideas analyzed

in the 1983 piece coauthored with Spelman. By highlighting her authorial positionality, and those of "the place of La Raza, la gente de colores . . . and where light and dark are highlighted," Lugones appears to return to themes of complexity and multidimensionality within framings of agency (1991, 35). In the year prior, Lugones also published "Structure/Anti-Structure and Agency under Oppression" in which she names the role of constructing practical syllogisms, a point that harkens to a multiplicitous framing of agency and positionality: "The relation between the practical syllogism and the rejection of the 'each person is one' claim is complex. At least some of the syllogisms of the different person one is in one world will be different in kind from those in another world: they may be servile syllogisms, or syllogisms that have intentions that cannot be understood in the world in which they are being put into action" (1990, 504). Although developing a more complex conception of practical syllogisms and of moral agency here than in the dissertation, Lugones appears to be demonstrating something related to her earlier 1978 project and that connects us to Dotson's and Anzaldúa's respective writings. Namely, in the dissertation, she aimed to show that there were important differences between what she called actual and ideal syllogisms, wherein a given person might imagine a set of appropriate reasons that lead to a particular morally appropriate action (framed through an ideal syllogism) and the actual reasons that motivate someone's particular action (whether morally appropriate or not). As such, Lugones appears to have an early interest in the slippage between imagining the set of appropriate reasons for action for another, and the limitations that arise when understanding what motivates or undergirds the presumed actual reasons for one's actions. In this sense, the dissertation may be considered an early precursor to what she calls "liberatory syllogisms" in 1990 in "Structure/Anti-Structure and Agency under Oppression." Akin to the critiques of representationalism that we find in Anzaldúa, Lugones's early attention to ideal forms of reasoning appears to suggest that she rejected isolationist and insular notions of cognition and the structuring of epistemic accounts of human actions. Agency and forms of reasoning are processes of material relation on this view. Yet, like Dotson's demand to better approximate the bonds of one's oppression, Lugones seeks, too, to expand and explore the interconnectedness among our actions and normative engagements with one another, including how we interpret the reasons for one another's actions and the categories that we seek to overthrow.

Along these same lines, in her 2003 chapter on "Tactical Strategies of the Streetwalker/Estrategias Tácticas de la Callejera," Lugones frames an intersubjective form of intentionality that challenges representational readings of action and that reasserts a framing of multiplicitous agency. She explores Michel de Certeau's conception of spatiality to extend her discussion of agency in *Pilgrimages/ Peregrinajes*. De Certeau's work highlights different ways in which we can describe the actions of people moving across a given terrain. Notably, some theorists will take a bird's-eye view, that is, a view from above, that attempts to trace the reasons for specific movements across a given terrain. In contrast to this, other theorists will take a street-level view, a view that sees the micro-interactions and expressions of solidarity and negotiation that occur in the day-to-day lives of people. Yet this view can sometimes occlude the larger political implications of one's actions. From this view, the patterns of resistance that may be part of a larger pattern of refusal, insistence, and so on may be harder to understand. Between these two conceptions of agency—between top-down strategies and street-level tactics—Lugones proposes tactical strategies. Tactical strategies, as Mariana Ortega describes them, point to the dispersion of intentionality *between* subjects, rather than *in* any one of them (Ortega 2016, 107). In this sense, Lugones offers a relational account of selfhood that interprets the syllogisms or patterns of reasoning that we construct as a collective task in meaning-making. Akin to what we find in Anzaldúa's discussion of autohistoria-teoría and Dotson's criterion for better approximating the bonds of oppression of another, the significance of one's understanding of self or others, or even the meaning of one's own actions, are drawn from collective resources, not private, individualized, and insular sets of epistemic, hermeneutic, or moral resources.

Moreover, Lugones's early attention to the capacity to recognize and describe resistant networks—networks of action that are often historically neglected or erased due to dominant colonial, gender, and racial formations—adds an important layer to what she later calls the "dark" and "light" sides of the modern/colonial gender system. In this sense, we can read her later work on the function of white heterosexuality as what she calls "not merely normative but as constitutively perverse" as it, via the violence of Eurocentric modernity/colonialism, has sought to erase and simplify an array of erotically embodied forms of relationality (2007, 187–188). As such, Lugones's work provides a robust contrasting conception of how to explore the history of kinship, embodiment, and desire across contextual and multiplicitous sites of colonial violence and resistance. Rather than reading through, merely, the light side, which is that of the category of Anglo heterosexualism, the work she highlights by Paula Gunn Allen (Laguna Pueblo) (1992) and Oyéronké Oyéwùmí (1997) reads against the grain of the colonial/modern gender system to specify social and embodied relationships that exceed and confound the light side's heteronormative binary. In this sense, Lugones's work encourages her readers to seek new ways to create liberatory syllogisms, that is, ways to interpret the actions of colonized and oppressed peoples beyond the constraints of gender binaries imposed by Eurocentric cultural imperialism or racial demarcations that presume heterogeneity. She invites us, across her work, including her dissertation writings on particularity/generality, to seek ways to reinterpret the actions of others, ourselves, and our ancestors in ways that do not subsume our/their lifeworlds to that of specific individual or group norms, desires, and lived experiences.

Thus, returning to Dotson's framing of the "internal" character of ambivalent insurrectionist acts, we can interpret the construction of moral judgments and patterns of reasoning through Lugones's approach to liberatory syllogisms. Under such a view the use of identity categories, processes that appear to transvaluate identities categories and the material structures of oppression, can be interpreted, akin to how we read autohistoria-teoría, as invitations to others to create and participate in meaning-making processes. Such a view avoids ontologizing the insularist and isolationist tropes of assuming specific patterns of neural activity or individual intentionality. Rather, the construction of a liberatory syllogism is itself an action in the world, and, like our self-descriptions, it is also open to conditions of normative uptake and contestation. This then means that our actions and their respective interpretations are also open to epistemic ambivalence.

Agential Framings of Ambivalence

From Dotson's work, we can take up the critical task of epistemically situating the range of potential relations, including patterned oppressions, that people face, and to which they may be connected. This is not simply a generosity of motivational interpretation, but rather an attempt to build coalition from shifting frames of reference to interpret actions across category configurations, as Lugones suggests. This requires digging into contextual and historical resources and seeking patterns across time for how linked oppressions and resistance may be enacted. One method for doing this can be found in what José Medina calls "chained actions" (Medina 2012, 225). Chained actions, Medina writes, "are actions that echo or resonate with one another, actions that overlap and share a conceptual space or a joint significant, actions that can be aligned and have a (more or less) clear trajectory" (225). His work harkens to the deeply multiplicitous ways in which actions "resonate" or "echo" across varying sites of political and normative space. In this way, Lugones's writings on liberatory syllogisms and Dotson's augmentation of the criteria for an insurrectionist ethics offer an interpretive lens to revisit Anzaldúa's own writings on ambivalence and agency.

One critical place where Anzaldúa addresses issues of agential interrelatedness and ambivalence is in "Let Us Be the Healing of the Wound: The Coyolxauhqui Imperative—la sombra y el sueño" (2002). In that piece, Anzaldúa grapples with the retaliatory military actions of the United States in the wake of the 9/11 attacks by members of al-Qaeda. She notes: "Championing the show of power and the use of fear and force to control, we became the terrorists. We attacked Afghanistan, a nation that had not attacked us—the nineteen terrorists belong to the transnational Al-Qaeda terrorist network, most from Saudi Arabia" (Anzaldúa 2009, 305). Using the pronoun "we" throughout this piece, she marks her complicity with these actions, as collective actions carried out by the U.S. military. She also lists the U.S. support of South African apartheid, death squads in El Salvador, the Allende dictatorship in Chile, and the Israeli occupation of Palestine, among other forms of violence that the United States has bolstered worldwide (306). While many of Anzaldúa's earlier writings do address elements of border militarization, this work is broader in scale, focusing on military actions and the foreign policy of the

United States. She notes that the United States has attempted to position itself as a "victim" that is justified in its retaliatory actions against Afghanistan, and that President George W. Bush boosts a self-image as "gunslinging at high noon, bragging that he'll bring in Osama Bin Laden 'dead or alive' and save the world for us" (307). Interestingly, she describes this mentality, including a hubristic desire to save Afghan women and the racial profiling that torments Arab and Asian Americans in the wake of 9/11, as "a Bush-type raptor within our psyches" (307–310). This is what she calls a "collective shadow" or "our sombras—the unacceptable attributes and unconscious forces that a person must wrestle with to achieve integration" (309). As we explore in the next chapter, such integration is not a form of completeness, but rather contingent transformations or reassemblages of meaning. For now, it is important to note these "unacceptable attributes" that are self-identified with a collective sense of selfhood in her work. Nepantleras, she states, are those who are in a position to facilitate crossing through forms of collective harm, shame, and anger. They "guide us through the transformation process—a process I call conocimiento" (310).

I interpret this call for nepantleras and the process of cono-cimiento as one of a perspectival shift toward increased interrelat-edness and connectivity. As we discussed in the previous chapter regarding teotl, and akin to Keating's reading of a relational ontol-ogy or "metaphysics of interconnectedness" that we discussed in the introduction, Anzaldúa's positioning of nepantleras is a call for exploring the deep "cracks" between organizations or arrangements of meaning. In the context of the essay "Let Us Be the Healing of the Wound," this refers to responses to traumatic events, when the presumed stability of the world "cracks" and with it the forms of orchestrated cohesiveness and normative expectations that existed before. Such sites of instability, vulnerability, and perpetual insecurity are akin to what Ortega describes as cases of "not being-at-ease in a world" (Ortega 2016, 82). Ortega states that a "thick sense of not-being-at-ease . . . can be rather painful and confusing, the uneasiness has to do not only with not knowing the norms and not having a sense of shared history in this particular world (a thin sense of not-being-at-ease) but with the additional experience of being confused as to the kind of person that I am" (82). This sense of instability is a kind of existential ambiguity, what Anzaldúa describes as being in a state of *nepantla* wherein the border and conflicting or negotiating governing authorities create a multiplicitous "edge of barbed wire" that provides no continuity regarding a person's normative status in a given place (Anzaldúa 1999, 35). Those who have learned to navigate those cracks by building bridges and developing new connections would then be nepantleras.

Reading Anzaldúa through the lenses above provided by Harris, Dotson, and Lugones offers a means to consider how her notion of the *borderlands* and *nepantla* point to forms of agential ambivalence. In this, understanding the negotiations that arise from "cracks" in hermeneutic, moral, or existential worlds of sense require the work of nepantleras. Namely, what Anzaldúa calls "alliance work" in "Bridge, Drawbridge, Sandbar, or Island: Lesbians-of-Color Hacienda Alianzas" (1988) "occurs in bounded specific contexts defined by the rules and boundaries of that time and space and group" (Anzaldúa 2009, 143). Such a deep form of contextualism ripples throughout her work, and thereby places Lugones's reading of liberatory syllogisms within a deep historical thread of Latinx feminist praxis. To clarify, Anzaldúa considers four modes of connection or disconnection that individuals or groups may adopt within spaces of deep divide and struggle. In this piece, she, as Lugones does also does throughout the 1980s and 1990s, considers coalition building within feminist spaces, in this context, the National Women's Studies Association. She points specifically to the conflicting aims of white lesbian separatist feminists and women of color feminists who reject separatism. Within this context, she notes four ways in which their interactions may occur: serving as a bridge, a drawbridge, an island, or a sandbar. Bridging is a form of chosen or imposed mediation. A drawbridge positionality means allowing an opening and retreat from engagement across differing political struggles—"Withdrawing, pulling back from physically connecting with white people" (147). "Being an island," she proposes, "means that there are no causeways, no bridges—maybe no ferries, either—between you and whites" (148). This is the creation of spaces that seek to delimit who is able to work in coalition. Such work is hard to sustain, she notes, because of the mutual interdependencies among differing communities for survival. In this sense, she writes that "there are no lifelong islands because no one is totally self-sufficient" (148). Lastly, sandbars are those fluid forms of bridging between island and mainland that ebb and flow with the tide. They are perhaps only visible or known among some who navigate within such contexts, and are impermanent and shifting.

Anzaldúa offers these four positionings in this 1988 piece to think through solidarity work among feminists; however, I propose that we can broaden her ideas here to consider agential positionings in response to ambivalence. As such, these four modes of engagement can be models for thinking across agential positionings and developing liberatory syllogisms that better seek to approximate the bonds and range of oppressions that another person may confront. For example, *bridging* an agential divide is to seek ways to approximate the bonds of oppression that connect struggles against racism and sexism. Dotson's focus on Garner is one such example of a bridging form of agential positioning, in that understanding Garner's relationship to her infant daughter and the terrifying futures for many Black women and girls becomes a crucial facet of developing liberatory interpretive strategies to explain her actions within an insurrectionist ethic.

Other positions are those of *drawbridges* in which the desire to disconnect differing forms of agential striving may be important for community stability and safety. In this, as Anzaldúa notes, the need to withdraw or bracket certain patterns of connectedness can be crucial for community and personal survival. For example, as we address more directly in chapter 5, acknowledging or affirming mixture, as a framing of mestizaje does, risks introducing additional forms of vulnerability to communities who are being threatened with erasure and marginalization. As such, Deborah Miranda (Ohlone–Costanoan Esselen Nation of California), Andrea Smith, and other scholars of Indigenous Studies note that Native peoples impacted by the logics of purity from the settler United States risk political vulnerabilities by heralding mixture as a model of Indigenous communal identity (Miranda and Keating 2002; Smith 2011). In this, drawbridge agency appears necessary as a survival strategy to affirm both Chicanx and Indigenous shared survival. At times, racial and cultural mixture are important to highlight; at other times, this acknowledgment comes at a cost to communities struggling for land sovereignty and self-determination.

Another form of agential response is what Anzaldúa suggests as "island" agency whereby distinction and difference are crucial for a given action or form of struggle. In this sense, the risk of connection or association is too great, despite the existence of underlying ecological relations between islands, waterways, and shores. Anzaldúa notes that such island positionalities cannot be permanent, given that total self-sufficiency is impossible. Yet some framings of action may require long-term stable distinction in order to preserve and maintain the continued relevance and importance of a given act. For example, Medina describes forms of individuation that often accompany the widespread recognition of heroic acts among antiracist struggles. He cites Rosa Parks's 1955 refusal to move to the back of a segregated public bus in Montgomery, Alabama as one such individuated form of action. As a seemingly agentially isolated event, Parks's act becomes emblematic of a Black woman's refusal to comply with Jim Crow segregation, or one woman's struggle against a racist system that perpetuates violence and humiliation on Black Americans across the U.S. South. This can be a framing of "island" agency in the sense developed from Anzaldúa's work, which, in terms of the narrative of Rosa Parks, grew in terms of popularity and added to a form of public epistemic stability in the United States regarding singular instances of Black resistance. Yet, as Medina shows, Parks was not isolated in this action (Medina 2012, 235). She had, in fact, resisted bus segregation prior to this act, and had worked and trained with other activists against Jim Crow segregation. Her act is thus importantly *not* disconnected from other actions by Black organizers in the U.S. South. As such, the separation necessary to build a collective narrative for Parks effectively cuts her activism off from further methods of better "approximating the bonds" of the range of oppressors that Parks and others at the time faced. For example, Claudette Colvin's similar refusal to move to the back of the bus in Montgomery in March 1955, months before Parks's action in December, did not become a prominent symbol of civil disobedience. Colvin was, according to Terry Lovell (2003), "too dark-skinned, too 'rough' in class terms, too young, too loud, and pregnant and unmarried" to serve as the public face of Black resistance to bus segregation in Montgomery (12). As such, Black leaders at the time chose to overlook Colvin and other Black women who were resisting Jim Crow because they were seeking a more "suitable candidate to be the standard bearer" for challenging Jim Crow segregation (9). Accordingly, isolationist attempts like this one, while attempting preservation and impact within racialized political spaces, are also risky, and may end up, for example, perpetuating narratives of respectability, uniqueness, and individualism that may lead to further harms for those who remain negatively impacted by the norms to which they contribute.

Another example, under this "island" form of agential interpretation, would be the prioritization of the 1969 Stonewall Rebellion and the isolation of this event from prior queer and trans resistance of the time, including the 1969 Compton's Cafeteria uprising in San Francisco and the protests following the Black Cat Raid in 1967 Los Angeles. Isolating Stonewall from these other uprisings, as well as distancing the commemoration of the 1969 event from the gay infrastructure already extant within New York City, including the Mattachine Societies of New York and the East Coast Homophile Organization's event from 1965 to 1969 called the "Annual Reminder," risks covering over the ways in which queer and trans of color communities in resistance have shaped history, and the ways in which such communities of color have been renarrated by white gay organizers since (at least) the 1960s (Armstrong and Crage 2006, 736). That is, while white organizers saw an opportunity for commemoration and public attention for gay rights, other queer and trans resistance movements allied with antiracism and anti-police-violence within communities of color, such as those following the Black Cat raid in Los Angeles, were largely overlooked (734). This perpetuates a narrative that queer and trans justice movements have largely been white-led movements, rather than considering the interconnected forms of struggle that LGBTQ communities of color have waged across history.

Lastly, sandbar agential framings are those potential connections that may appear disconnected or unrelated, but that share some underlying chained relations. Such agential framings shift depending on the ebb and flow of historiographical information and epistemic demands for further interrogation. As Gaile Pohlhaus Jr. (2012) has argued, given the plurality of epistemic resources among differing communities of knowers, there are some hermeneutic resources that have long been available to nondominant communities, but that are willfully disregarded or denied by those in dominant communities (728). For Latinx communities who understand our deep histories of resistance to U.S. imperialism, for example, it will not be difficult to understand how twenty-first-century forms of U.S. military interventions in Central America trace long-term routes of U.S. domination in the region. Recalling the stories of my Tío Joaquín and bisabuela

Josefa, for example, their critiques and acts of resistance to U.S. presence in Nicaragua echoes through my interpretive framings of U.S. military actions in Latin America today. Thus, while a diasporic project of Central American–descended philosophers in the United States is, perhaps, still in the making, we may also carry histories of meaning and epistemic resources that create temporal and shifting "sandbars" of meaning between, for example, our own public condemnations of U.S. interventionist practices in Latin America. In this manner, the work of Central American feminist philosophers such as Linda Martín Alcoff, Mariana Ortega, and I appear, at times, to share in a collective project of critique and movement building. Such linkages are not always obvious, but they may be part of a broader epistemological and hermeneutic ecology that shapes our political and normative relations within Latinx feminist philosophy.

We can note, then, from these four agential framings that none of them unequivocally solves issues of ambivalence. Rather, the "something else" that Anzaldúa describes emerges from each possible mode of agential connection and requires us to delve into new possible liberatory syllogisms that can potentially account for why a given explanation for action may reflect a "withdrawal" model (drawbridge) or "isolation" model (island), rather than a bridge model or a provisionally and partially available form of agential connection (sandbar). The "something else" is the possibility for unearthing new connections, or, as Anzaldúa suggested, "nothing is thrust out, the good, the bad and the ugly, nothing rejected, nothing abandoned" (Anzaldúa 1999, 101). Akin to the insurrectionist project that Harris and Dotson describe, and threaded through Latinx feminist theory as seen through Lugones's writings, Anzaldúa's offerings on agential ambivalence call for novel interpretive strategies that strive toward new collective webs of meaning and material connection in the face of the "ugliness" of the ever-present possibility of complicity within systems of oppression. Accordingly, in the following two chapters, we explore some critiques of Anzaldúa's work, including critiques within disability studies and Indigenous studies, to grapple with sites of ambivalence that circulated within her own writings. With this, I hope to create space for us to consider her work anew, and from a multiplicitous register that allows for configurations of her engagements with a deeply coalitional project.

Chapter 4

Putting Coyolxauhqui Together

The form of multiplicitous agency that we have been developing thus far has demonstrated Anzaldúa's commitments to a relational model of action and meaning that relies on distributed, interdependent, and collective characteristics of agential communities. In the previous chapter we examined an interpretive approach to generative ambivalence that functions throughout her work, and we sought to underscore how the demand to situate the range of oppressions that agents experience can be bolstered by creating new liberatory syllogisms. The following two chapters now extend the models of multiplicitous agency and productive ambivalence that we have been building to explore how such relational understandings function within discussions of embodiment, resistance, and coalition building. Accordingly, these last two chapters outline several contextualized and historicized possibilities for coalitional struggle within Anzaldúa's own work to engage questions of action and to interpret how actions and meanings matter to nepantleras, that is, persons involved in agential communities. Specifically, the following two chapters turn to issues within disability theory, transgender critique, and Indigenous studies to underscore the complexities of Anzaldúan multiplicitous agency. However, to avoid what Aurora Levins Morales has cautioned as a "canonization" of Anzaldúa, the following two chapters, while drawing out notions from her work, also seek to critique and augment Anzaldúa's corpus to build stronger relations of solidarity between Latinx feminisms and areas of political analysis such as disability justice, critical trans politics, and Indigenous sovereignty movements, all topics that were undertheorized within Anzaldúa's own writings (Levins Morales 2013, 3).

A number of scholars within disability studies have made a significant impact on theories of embodiment, questions of human sociality, and genealogical interventions within the biomedical discourses that have framed contemporary conceptions of human biology, cognition, nature, and rationality.[1] Within Anzaldúa's reception literature, a number of theorists have noted her relevance for disability theory and disability justice (Bost 2010; Levins Morales 2013; McRuer 2006; Minich 2014). Specifically, in this chapter I revisit Anzaldúa's work to examine how her approach to multiplicitous agency functions in the context of issues within disability justice, including where in her work we find resources for thinking through disability as an organizing framework for embodiment and structural systems of oppression. Her approach to agency that rejects individualism, imperialism, isolationism, and insularism functions well, I argue, within a disability justice framework. Accordingly, I turn to Anzaldúa's work to interpret her as a disability theorist *de la frontera* to show the mutual imbrication of disability and the relevance of multiplicitous agency for issues relevantly linked to disability justice.

To carry out this analysis, I first demonstrate how Anzaldúa has been taken up by disability theorists, including her interpretation as a *crip theorist* (McRuer 2006). Then, I delve directly into her texts to show an area of her corpus that offers productive resources for working through forms of agential ambivalence within disability justice. Most notably, I underscore her approach to what she describes as a renarration of the Mexica/Aztec figure of Coyolxauhqui, as well as her discussions of her own embodied experiences of pain, shame, and medicalized intervention. I then conclude this chapter by demonstrating how these areas of analysis within her body of work provide coalitional possibilities for agential communities within disability justice. These include how her approach to multiplicitous agency remains relevant for critiques of environmental racism, for understanding the stakes of identarian forms of political mobilization, and for understanding the complicated nature of gender-based violence.

As a personal aside, I would like to clarify for the reader that I do believe that disability has shaped the contours of my life, perception, and understanding of the world. My relationship to disability is, in part, shaped by my understanding of my own body, chronic illness, and many of my loved ones who, although perhaps not personally identifying as "disabled," have been considered under this label by various medical, governmental, and carceral institutions at different times in our family's history. These networks of relations to disability include my relationship with my abuelo, Pápa Juan, a "wandering soul," as my tío Juan Eduardo calls him, whose humor, adventurous spirit, and penchant for poetry and drink often surface in our family lore. I can recall the booming sounds of the local Spanish-language station that emanated from the fuzzy-screened TV in his room, the blurred image on the screen irrelevant as we quietly listened to the score of a soccer match or the evening news. From his presence in my childhood, I consider a large part of my aural orientation to the Spanish language developing from these early experiences with my grandfather. That he lived with us during a time when he was struggling with health complications due to diabetes and glaucoma also made me vaguely aware of the caretaking labor that my mother took on, as she and he negotiated their life and daily routine together. From their relationship, I likewise began to learn of the pain of loss, sacrifice, and deep interpersonal traumas that can stem from disagreements about what proper caretaking looks like. These relations, I believe, taught me early lessons about interdependence, the emotional and physical labor of caretaking, and the ways in which structural harms may filter into practices of care.

I also grew up bearing witness as my mother strategically maneuvered life without health insurance, including the negotiation of sliding-scale payments and hospital bills, and I continue to learn from her resourcefulness and administrative acuity. I also learned of substance use from an early age, and saw the immense destructiveness that these conditions can bring, such as the criminalization, punishment, and shame that can follow patterned substance use. From these experiences, I came to detect differences regarding how my parents—long-separated but living in the same city—were impacted by what Shelley Tremain (2017) might consider a facet of the "apparatus of disability" in their day-to-day lives. While there were times that the risks caused by substance use were present to both of my parents, the consequences always seemed to more directly, more severely, and more frequently impact my mother, whose brownness, gender, and working-class status render her more likely to face scrutiny and surveillance. Growing up in these two worlds, with my mother, a working-class first-generation Central American woman, and the middle-class life of my father, a white Southerner, offered me an early lesson in how differential access to resources works, how vulnerability to state and sexual violence works, and how most medical institutions and therapeutic settings are not designed with the needs of people of color in mind. In these ways and others, I consider disability to have always shaped my life, and I continue to learn from and lift up the hard-fought dignity, care, and resources that disabled people bring into the world. In these ways, a future with disabled people and the continued flourishing of a multiplicity of bodyminds is a future that I fight for and desire. With this, I hope this analysis of Anzaldúa's work and the broader book contribute to a project that helps to collectively build such a future.

Crip *Atravesadas*

To better understand Anzaldúa's relevance within disability scholarship, it will be helpful to briefly scaffold some of the contemporary strands of disability studies that bear theoretical affinities with the Anzaldúan themes that we have explored in previous chapters. For example, questions regarding the relationship between embodiment and agency have been central within philosophical studies of disability for decades (Wendell 2013; Siebers 2008; Garland-Thomson 2011). One strand of this critique challenges the erasure of agency among disabled people, including societal patterns of violence, paternalism, romanticization, and ostracization that have negatively impacted disabled people (Young 2015; Garland-Thomson 2009; Johnson 2003). For example, activist and comedian Stella Young's critique of what she calls "inspiration porn" directly responds to the ways in which able-bodied people rely on mischaracterizations, generalizations, and the objectification of disabled people to make themselves feel inspired and affirmed (Young 2015). In this framing, Young notes how the particularity of disabled people's understandings of themselves is erased or exploited by able-bodied people for their own affective investments.

Other critical orientations within disability studies focus on issues of impairment and history, including critiques of the assumed morphology and functionalism implicit within the biological and medical sciences (Tremain 2001, 2005, 2017; Mitchell and Snyder 2015). For example, one Foucauldian strand of this critique can be found in Mitchell and Snyder's work (2015) on "ablenationalism." They draw specifically from Jasbir Puar's (2007) notion of "homonationalism" as a relational nexus that considers forms of LGBT political inclusion (e.g., same-sex marriage and LGBT-friendly tourism) as sharing in the cultural homogenization and foreign policies of nation-states. Like homonationalism, in which specific persons considered under the "LGBT" umbrella are modeled and valorized within the domestic policies of a given nation-state, ablenationalism likewise creates forms of exceptionalism and valuation that present some persons as worthy of national protections and inclusion (Mitchell and Snyder 2015, 13–14). The aims of neoliberal policies and patterns of exceptionalism thereby create notions of "deserving" and "undeserving" disabled people, which effectively reifies patterns of normalization and existing matrices of structural violence, including white supremacy, heterosexism, and global capitalism. Ablenationalism focuses on rights-based forms of inclusion within domestic and foreign state policy that create notions of a racialized, sexualized, disabled, and gendered bourgeois citizen who is considered a justified and rightful recipient of state protections. In this sense, this framing of disability shifts away from individualized models of impairment, for example, and focuses on patterns of distribution and forms of subjectification (rather than individualized agency).

Additionally, phenomenology has provided tools for disability theorists to analyze motility, pain, illness, perception, and other embodied aspects of experience (Toombs 1987, 1988, 1995; Carel 2008, 2011, 2012; Salamon 2012; Scully 2012; Svenaeus 2000a, 2000b; Wieseler 2018). "Embodiment," in the sense employed in phenomenology, often refers to the lived body as it is experienced first-personally. This perspective is contrasted with (sometimes tacit) conceptions of embodiment that consider the body as an object from a third-person perspective. Within the phenomenology of disability, issues of temporality, motility, and gendered and racialized comportment have become central, and the emphasis on first-person experiences is a key political insight that underscores the epistemic and hermeneutical resources of disabled people.

Given these distinct and important methodological approaches to disability, there are a number of significant ways to engage these areas of analysis within disability studies and Anzaldúa's work on issues of embodiment and the agential framings of intersubjectivity. Noting such affinities, for at least the past two decades, Anzaldúa's readers have interpreted her work in light of its relevance for thinking through issues within disability (Bost 2010; Levins Morales 2013; McRuer 2006; Minich 2014; Piepzna-Samarasinha 2018). For example, Julie Avril Minich has noted the shared concerns between the fields of border studies, including Anzaldúa's work, and those of disability studies. The two fields, she states, "share a concern with the ways in which social landscapes are built to restrict freedom of movement" (Minich 2014, 25). From this lens both border studies and disability studies examine how social landscapes challenge the assumed givenness or naturalness of forms of able-bodied motility. Also, in a similar vein, Robert McRuer states that Anzaldúa's framing of oppression locates her within a *queer crip* thread of scholarship. He writes that her "career-long considerations of terms and concepts that might, however contingently, function to bring together as they threaten to rip apart los atravesados: 'The squint-eyed, the perverse, the queer, the troublesome, the mongrel, the mulato, the half-breed, the half dead: in short, those who cross over, pass over, or go through the confines of the "normal" place her work well within the framings of a politicized disability critique such as crip theory'" (McRuer 2006, 38–39, quoting Anzaldúa 1999, 25). Moreover, McRuer argues that Anzaldúa's work resists simple identarian constructions of social positioning and agency. Instead, he reads her work as consistent with crip theory in that it offers a methodology for examining sites and forms of cultural production that extend beyond what is often readily identifiable as "disability." In this sense, as we explore further here, the critiques found within her work of individualism, isolationism, and insularism discussed in chapter 1 support such a reading offered by McRuer.

In a related vein, Suzanne Bost's (2010) work on Chicana feminism and disability argues that Chicana feminist work challenges the neat dichotomies between "us" and "them," between those who are clearly oppressors and those who are oppressed. Similar to what we discussed in previous chapters regarding Anzaldúa's framings of nos/otras, autohistoria-teoría, and ambivalence, Bost's emphasis on disability within the works of Chicana authors like Anzaldúa, Cherríe

Moraga, and Ana Castillo offers "a politics that is strengthened by its mixing of cultures and its openness to continual change brought on by incorporating difference" (Bost 2010, 27). Bost interprets such changes as material, political, medical, and aesthetic forms of transformation, and reads Anzaldúa's work as inscribed by relations to pain and illness. Specifically, pain is not rejected or denied within Anzaldúa's work, but rather, pain is infused within Anzaldúa's lyricism and the content of her work (86). "Disability" is thereby not a fixed term for people or identities, according to these readings, but rather it constitutes a set of relations by which agents experience and negotiate the world. Even so, however, the term "disabled," Bost notes following the work of Siebers (2006), "is still a significant marker of social location, though not a totalizing way of understanding subjectivity or political filiation" (25). Thus, as we discussed in previous chapters, nos/otras as a demonstration of multiplicitous agency seeks to retain an emphasis on social locations without reducing or ontologizing the agential source or sense of interiority of a given speaker or actor.

Importantly, Anzaldúa directly addresses her relationship to identifying as disabled in a 2003 series of email exchanges with AnaLouise Keating, who was, at the time, discussing Anzaldúa's writings with a student working on themes of disability in her university course. Anzaldúa is cautious about taking on the label of being "disabled" or "diabetic," although she notes that she welcomes the students to read her within the context of disability studies. She states that she is worried about "generic/cultural slices-of-the-pie terms" that may reduce identity and experience (Anzaldúa 2009, 300). Yet she rejects a description of her relationship to disability as one of being "distanced" from disability:

> I feel an in-my-face, up-front-and-personal relationship with diabetes & its disabling complications. I can't escape it. I am concerned with my eyesight when I read, write, watch TV, or go to the movies. I have to pay attention to my blood sugar levels when I eat and exercise, when I stay up at night, when I socialize, & when I travel to do speaking engagements. The state of my feet is foremost in my thoughts at all times. When I forget some of these my body reminds me, sometimes painfully. (300)

Naming the everyday relationship that she has with disability, Anzaldúa continues to explain that she considers people with disabilities as "prone to develop la facultad" (300). By this, Anzaldúa refers to an aesthetic and epistemic concept whereby persons develop a sense for interpreting or perceiving the underlying complexity of their geopolitical spaces. This concept appears in many of Anzaldúa's writings, and a discussion of it is raised in her 1987 *Borderlands/La frontera*. In that work, Anzaldúa describes la facultad as a perceptual process whereby the interconnectedness of the world becomes "excruciatingly alive" (Anzaldúa 1999, 60). It is, in her words, "the capacity to see in surface phenomena the meaning of deeper realities, to see the deep structure below the surface. It is an instant 'sensing,' a quick perception arrived at without conscious reasoning" (60). While this description tends to prioritize la facultad through a visual sensory modality, her continuation of the discussion opens up further possibilities for interpreting her 2003 correspondence with Keating on disability. In particular, Anzaldúa notes that there are specific conditions under which people develop this kind of perceptive sensitivity. She notes that "those who are pushed out," "who do not feel psychologically or physically safe in the world," and "those who are pounced on the most" develop this kind of "acute awareness" (60). In this framing, la facultad becomes an embodied and critical orientation toward the world that is developed through difference, confrontations with harm, and displacement. Against ableism's patterned displacements, rejection, and neglect, Anzaldúa locates aesthetic and epistemic modes of orientation and perceptual awareness that help one to investigate systemic forms of political ostracization and population management. However, she also rejects labels that may lead to "slices-of-the-pie" models of identity wherein differential access to resources and affirmation are at stake.

On these matters, Levins Morales and Bost have read Anzaldúa's work as seeking to find the transformative and creative potential within disabled, chronically ill, and pained forms of embodiment. For instance, in response to Anzaldúa's refusal to identify as "disabled," Levins Morales notes that the reason for this may have been that Anzaldúa did not have the "strong, vocal, politically sophisticated disability justice movement led by queer working class women and trans people of color who understood [her] life" (Levin Morales 2013, 4–5). Such a community, Levin Morales remarks, could have been the normative bridge that might have led Anzaldúa to embrace disability as a home-making practice rather than refuse it. Levins Morales writes that Anzaldúa likely needed a disability justice movement that would hold her in her multiplicitous dimensionality and see "all the ways our bodies are made wrong, held responsible for our own mistreatment, blamed for showing the impact of oppression, all the ways out nature is called defective, are connected, rooted in the same terrible notions about what is of value" (5). In the context of a panel on disability and Latina feminism, Levin Morales offers a statement of hope and suggestion: "I think if we called on you to bring the story of your body to this circle, you would come" (9). This sentence, thus, finds in Anzaldúa's work a desire to build, create, and transform worlds of meaning and sense through the important resources developed from embodied experiences with pain, illness, environmental toxins, and negotiations with ableist institutions. Anzaldúa's work, as Bost also notes, viewed the materiality and experience of pain as a site from which to theorize selfhood, society, and history (2010, 29). This is what Levins Morales considers "the atlas of our skin and bone and blood" that embodiment and experience provide, and which disability studies has so carefully thematized (Levins Morales 2013, 10).

Accordingly, to extend some of this work that seeks to explore the relevance of Anzaldúa's work within disability studies, in the following section I turn to areas of her writings that show the relevance of her notion of multiplicitous agency within a disability justice approach by examining her framing of the Mexica/Aztec story of Coyolxauhqui.

Re-membering Coyolxauhqui

From the purview of the abovementioned interpretive threads, I propose, alongside many others, that we can read Anzaldúa's work for its relevance within a disability justice movement. More specifically, disability justice is a movement that began in the mid-aughts founded by Black, brown, queer, and trans activists, including members of the Disability Justice Collective such as Patty Berne, Mia Mingus, Leroy Moore Jr., Eli Clare, and Sebastian Margaret (Piepzna-Samarasinha 2018, 15). Against a disability rights framing, as Patty Berne notes, disability justice focuses on the relationship between "intersecting junctures of oppression," which include addressing white supremacy, settler colonization, housing insecurity, gender and sexual oppression, and incarceration, among other issues (20). Building from what Levins Morales states above regarding why Anzaldúa did not identify with the label "disabled," a disability justice framing is a movement that holds disabled people in their multiplicity, strength, and power, a movement that affirms and relies on the deep complexities of identity and social relations.

Leah Lakshmi Piepzna-Samarasinha (2018) has written extensively about disability justice as a movement and has also directed some of her writings to Anzaldúa's memory and presence in her own life. She writes that she and Gloria "meet in bed," combining both erotic suggestions of such a phrase with a rich description of her relationship to living and sleeping in her bed (182). She writes of her own relationship to fibromyalgia, "the name [she] choose[s] for the constellation of repeating cycles of fatigue, muscle pain that does not have an organic source, immune system meltdowns, shakiness, balance problems, and cognitive delay that hit [her] when [she is] stressed or doused with chemicals" (181). Piepzna-Samarasinha writes of an intimate relationship with how her body rests and experiences joy in her bed. She also discusses writing from her bed, a practice shared by many women of color, including Anzaldúa. In this, Piepzna-Samarasinha quotes Anzaldúa's statement in "Speaking in Tongues" that she "delves inward" while lying in bed and uses this inward movement to write (Anzaldúa 1983, 169). This relationship to disability, pain, and beds, Piepzna-Samarasinha states, makes both Anzaldúa and herself unable to hold 9–5 jobs or participate as "productive" members within the demands of global capitalism. Commenting on the ableism and exploitation of such racialized labor demands, Piepzna-Samarasinha states:

> Queer people of color never say we are disabled if we have any choice about it. We come from families who believe in being tough, in sucking it up. We do not want any more identities than we already have to wrestle with. Our bodies already seen as tough, monster, angry, seductive, incompetent. How can we admit weakness, vulnerability, interdependence and still keep our jobs, our perch on the

"this edge of barbwire" we live on? Why would we join
crips who are all white in the mainstream rights movement?
(Piepzna-Samarasinha 2018, 184)

In this passage, Piepzna-Samarasinha recognizes, as Levins Morales
does, the whiteness of many mainstream disability rights movements in
the United States and the United Kingdom, and marks the racialized
vulnerabilities that people of color have in relation to using "disabled"
or "crip" as a label. As such, Piepzna-Samarasinha too comments on
Anzaldúa's reluctance to identify as disabled, and also affirms that
her relationship to writing, to her bed, and to her queer of color
disability politics finds a source of shared affinities and longing within
Anzaldúa's work. She also writes of wanting to develop a movement
that bears witness to the beauty and pain of disability, and that resists
the shame, stigma, and disposability often attributed to disabled people.
In this way, Piepzna-Samarasinha shapes her book around a politics
that attempts to create space for disabled queer and trans people of
color to find a movement capable of holding and affirming them.
Building from this set of aims, I offer several additional elements of
Anzaldúa's work that demonstrate a series of resources for working
in and with a disability justice movement, including such complex
relations to illness, movement, medicalization, and joy.

One aspect of Anzaldúa's work that provides further resources
within a disability justice framework stems from her relationship to
Mexica/Aztec creation stories, and specifically her narration of the
Coyolxauhqui story. As noted in chapter 2, much of Anzaldúa's
work engaged stories, philosophical orientations, and the ontology of
Mexica/Aztec peoples. I return to some criticisms of her relationship
to these Indigenous histories in the following chapter, but for now,
I highlight several aspects of her reading of a Mexica/Aztec creation
story that reflects affinities with the aims of disability justice.

Anzaldúa refers in various places throughout her corpus to
the story of Coyolxauhqui. According to Keating, Anzaldúa's first
major engagement with the story in published form is her 1993
essay titled "Border Arte: Nepantla, el lugar de la Frontera." In
this piece, Anzaldúa describes walking through an exhibit at the
Denver Museum of Natural History titled "AZTEC: The World
of Moctezuma" (Anzaldúa 2009, 179). This essay is foundational

within Anzaldúa scholarship for many reasons, among which are her engagements with Mexica/Aztec historiography, the commodification of Indigenous art, and an analysis of art as a creative process. Regarding Coyolxauhqui, Anzaldúa recounts walking by the exhibit of "la diosa de la luna, Coyolxauhqui" and offers several interpretive lenses for Coyolxauhqui. For example, she writes of "the dominant culture's repeated attempts to tear the Mexican culture in the U.S. apart and scatter the fragments to the winds" (177). This language harkens to the archival evidence of her story that draws from a Mexica/Aztec worldview.

On this point, Jennie Luna and Martha Galeana (2016) note that the extant stories of Coyolxauhqui largely stem from the anthropological exploration of the *Florentine Codex*, a sixteenth-century study of Mexica/Aztec cosmology (12). Carried out under the direction of a Franciscan priest, Fray Bernardino de Sahagún, and a team of Nahua scribes, this group created a codex that depicted a number of creation stories and histories of Mexica/Aztec peoples, and among them was the story of Coyolxauhqui. According to the *Florentine Codex*, Coyolxauhqui, depicted in relation to the moon, is the daughter of Coatlicue who is depicted as the earth-mother with a serpent skirt. The story suggests that, one day, Coatlicue was sweeping the temple of Coatepec and found some hummingbird feathers and placed them in the sash of her belt (12). The feathers, as some scholars have noted, symbolize "divine semen," and from these feathers Coatlicue became pregnant with a child, Huitzilopochtli, who was rumored to bring war with him (Carrasco 2012, 73). Upon hearing this, Coyolxauhqui, worried about the oncoming of war, informed her brothers, the stars, and, together, they planned to kill Coatlicue before the birth of Huitzilopochtli. Coatlicue received word of this plan and feared for her life. Likewise, Huitzilopochtli while still in Coatlicue's womb hears of Coyolxauhqui's plan. When Coyolxauhqui approaches Coatepec, where Coatlicue resided, Huitzilopochtli emerged from Coatlicue as a fully grown adult and defeats both the star army and Coyolxauhqui. The manner in which Coyolxauhqui is killed is significant in that Huitzilopochtli cuts off her head and limbs, and tosses her head into the sky, where it then remains as the moon, offering comfort to her mother Coatlicue. Her dismembered body is then tossed to the bottom of Coatepec hill.

In 1978, a stone disk of Coyolxauhqui was found near the base of Templo Mayor, once the center of Mexica/Aztec life in Tenochtitlan; the disk illustrates Coyolxauhqui's dismembered body and her cheeks painted with bells on them. The monolith was found by electrical workers digging near the Metropolitan Cathedral in what is today Mexico City (Carrasco 2012, 71). The stone is estimated to have been created around 1500, prior to Hernán Cortes's conquest of Tenochtitlan in 1519. When the stone was unearthed in 1978, it appeared to confirm the story of Coyolxauhqui offered in the *teocuicatl* (divine song) of the *Florentine Codex*.

In an article offering an alternative telling of the Coyolxauhqui story, Luna and Galeana (2016) note that the *Florentine Codex* is not the only archival trace of this ancient figure. Rather, they argue that, unlike the monolith and the codex, both of which have been read through the interpretive lenses of an anthropological gaze and a mythic figuration of Indigenismo within Mexican historiography, *danzantes mexicanas* (known also as "Aztec dancers") offer another way to interpret Coyolxauhqui's story (9). The moon, on their reading, is considered an "eternal dance" in that it is constantly in flux (waxing and waning), and Coyolxauhqui's story demonstrates the movement of time and the regeneration of energy (23). "The cascabeles/bells on her face and wrists rattle and make music as she dances through space," they write (23). Moreover, they turn to the Nahuatl meaning of her name, Coyolli + xauh + qui, which can be translated as "face painted with bells" (*coyolli* meaning bells, and *xahua* meaning to paint oneself) or "one who picks the coyoles" (*coyolli* meaning a ceremonial palm leaf, and *xahua* meaning to dig or pick up) (15). They also note the relationship that she bears with the waxing and waning of the moon, and of blood, which spews from her arms and legs (24). Accordingly, they read Coyolxauhqui as a "Celestial dancer" (23). This view of her as a ceremonial figure is contrasted with that of a goddess—a notion, they state, that relies too heavily on Christian deism (14). Coyolxauhqui is, on their reading, a depiction of a ceremonial relationship to birth and life, including an embodied relation to bleeding and menstruation.

Luna and Galeana also discuss Chicana feminist interpretations of the Coyolxauhqui story, commenting on both Anzaldúa's and Cherríe Moraga's respective readings. They note that both

Moraga (1993) and Anzaldúa were in search of stories of women in Indigenous communities within Mesoamerica that would honor and strengthen perceptions of Chicanas in the present (Luna and Galeana 2016, 16). Yet Luna and Galeana's readings of both Moraga and Anzaldúa largely only consider Coyolxauhqui as a figure of dismemberment, and her story is only considered relevant, they claim, in the service of desires to become "whole" again. They note that these figurations of Coyolxauhqui as a powerful Indigenous woman torn apart by another harkens to colonial conquest and the continued marginalization and violence that Indigenous women and Chicanas face. Moreover, Huitzilopochtli's killing of Coyolxauhqui, the story of a brother killing a sister, likely registered to many Chicanas who were battling with sexism and erasure within the Chicano rights movement of the 1960s and 1970s (17). Luna and Galeana critique this interpretation by rejecting a reading of Coyolxauhqui as the wounded and "dismembered" woman. Rather, she is, on their interpretation, already "whole" and a powerful woman "engaging in cycles of menstruation, reproduction, labor, and birth" (8).

While there are a number of powerful insights within Luna and Galeana's reading of Coyolxauhqui, their sources within Anzaldúa's corpus do not extend beyond *Borderlands/La Frontera*. Also, although Coatlicue does appear in *Borderlands/La frontera*, Coyolxauhqui does not. The authors appear to acknowledge this and refer instead to Anzaldúa's conception of the borderlands as a space of continual fracturing, splintering, and dismemberment. This is, then, an interpretation that they link to Chicana interpretations of Coyolxauhqui and the potential of this story for forms of regeneration and transformation offered through a relationship to pain. Thus, while their account is helpful for showing some potentially limited framings of Coyolxauhqui's story for Chicanx communities seeking connection to embodied pain and cyclical relations to blood and menstruation, their analysis misses crucial insights from within both Anzaldúa's own writings and from a disability justice perspective that seeks transformation and critique *within* relations to pain.

The majority of Anzaldúa's own writings on Coyolxauhqui emerge after her 1987 publication of *Borderlands/La Frontera*, and, as mentioned above, Keating and others have described her as shifting her interpretative lens since that period. Specifically, Anzaldúa's commentary on Coyolxauhqui in "Border Arte" emerges in the context of considerations about the commodification of Indigenous art, history, and iconography. She writes that the very museum that she is walking through offers a "slick, prepackaged exhibition costing $3.5 million" (Anzaldúa 2009, 177). This "exemplifies [the] dismemberment" of Coyolxauhqui, Anzaldúa remarks. Here, she shares the critique of Luna and Galeana, as well as of other Indigenous and decolonial scholars who have critiqued the romanticization and commodification of Indigeneity. Such a critique is apparent elsewhere in her work as well, as we mentioned in her rejection of anthropolitical conceptions of the "primitive mind" in chapter 1. Additionally, she states in a 2003 interview for *Studies in American Indian Literatures* that her use of Indigenous cultural figures and terms, including her own references to Coyolxauhqui, are acts of remembrance rather than simple acts of appropriation or commodification. Anzaldúa expresses a skepticism about the use of Indigenous stories and cultural production for financial gain or prestige. In this sense, she appears to consider her framing of Coyolxauhqui as serving other ends. That is, as Scott Lauria Morgensen has noted while acknowledging her problematic absence of engagement with present-day Mesoamerican Indigenous authors, artists, and communities, her relationship to Mexica/Aztec stories is "marked by the hunger of a queer feminist Chicana critic defying white supremacy and settler colonialism by reaffirming her Indigenous heritage on lands her peoples traversed prior to conquest" (Morgensen 2011, 183). In this sense, her references to figures like Coyolxauhqui can be thought to serve critical ends, a topic I return to in the next chapter, even if she herself should have engaged more carefully with the contemporary work of Indigenous Mesoamerican authors, artist, and activists. This might include, then, the Indigenous activists, scholars, and *maestras* of dance that Luna and Galeana engage in their interpretation of the Coyolxauhqui story, such as Temitzin Solórzano, Axayacatl Solórzano, and Arturo Meza Gutiérrez.

Other framings of the story of Coyolxauhqui in her work include what she calls the Coyolxauhqui *imperative*, which she describes as "the path of the artist, the creative impulse . . . basically an attempt to heal the wounds" (2002, 292). In "Let Us Be the Healing of the Wound: The Coyolxauhqui Imperative—la sombra y el sueno" (2002), she elaborates the Coyolxauhqui imperative within the context of the fall of the World Trade Center on September 11, 2001.

She writes, "The day the towers fell, me sentí como Coyolxauhqui, la luna" (303). Elsewhere in the essay, she states:

> The Coyolxauhqui imperative is to heal and achieve integration. When fragmentations occur you fall apart and feel as though you've been expelled from paradise. Coyolxauhqui is my symbol for the necessary process of dismemberment and fragmentation, of seeing that self or the situations you're embroiled in differently. It is also my symbol for reconstruction and reframing, one that allows for putting the pieces together in a new way. The Coyolxau[h]qui imperative is an ongoing process of making and unmaking. There is never any resolution, just the process of healing. (313)

This interpretive framing of a process of healing without resolution suggests a reading that challenges some aspects of the Luna and Galeana interpretation. Drawing from our reading in previous chapters of Anzaldúa's notions of multiplicitous agency and ambivalence, Anzaldúa's own relationship to healing is not one of totality or finality. Rather, multiplicitous agency suggests orchestration, rearrangement, and perpetual movement—both embodied movement and in the normative accounts we provide to explain action. In this sense, Coyolxauhqui is not "whole" because she is final, complete, or "accurately" re-created. Instead, her story is one of action, of creation, and remaking from the available resources within one's historical, cultural, and communal relations. From this reading, like the Luna and Galeana interpretation, Anzaldúa's Coyolxauhqui imperative is also suggestive of regeneration, creation, and life.

Anzaldúa's own relationship to Luna and Galeana's analysis of Coyolxauhqui as a figure for birth and menstruation, however, is also complicated to take on from an Anzaldúan framework. That is, we can approach these issues from within the patterned resistance that Anzaldúa voiced throughout her life to a predetermined future of childrearing and domesticity. In *Borderlands/La Frontera*, for example, she writes of Chicana mothers telling their daughters and sons to expect women to be the sole caretakers of their families and to be submissive to their husbands (1999, 38). She states: "Educated or not, the onus is still on woman to be a wife/mother. Women are made to feel total failures if they don't marry and have children" (39). She identifies strongly as rebelling against these valuations and expectations of Chicanas. Moreover, as a queer Chicana, she notes her own fear of harsh rejections from her family because of her queerness: "We're [queer Chicanas] afraid of being abandoned by the mother, the culture, *la Raza*, for being unacceptable, faulty, damaged" (42). In this sense, Anzaldúa's queer positioning to heteronormative expectations of motherhood and childrearing may have distanced her interpretive relationship to Coyolxauhqui as a figuration of pregnancy and reproduction, as Luna and Galeana propose. Thus, Anzaldúa may depart or retell the Coyolxauhqui story as a form of queer regeneration, a kind of response to pregnancy and birthing expectations, that shaped Coyolxauhqui's relationship to her mother, Coatlicue.

Read in this light, Coyolxauhqui's anger caused by Coatlicue's impregnation with Huitzilopochtli diverges from the Mexica/Aztec worldview of a warring relation of the moon with the sun. Instead, we may read Anzaldúa's reading of Coyolxauhqui as an anger about the potential fear and stigma caused by demands for reproduction for queer Latinxs, and the communal destruction that she alludes to when she describes people of color feeling "disposable, perpetually unsafe, and torn apart like Coyolxauhqui" (Anzaldúa 2002, 308). Her reading thus connects us to a strand of critique within the reproductive justice movement, a movement that, alongside disability justice, commits itself to rejecting medicalized paradigms for interpreting the lives of people of color. As a movement formed and led by women of color in the 1990s, the basic framework of reproductive justice, as described through the landmark reproductive justice organization SisterSong, is to defend "the human right to maintain personal bodily autonomy, have children, not have children, and parent the children we have in safe and sustainable communities" (SisterSong 2019). Among the issues addressed through this framework is the discourse between prolife efforts to repeal and restrict access to abortions, and prochoice efforts to ensure safe and nonstigmatizing options for people to make a decision about whether or not to terminate their pregnancy. Importantly, a reproductive justice framework brings into purview the long history of eugenics and population control efforts through state and medical institutions, including forced sterilizations and selective abortion. Additionally, as Loretta Ross (2006) states, reproductive justice efforts seek to transform the societal conditions of racism, heteropatriarchy, capitalism, anti-Semitism, and religious fundamentalism that have long sought to diminish the lives and futurity of people of color, queer and trans people, religious minorities, and poor people across the globe (54). We can thereby place Anzaldúa's reading of Coyolxauhqui within this frame to see how her work, while diverging from Luna and Galeana's reading of the ceremonial role of Coyolxauhqui for reproduction, labor, and birth within a Mexica/Aztec worldview, brings into the frame a relationship of reproductive multiplicitous agency for queer people of color.

Additionally, and as we further explore below, Anzaldúa's relationship to an endocrine condition that led her to begin menstruation from infancy, experience early-onset puberty as a child, and to undergo a hysterectomy at the age of thirty-eight, may have provided her with an intimate relationship with menstruation that differed from the depiction offered by Luna and Galeana. That is, in a 1982 interview with Linda Smuckler, Anzaldúa writes that she lived in great pain prior to her hysterectomy, and that this pain impacted her everyday life, including her sexual and romantic relationships (Anzaldúa 2000, 34). Thus, the relationship to pain that Luna and Galeana critique within Anzaldúa's orientation within *Borderlands/ La Frontera* appears as part of her relationship to menstruation. That is, they consider Chicana readers of Coyolxauhqui's story to have overlooked the positive relationship that women have to menstruation, and at one point in their article they refer to how "the woman's uterus 'dismembers' and liberates the precious fertile blood that could have potently turned into placenta. A woman's uterus is also Coyolxauhqui" (Luna and Galeana 2016, 21). Yet their reading overlooks the painful and often conflicted relationships that people may bear with menstruation, including disabled and trans people who menstruate and the immense sites of shame and fear that such an embodied experience can cause.[2] Additionally, and importantly, Luna and Galeana's framing of "the science of menstruation" ignores how endocrine disabilities, gender variance, and other forms of nonnormative embodiment, like those experienced by Anzaldúa, may shape one's orientation to menstruation. Luna and Galeana thus, perhaps unintentionally, normalize and attempt to naturalize a process of menstruation, and leave out a number of queer, trans, and disabled relations to menstruation.

Disability and the Coyolxauhqui Imperative

As such, I propose that we consider Anzaldúa's reading of Coyolxauhqui from within a disability justice framing that attends carefully to the multiplicity of racialized and gendered bodies. From a disability justice framework, such a reading of Anzaldúa's retelling of the Coyolxauhqui story, I propose, serves as a critique of ableist tropes of objectification and fascination with disability. For example, in a study of phenomenological approaches to disability, Christine Wieseler (2018) points to two common narratives that negatively impact disabled people: tropes of tragedy or heroism (86). Depictions of disabled people as helpless and deserving of pity is one way in which disabled people have been commonly presented in differing film, television, literary, and public health campaigns (86). The second common depiction of disabled people includes an overcoming narrative or "supercrip narrative," to borrow a phrase from Eli Clare (2009), in which disabled people are viewed as exceptional, outstanding, or as worthy of praise for the difficulties that they have overcome. Both of these framings of disabled people—as heroic or tragic—Wieseler argues, fail to "provide realistic accounts of the everyday experiences of disabled people, and they tend to individualize disability rather than to consider the importance of social context" (86). Such a social context, Wieseler proposes, must consider a fuller range of the existential dimensions of disabled life under conditions of structural racism, sexism, heteronormativity, and capitalism. Threading out this insight within disability studies, Wieseler turns to resources within phenomenology that guide her reading, specifically, of experiential descriptions of amputees and people who fall under the medicalized label of body integrity identity disorder (BIID), that is, people who desire forms of bodily alteration that include paralysis, deafness, blindness, or the amputation of limbs (90). Specifically, Wieseler argues that the current literature on amputation and BIID omits the everyday experiential descriptions of living as a disabled person. Such descriptions, she avers, may illustrate how amputees, for example, understand their bodies not simply as an individualized relation regarding the state of an assumed-to-be "objective" body. Against such an account and drawing from Havi Carel's writings (2012) on illness and phenomenology and Nikki Sullivan's writings (2014) on BIID, Wieseler proposes that interpreting amputation and BIID through a lens that considers "impairment as one component of a person's life as a whole" is a more useful framing than an individualized model of amputation as pathology or loss. Being an amputee or desiring to be an amputee is about being in the world, including the social relations that one inhabits as an amputee (102). While there is no *one* set of existential possibilities for such forms of being in the world, Wieseler notes that there are possibilities for connections among amputees and people who desire amputation, and that future research on living as an amputee in connection with research on BIID would benefit from a phenomenological approach that is able to better interpret the full range of racial, gender, and class-related divisions within the lives of amputees. Highlighting such work and the potential connections between amputees and people who desire amputations, she also notes, will help diminish some of the tragedy and overcoming narratives that disabled people experience and may offer ways to more concretely engage the everyday experiences of disabled people.

From Wieseler's work and a disability justice perspective, we can find resonances between Wieseler's framing of amputation and BIID and Anzaldúa's interpretation of the Coyolxauhqui story. That is, like Anzaldúa's Coyolxauhqui narration, Wieseler's account suggests that some potential phenomenological descriptions of amputees and people who desire to be amputees will involve a broader social set of relations that frames one's orientation to their body. That is, against a view that one's relationship to bodily structures is one of simply a lack or pathology, considering amputation as a figuration of being in the world brings together a sense of social relationality along with one's intimate orientation with their own body. Akin to Anzaldúa's Coyolxauhqui story, the task of describing the orientation that one has to their own body is a social task that harkens to a set of cultural and historical relations that render a retelling of that orientation meaningful and able to be understood by others. Anzaldúa's writing of the process of re-membering is thereby not simply a form of heroism or tragedy regarding the figure of Coyolxauhqui, although elements of both tropes are present in her work at times. Rather than viewing Coyolxauhqui as requiring wholeness in a sense that demands "fixing," "curing," or reconstructing one's body to an assumed state of nondisabled or unpained life, we can read her as suggesting that re-membering is an orientation to the relations that one has to one's body and the world that requires an interpretive and socially rich community for its meaning and affirmation. Within this, identifying and living as "disabled" is one such possibility. Yet so too are dense complicated networks of shame, fear, and everyday vulnerability that can accompany identifying as disabled, as we hear Piepzna-Samarasinha state above regarding Anzaldúa's reluctance to identify as disabled.

Regarding a reorientation to one's body, in her 2002 essay "now let us shift . . . the path of conocimiento . . . inner work, public acts," Anzaldúa offers a reading of responses to trauma and forms of healing that can follow such trauma. One of the stages of transformation following trauma that she lists is "putting Coyolxauhqui together . . . new personal and collective 'stories' " (Anzaldúa and Keating, 2002, 558). In this section of the text, she describes ways of questioning one's own beliefs and shedding one's former "bodymind and its outworn story like a snake its skin" (559). Delving into personal and collective fears, insecurities, and relations with one's embodied self and the world is part of this process. Yet she also sets the location of this section as "returning from the land of the dead, you wake up in the hospital bed minus your ovaries and uterus. Scattered around you en pedazos is the old story's corpse with its perceptions of who you used to be" (558). Thus, for Anzaldúa, Coatepec, the sacred mountain where the battle between Coyolxauhqui and Huitzilopochtli took place, appears as the phenomenological center of her own embodied being. However, her understanding of oneself is "scattered around . . . en pedazos," suggesting here that her relationship to her understanding of that body is, like Coyolxauhqui's body, broken apart and fallen from Coatepec, from her own current center of embodied orientation.

Paul Scolieri (2004) notes that the depiction of Coyolxauhqui on the monolith found at the bottom of the Templo Mayor presents Coyolxauhqui as both perpetually falling and fallen: "The stone's form compounds at least two temporal relations: the cylindrical stone sculpture seems to suspend Coyolxauhqui in a permanent state of rolling, yet its carved facade entombs the goddess, immortalizing her body's crash into the earth" (93). Falling bodies, within a Mexica/Aztec worldview, is an act of unmaking and remaking, and other creation stories within the *Florentine Codex* note that falling "serves the purpose of fostering transformation . . . and order" (95). In this sense, Anzaldúa too may be referring to healing as a form of organization or stability. However, as we note throughout, such stability is impermanent and dynamic, and she directly notes this in her description in "now let us shift" (2002). She states that this step entails seeing through "the illusion of permanence—the fantasy that you can pull yourself together once and for all and live happily ever after" (Anzaldúa 2002, 562). Commenting on the perpetual regeneration of the self, she writes that "tu autohistoria is not carved in stone but drawn on sand and subject to shifting winds" (562). This means that multiplicitous selfhood entails "rework[ing] your story" and "invent[ing] new notions of yourself and reality—increasingly multidimensional versions where body, mind, and spirit interpenetrate in more complex ways" (562). The stage of "putting Coyolxauhqui together" then is an acknowledgment of a relational and increasingly multidimensional version of relations to one's embodied orientation in the world (including perhaps the construction of new liberatory syllogisms and accounts for action, as I described in chapter 3). Although Anzaldúa curiously contrasts stone and sand in this passage regarding the assumed permanence of one's re-membering, she has not failed to pick up on themes of regeneration and creation alongside relations to pain and embodied multiplicity within the Coyolxauhqui narrative.

Further connecting this work with disability theory, Wieseler notes that a Merleau-Pontyan framing of phenomenology adheres to a relational ontology rather than an individualizing one, and that the body is central for being within such an approach (84). If we focus on Nahua ontologies, we likewise find a world of relations rather than individuals, and within Anzaldúa's work we find her theorization of the Coyolxauhqui imperative as assuming the centrality of the body as well:

> All of life's adventures go into the cauldron, la hoya, where all fragments, inconsistencies, contradictions are stirred and cooked to a new integration. They undergo transformation. For me esta hoya is the body. I have to inhabit the body, discover its sensitivity and intelligence. When all your antenna quiver and your body becomes a lightning rod, a radio receiver, a seismograph detecting and recording

ground movement, when your body responds, every part of you moves in synchronicity. All responses to the world take place within our bodies. (Anzaldúa 2009, 292)

This passage affirms the insights that Wieseler notes in her development of a phenomenology of disability. For example, Anzaldúa appears to share with Merleau-Ponty the centrality of agency and action from within an embodied orientation to the world. Yet such a world is not individualized, it is constantly in motion in relation to a world as well, including others with whom one is in community.

Read in this register, Coyolxauhqui's relationship to wholeness for Anzaldúa is one of relation, between the moon and the sun, between desire and duty, between war and fear, and between erasure and expression, as the "imperative" that she draws from the story is one of writing and retelling. For example, she sets the stage of her analysis of the Coyolxauhqui imperative in "Let Us Be the Healing of the Wound" (2002) within the post-9/11 U.S. outrage and fear, and within the context of the racialized targeting of Muslims, Arabs, and other communities of color harmed by the backlash of the event. Anzaldúa focuses explicitly on communities of color and writes of the continued harms such communities experience: "So that white Americans can keep their illusions of safety and entitlement unmarred, our government sets up oppressive measures such as racial profiling which make people of color feel disposable, perpetually unsafe, and torn apart like Coyolxauhqui" (308). Feeling disposable and unsafe due to racism is a form of "dismemberment" in Anzaldúa's work. As such, this too is a relation, a relation to the threat of state violence and public persecution. Akin to the form of ablenationalism by Mitchell and Snyder (2015) mentioned earlier in this chapter, Anzaldúa presents a keen awareness of the orchestration of human relations that treats populations of color as disposable outcasts and undeserving of state protections. As she wrote in her email exchange with Keating, the "slice-of-the-pie" framings of identification, resources, and respect are dangerous in a world that constructs itself by rendering some populations expendable. Accordingly, we can find in the Coyolxauhqui narrative provided by Anzaldúa an analysis of societal fracturing and multiplicity, as well as one's embodied relationships to creative retellings and reorientations. Returning to Piepzna-Samarasinha's letter

to Anzaldúa from the world of their beds, they both demonstrate
the possibility for painful longings and creativity through relations
with disability. As I offer in this reading of Anzaldúa's work, the
Coyolxauhqui narrative is not a simple story of reintegration or
rebuilding in light of trauma. Rather, it is an embodied orientation
toward building multiplicitous relations with the world.

Multiplicitous Coalition Building

After tracing the interpretive threads above of Anzaldúa's Coyolxauhqui narrative, this section turns to three further possible areas
within her work for coalition building toward disability justice. These
areas for multiplicitous coalition are found in Anzaldúa's critique of
environmental racism, her rejection of identarian framings of political mobilization, and the relevance of the Coyolxauhqui story for
interpretations of gender-based violence.

First, regarding both identarian politics and environmental racism, Joni Adamson (2012) has linked Anzaldúa's framings of illness,
medical intervention, diabetes, and bodily pain to the transnational
agricultural industries that shaped Anzaldúa life and those of many
others in the border zones of the Rio Grande Valley. Notably, both
diabetes and various endocrine conditions have been linked to the
use of DDT and arsenic in pesticides used across agricultural sectors
in Texas (18). In fact, agricultural labor movements, critics of environmental racism, and Indigenous and Chicanx resistance movements
have been deeply intertwined with the politics of southern Texas as
well. Adamson, specifically, examines the work of Ndé Lipan Apache
scholar-activist-author Margo Tamez in relation to border militarization, environmental degradation and toxicity, and Indigenous-Chicanx
solidarity. Adamson turns to Tamez's poetry and the long traditions of Ndé Lipan Apache resistance to the industrialization and
militarization of Indigenous lands along the Rio Grande. Adamson
also notes the broad alliances among Indigenous communities and
Chicanx communities in Tamez's work. For example, both Tamez
and Anzaldúa write in their respective works about their families'
experiences as laborers in the agricultural industries in South Texas,
and, as Adamson describes, the "the human costs of diaspora and

detribalization in terms of sexual and gender violence and literal contact with toxins" (17).

Through this lens, we also see that both Tamez and Anzaldúa struggle against notions of authenticity and the stereotypical expectations for Indigenous and "ethnic" writers (17), and both reject simplistic identarian moves that reinscribe patterns of thought, affect, and habits that seek to flatten the meanings of particular Indigenous or ethnoracial identities. In an interview with Lisa Alvarado, Tamez writes that many publishers of Indigenous literature want to market books by Indigenous women that present them as "flat caricatures who are submissive and placid, complacent non-actors in their own destiny" (Alvarado 2007). To resist this tendency, Tamez describes her collection of poetry, *Naked Wanting*, as primarily a book about "decolonization, patriarchy, sexism, oppressive traditionalism and indigenism, miscarriage related to DDT and Toxaphene, indigenous women's labor and reproduction as sites of many colonization projects, erased histories" (Alvarado 2007). In this sense, Tamez's framings of environmental degradation and border militarization are persistently linked to Indigenous land claims and rejections of settler state narratives of futurity.

Similarly, throughout her writings, Anzaldúa criticizes efforts to homogenize or reduce experiences and authorial positionings of Chicanxs to reified stereotypes or identities. In the published email dialogue with Keating on disability mentioned above, Anzaldúa writes that the forms of nepantlism that she seeks would not reify particular identarian norms. Rather, she writes: "I'd like to create a different sense of self (la nepantlera) that does not rest on external forms of identification (of family, race, gender, sexuality, class, and nationality), or attachments to power, privilege, and control, or romanticized self-images" (Anzaldúa 2009, 302). In this sense, both Tamez and Anzaldúa critique narratives of collective transformation that rely on unified forms of identification that place authorial agency within existing tropes of race, gender, and other social identity markers.

If we were to read Anzaldúa more conservatively on this matter, she might appear to be advocating a rejection of forms of identification with racial and gender categories that are often important strategic tools used to counter state power and control. For example, important race-based movements, such as those advanced by the Black Liberation Army and the Brown Berets, have relied on racial identification and solidarity to resist racism, class violence, and imperialism. Yet Anzaldúa's writings on "The New Mestiza Nation" (written and revised from 1992 to 2001) suggest a more politicized approach to interpreting the functions of identity-based strategies. Specifically, her essay "The New Mestiza Nation," as well as a number of lectures that she delivered throughout the 1990s, provide a richer account of struggling with institutional and political demands that can co-opt identity-based movements and the dangers of being wedded to those demands.[3] For example, in "The New Mestiza Nation," she describes a kind of "radical multiculturalism" that is contrasted with other responses to pluralism within academic and public discourses. That is, while some people may acknowledge the reality of a plurality of communities and experiences in the United States, many "white supremacists, right-wingers, the advocates of family values, and academic elites" also often seek to preserve hegemony and systems of oppression by using frameworks of "political correctness that silence dissenting voices" (Anzaldúa 2009, 203). "Radical multiculturalists," on the other hand, she writes, "seek to split open the fantasy of a monocultural nation, interrogate the history of internal and external colonialism by the U.S. government, and protest U.S. wars against the Third World and imperialist domination of the Americas" (203). Continuing, Anzaldúa points to the difficulty of maintaining this form of radical resistance within academic and teaching professions:

> The new mestiza finds herself inside the ivory tower, inside white-colored walls. It is hard to get through that gate and many do not make it. But once she passes through that gate, she becomes a sort of Trojan horse, a Trojan mula who has infiltrated in order to subvert the system, bringing new ideas with her. . . . Overwhelmed by her multiple tasks, she often ends up seduced and subverted by the system instead of subverting it. If she is a progressive white teacher, she has to fight not only her own white sisters, but also those people of color who think, "What is that gringa doing with our stuff?" As a faculty member of color she does double, triple, quadruple work. She becomes a Trojan mula, stumbling with all this baggage. And sometimes the academy starts chipping away at her

walls as she rams the academy's walls with her head to make room for others like herself; she ends up on the floor with a bloodied head as she comes up against classrooms where she and her communities are completely invisible. The mestiza must constantly find the energy to develop strategies, meet with people, form organizations, and build coalitions. (207)

Her descriptions here of the many obstacles and dangers of preserving stances that challenge systemic oppressions such as white supremacy and heteropatriarchy suggest that, similar to Tamez and others, Anzaldúa reads deep linkages between the functions of identity-based work within academic and scholarly production. Moreover, she notes the patterned skepticism and fatigue that often accompanies antiracist and antisexist work in the academy and that becomes an obstacle to continued solidarity and activism.

Directly to this point, she writes that after degrading experiences that demoralize and discourage resistant activity within universities, academia continues to reap benefits from people of color:

After the first, second, or third year in college, or by the time the mestiza is in graduate school, chances are she has been stepped on a lot—she has boot tracks on her face. Her head is already bloodied from going up against the walls. I call this *Pisando su sombra*, and it takes its toll. She may get subverted instead of doing the subverting. In such instances, her mind and imagination are taken over, and the mestiza is internally colonialized: She is mined for her art, words, writing, and music, for her clothes, hair, and the way she walks. She is mind-mugged, violated intellectually as she faces the crisis of representation for women of color, queers, and other mestizas. (207)

Noting what she calls a "crisis of representation," Anzaldúa remains deeply skeptical of the reliance of identarian configurations within institutions that seek to benefit from "inclusion and diversity" initiatives that, while incorporating people of color, undermine our abilities to subvert or transform those institutions. We can thus connect Anzaldúa's discussions of disability and identity-ascription to a broader political critique that includes the co-optation of identities used by institutions and governments that seek to control oppressed communities, and that render identity-based movement-building as a complex negotiation of political projects and goals.

Additionally, given crip theory's own resistance to simple identarian moves and the functions of state power, we can recall McRuer's invocation of Anzaldúa as a crip theorist. Specifically, we can interpret Anzaldúa's critique of national borders, as well as the violence of gender and racial categorizations that degrade and confine experience and embodied desires, alongside Tamez and other activists, authors, and educators who have been marking the mutual imbrication of the militarization of border zones and the complexities of disability and ablenationalism. Tamez reads the toxicity, illnesses, and trauma caused by national borders as of a larger piece with the control and erasure of Indigenous communities and people of color. Moreover, both Anzaldúa and Tamez remain skeptical of identarian-based solutions to addressing those harms and see the work of bodily affirmation and coalition as necessary to avoid agential isolationist and individualizing tendencies within academic, activist, and public discourses.

We thus find a number of aspects of Anzaldúa's work that resist the forms of agential isolationism, individualization, and imperialism that maintain matrices of state power and harm disabled people. This entails a degree of ambivalence, as we have noted in the previous chapter. However, on this point, commenting on the relationship between transness and disability, Eli Clare has noted that perhaps we should "lean towards places where we name our bodily differences, even through our ambivalence, grief, and longing, in ways that don't invite and encourage shame" (Clare 2013, 263). Clare suggests that beyond desires for inclusion within patterns of gender, morphological, or medical "normalcy," there are ways to affirm each other in the familiarity of our own bodies (265). We can develop a "politics that will help us all come home to our bodies," including in our multiplicity and embodied particularity (265).

Given the functions of disability discussed above, finding sites of contestation, critique, and affirmations of embodiment and desire *within* disability remain important facets of this analysis. As such, Anzaldúa's writings on pain and embodied affirmation reject simple "cure" narratives that seek an overcoming or rejection of disability.

Instead, as Piepzna-Samarasinha, Bost, and Levins Morales attest, Anzaldúa's work provides affirmation of the complexities of pleasure, creativity, and pain within disability. When read in this way, and through the connections between Tamez's and Anzaldúa's writings on environmental toxins, exploitative labor, and land sovereignty at the Mexico-U.S. borderlands, we can strengthen the strand of critique of environmental racism in her work. For example, Priscilla Soli Ybarra (2009) has read Anzaldúa's conception of borderlands as a framing of a bioregion. Ybarra finds careful descriptions in Anzaldúa's work of the degradation of the land and waterways of the Rio Grande Valley, and how the author connects this to the colonial devastation wrought on the inhabitants of those lands for centuries. She also notes that Anzaldúa was aware of how the devaluation of the Mexican peso in 1982 had severe economic effects on the communities that rely on agricultural and manufacturing industries in the Valley (186). Anzaldúa writes: "The borderlands depression that was set off by the 1982 peso devaluation in Mexico resulted in the closure of hundreds of Valley businesses. . . . Because the Valley is heavily dependent on agriculture and Mexican retail trade, it has the highest unemployment rates along the entire border region; it is the Valley that has been hardest hit" (Anzaldúa 1999, 112, quoted in Ybarra 2009, 186). From this framing, as Ybarra notes, Anzaldúa links the poverty experienced by Chicanx communities in the Rio Grande Valley to their relations with farming, economic policy, and the land. However, as Ybarra proposes, the farming industries that Anzaldúa's own family and so many other Chicanxs and Native peoples relied on during this period "motivated a trend to clearcut the land for farms—some of which did not materialize. This resulted in clearcut lands that exposed topsoil to destructive erosion" (Ybarra 2009, 187). From this framing, Ybarra reads Anzaldúa as sensing a deep relationship between the stability of her family and communities and care for the land.

Additionally, I find Anzaldúa's analysis of a relational ontology that uses ecosystems as a framing for agency as another important theme that responds to conditions of environmental racism. She describes nos/otras as a "living ecology" in which we are interdependent with one other and the world around us. This worldview resonates with Tamez's framing of the Ndé extended kin relations within the borderlands:

Ndé are actors in a resurging revolutionary consciousness across the region; Ndé popular constructions (denouncements, posters, artwork, song, poetry, film) demonstrate the resilience and persistence of more than four centuries of forging alliances with Tlaxcaltecas, Nahuas, Coahuilas, Purepechas, Mescaleros, Jumanos, Kickapoos, and urban Xicanos—all Mexico border region indigenous peoples in extended kinships impacted by the wall. Drawing from the taproots of this history, Ndé have galvanized a multiplural indigenous reality, challenging identities imposed by state and oligarchic wardens upon indigenous peoples: "Mexicans," "Latinos," "illegals," "foreigners." . . . Ndé's inherent relationship to a homeland [are] not bounded by borders, nor based in biological "Native" authenticity, ethnicity, or race. Rather, it is bound up in a worldview of kinship, remembrance, and the recovery of mother tongues, first foods and water governance, and gender complementarity in self-governance. (Tamez 2012, 59)

Such a Ndé form of relationality, rooted within the Rio Grande Valley, demonstrates complex extended communal relationships between Indigenous and mestizx communities in the region. As Tamez asserts here and elsewhere in her work, forging memory to "mother tongues, first foods and water governance" are central to these forged alliances, as is "gender complementarity in self-governance."

Given this emphasis in Tamez's work, gender justice is framed as a pivotal facet of environmental justice. That is, Tamez links solidarity work in the borderlands explicitly to issues of gender and bodily self-determination. Pivoting to Anzaldúa's work, among her readership, Coyolxauhqui has also been used as a figure to address dimensions of sexual and gender self-determination, including the condemnation of gender-based violence in the borderlands. For example, authors and artists such as Jane Caputi and Alma López have both created works that draw from the image of Coyolxauhqui to theorize the mass murders of women in Ciudad Juárez (Caputi 2010; López 2003). Interpreting López's image, titled *Coyolxauhqui's Tree of Life*, which was created for a 2003 conference on "Maquiladora Murders," Caputi reads López's depiction of Coyolxauhqui as a symbol that requires viewers to re-member the violent genocidal forces behind the ritualistic killing, rape, and torture of women working in the maquiladoras of the borderlands. Coyolxauhqui, as brutally murdered by her brother, is symbolic of what Caputi calls "gynocide" (Caputi 2010, 279–280). Gynocide, Caputi proposes, is not an attempt "to destroy all women, but to destroy women as a spiritual, political, and cultural force and to obliterate women's group identity, with a shared history, responsibility, consciousness, and sense of values and purpose" (280). From this framing, Coyolxauhqui becomes a symbol of the patterned genocidal violence against Indigenous women and women of color who have sought to preserve, protect, and value relations among women and femmes. This figuration of violence enacted against those considered part of this group is distinct in that it does not rely on individualist identarian framings of inclusion/ exclusion. Rather, the figuration of Coyolxauhqui used by López and Caputi is a symbolic and narratological framing of the targeted violence impacting specific racialized and exploited groups of women and femmes in the borderlands.

Within this context, Jasbir Puar's (2017) analysis of the concept of "debility" becomes a relevant lens through which to interpret such multiplicitous sites of corporeal relations of women and femmes in the maquila industries of the borderlands. Specifically, Puar notes that the boundaries of "disabled" and "nondisabled" shift across differing geopolitical and historical spaces (xiv). Accordingly, differences in the labor demands of global capitalism, differences in corporeal relations to land, terrain, or waterways, and differences between the legal, administrative, legislative, and institutional frameworks across geopolitical sites shape how "disability" surfaces. Across some sites, wherein "disability" and "difference" produce rights-bearing, protected classes of people, "disability" becomes a mode of distribution of resources, whereas elsewhere such forms of resource allocation may not be available. Aligning with the work on the biopolitics of disability by Mitchell and Snyder (2015), Puar notes that an assemblage of disability can frame a "privileged category by virtue of state recognition," and that "disability" can sometimes name "that body or that subject that can aspire both economically and emotionally to wellness, empowerment, and pride" within the nation-state (Puar 2017, xvi). However, for people worldwide who do not enjoy such state recognition by virtue of their race, gender, caste, status as wage laborers, religion, and so on, Puar turns to Julie Livingston's (2006) description of "debility"

(Puar 2017, xvi). Debility describes a range of "chronic illness and senescence" that are "not regarded as disabilities: indeed they [are] 'normal' and in some cases even expected impairments" (Livingston 2006, 113, 120, quoted in Puar 2017, xvi). In this manner, the gynocide of maquiladora workers noted above in works by Tamez, López, and Caputi speak to jointly state-constructed (Mexico and U.S.) patterns of debility-impacted women and femmes living and working within industrial capitalist zones of the borderlands. While a number of journalists, scholars, human rights groups, and activists, including movements such as ¡Ni Una Más!, have called public attention to the forms of sexual violence, murder, exploitation, and environmental toxicity impacting maquiladora workers in the borderlands, there remains the patterned silence of their lives. That is, as Alicia Gaspar de Alba (2010) argues, recognition of the lives of maquiladora workers only emerges *after* their deaths (4). This failure to acknowledge or fight for the lives of workers in these industries of the borderlands could thereby be described in terms of debility, as an assumed or inevitable confrontation with bodily and psychological harm.

Within this purview, the environmental toxins and harsh work conditions that many maquiladora workers confront also contribute to poor health outcomes for workers in these industries (Adell 1999). In this vein, Gaspar de Alba frames the refusal of Mexico and the United States to investigate, prosecute, or prevent these forms of patterned violence as a complicity with their perpetuation (Gaspar de Alba 2010, 8). Thus, killings, sexual assaults, psychological devastation, excruciating labor demands, and environmental toxicity frame the conditions of debility that impact maquila workers in the borderlands. This notion, then, of conditions of debility, not disability—due to the lack of state protection and provisions—frames the range of economic, political, social, and racial dynamics that forms an assemblage or multiplicitous set of relations that is being narrated by agential communities including Gaspar de Alba, López, ¡Ni Una Más!, and organizations based in Ciudad Juárez like Casa Amiga Esther Chávez Cano and Centro de Protección Mujer a Mujer.[4]

Shifting, then, to Anzaldúa's writings and Tamez's calling in of Nahua relations within the Indigenous communities of the Rio Grande Valley, we can revisit Anzaldúa's own relationship to Nahuatl and the Mexica/Aztec ontology that she evokes in her work. Namely, although the Chicano rights movement has sought out Mexica/Aztec imagery for its own revaluation and relations to land and place, Tamez cites Ndé relations with Nahua and many other Native and Chicanx communities who share critical strategies for challenging white supremacist and heteronormative gender violence in a way that retells Anzaldúa's relationship to these stories and their place within the community in which she was raised. Within Tamez's framings of the borderlands, we can contribute a disability analysis of the environmental degradation and patterned violence impacting Native peoples and communities of color in the Rio Grande Valley. Namely, the settler colonial devastation caused by the division of Native lands and the colonial naming of mixture and purity are two forces of division, two elements of nos/otras that Tamez, like Anzaldúa, rejects. Moreover, the patterned gender violence named through López's and Caputi's framing of Coyolxauhqui signals the specific constellations of conditions that perpetuate gynocide.

Toward this latter end, Melissa Wright (1998) has put Anzaldúa's work in direct conversation with ethnographic research that she conducted with women working in the maquilas of the Mexico-U.S. borderlands of El Paso and Ciudad Juárez. Although Wright did not address Anzaldúa's later writings (given the publication of Wright's article in the late 1990s, over ten years before more of Anzaldúa's work would be compiled and made more widely available in print), Wright does begin a complex conversation about how Anzaldúa's conception of the "new mestiza" might frame the political subjectivity of the women with whom she worked. Wright argues that "maquiladora mestizas," a name for a specific political positioning, have come to understand and navigate the class, racial, and gendered conditions of the borderlands. Specifically, she traces the agential practices of two women, Rosalía and Cynthia, who attempt to climb through managerial and engineering ranks within a motorboat manufacturing maquila in the borderlands of El Paso/Ciudad Juárez (1998, 120–127). Their stories demonstrate how the two women faced patterns of white racial and gendered assimilation, including how they dressed and spoke. Additionally, they had to distance themselves from being considered "just another Mexican woman" by "play[ing] hardball," preventing labor strikes, and publicly distancing themselves from wage-laboring *mexicanas* working in the factory (120–127). Additionally, both were asked to choose between being "American" or being "Mexican," which were comments that encompassed not simply their choice of dress and gender presentation but also their work ethic. Cynthia states, for example, "Mexican culture really doesn't teach them how to respect their jobs. My family is Mexican but when it comes to work, we've got the American work ethic" (126). In response to such forms of assimilation and pressure, Rosalía attempted to challenge existing stereotypes of Mexican women as unprofessional or unsuited for managerial roles, and Cynthia refuses to disavow her *mexicana* identity within the workplace, which eventually leads to her resignation when she is overlooked for a promotion in the company.

Wright notes in several places throughout the essay that these forms of political subjectivity are not likely what Anzaldúa had in mind when she began theorizing new mestiza consciousness (Wright 1998, 115, 124, 129). Accordingly, Wright interprets Anzaldúa's new mestiza as seeking unification across the borderland and the formation of a mestiza political positioning that resists the normative and affective divides that these women face. She asks whether the probusiness maquiladora workers that she has been interviewing could be interpreted as Anzaldúan new mestizas, specifically, because "the joint effects of their self-inventions, or resignifications, also work to exclude other *mexicanas* from the material and social benefits accruing to maquiladora managers" (129). Wright concludes that their actions and descriptions of their actions (from themselves or others who know them) demonstrate a knowledge of the racial, cultural, and gendered demands on them, and negotiate how the border divides and distances people living in its proximity.

Wright appears to consider this a stretching or tension within Anzaldúa's work. However, again, were we to turn to Anzaldúa's later writings on nos/otras and the divides that have "segregated *mexicana* from *mexicana*," we have a more nuanced approach available to interpret these stories (Wright 1998, 115). That is, like the bridge, drawbridge, island, or sandbar agential framings we discussed in the previous chapter, the probusiness maquiladora workers presented in Wright's ethnographic research are, perhaps, negotiating the economic, racial, and gendered conditions created by the maquila industries in the border region. This is not to champion their actions by any means, as the consequences for wage-laboring maquiladora workers are crucial in these settings, but it is to assert that *la herida abierta*, to borrow Anzaldúa's phrase, that is, the Mexico-U.S. border, creates conditions of scarcity, violence, and shame for women that impact their agential possibilities (Anzaldúa 1999, 25). Accordingly, some of the negotiations among communities under such conditions can be considered as attempting bridgework, as Cynthia demonstrated by refusing to change her style of dress and to disavow her Mexican identity. Likewise, however, we also see drawbridge or sandbar agential movements with Rosalía, wherein she notes "I will always be *mexicana*. . . . I translate policy. So I need to know what it means to cross the bridge every day, to have your kids in an American school and try to keep up with what they want. I am *mexicana* but I'm not the traditional version" (123). In this, Rosalía appears to link herself to being *mexicana* in some way, and perhaps for those grappling with her actions, we may seek to find further interpretive and epistemic resources to understand why she has withdrawn or removed her identificatory standpoint from "traditional" *mexicanas*, a painful move that negatively impacts wage-laboring *mexicanas*. Yet among the normative forces for her actions are that her employers demand that she Americanize, stating that she is "not qualified," "she's just a secretary," and "very Mexican[, meaning] a woman in that culture doesn't know what it's really like to play hardball" (121). This racialized sexism and classism creates *una rajadura* between women in border regions. Navigating these wounds, then, is better framed through agential multiplicity, with its understanding of fracturing, provisional status, and ambivalence, rather than a framing of political agency that simply values unification despite forces that are tearing communities apart. In this way, the material distribution of resources available through movement up the managerial ranks speaks likewise to the disability exceptionalism of Puar (2017) and Mitchell and Snyder (2015). If, for instance, we assume that access to corporate benefits are one such material advantage that divides managerial and wage-laboring maquiladora workers, then, as Puar states, "access to health care may well [be] the defining factor in one's relationship to the non-disabled/disabled dichotomy" (Puar 2017, xvi).

From this analysis, then, and drawing from the critical tools developed by the disability activists and writers described above, there are thus a number of ways to extend a disability critique within and through Anzaldúa's ecological understandings of critique, care, and struggle. Specifically, through her framing of the Mexica/Aztec Coyolxauhqui story and the themes I have highlighted from her broader corpus, we find ways to address the complexity of a disability justice framing, including the attention to systemic racism, sexism, and neoliberal governance within such a view. In these ways, Anzaldúa's conception of multiplicitous agency, including her conception of nos/otras, is an invitation for further coalitional work that seeks to address the intertwinement of disability with other structures of oppression, and helps us begin to shape strategies for negotiating those complex networks of relations in the future.

Chapter 5

Building Coalition *con Nos/otras*

To delve into another specific and complex set of circumstances through which to explore the relevance of multiplicitous agency, this chapter examines relationships between categories of gender and race by considering the relevance of Anzaldúa's work within the contexts of critical transgender politics, studies of mestizaje, and Indigenous sovereignty movements. As I outline in the sections below, the scope of this analysis does not seek isolated forms of agential interiority wherein gender and racial identities are interpreted as separable or unrelated. Rather, the aim of the coalitional politics analyzed here focuses on how framings of oppression, both from Anzaldúa's work and those of other authors studying gender and racial violence, can address the multiple and, at times, conflicting, norms of solidarity work that strive to maintain both race and gender within its purview.

As such, here, we begin by working through questions regarding the potential for coalitional politics among queer Latinx scholarship on mestizaje and affirmations of trans, gender variant, and Two Spirit communities. Anzaldúa's writings have been cited and utilized by transgender and gender variant scholars since (at least) the 1980s, and her work remains significant within research in the interdisciplinary field of transgender studies today. While a number of trans and gender variant authors have focused on her writings on mestizaje to analyze the constraints of the gender binary and gendered institutions, few of these theorists have explored the implications of her articulation of mestizaje for questions of Indigenous sovereignty, a topic on which she has received significant criticism. In this vein, this chapter turns to Anzaldúa's middle and late writings—including her concept of nos/otras—to develop coalitional resources that seek to strengthen critiques of settler colonialism within the context of a critical trans politics. To carry out this analysis, in the first section I clarify the term "critical trans politics" to underscore the form of coalitional politics that I use to address Anzaldúa's work, and then I briefly turn to some authors in trans studies who have utilized Anzaldúa's work. In the following section, I raise some concerns with some of these framings of her work vis-à-vis critiques within Indigenous studies. To address these criticisms, in the final section I return to conceptual resources within Anzaldúa's work to show some strategies that may begin to develop a coalitional politics within critical trans studies that draws from Anzaldúa's work.

Trans Theorizing and Anzaldúa's Writings

Regarding terminology, I use the phrase "critical trans politics" to emphasize a particular approach to thinking about political action and the affirmation of trans life that resonates deeply with relational approaches to identity but that retains a commitment to the importance of agential positionings. Namely, transgender studies, as an interdisciplinary field of study, demonstrates the linkages between methodological specificities of a field committed to trans life in the face of a long history of work within the empirical sciences *about* trans people but not made *by* or *for* trans people. Notably, Susan Stryker's introduction to *The Transgender Studies Reader* marks the relationship between "the study of transgender phenomena" and "transgender studies." Stryker's outline of the contours of transgender studies directs readers to the varying fields of analysis that have sought to examine gender variance, including sexology, biomedical ethics, and anthropology. Within much of these discourses, the varied forms of knowledge production *from* and *among* trans and gender variant people themselves have been excluded. Unlike much of the research in these fields, transgender studies focuses directly on the experiences of trans and gender variant people, told from our own agential positionings (Stryker 2006, 12). As such, broadly speaking, trans and gender variant peoples become understood as methodologically significant contributors to the production of knowledge about gender, culture, race, and so on within transgender studies.

Transgender studies therefore takes on the complicated dynamics of positionality, experiential knowledge, and institutional and cultural production within the context of the late twentieth and early twenty-first centuries as politicized sites of epistemological inquiry. Notably, the post–Cold War, post–civil rights, and often postracial lenses through which patterns of identification and knowledge production have been challenged are relevant to the study of trans issues. As Stryker argues (and I have gestured at in previous chapters), the late twentieth century also marks a time in which debates regarding objectivity, relativism, postmodernity, coloniality, neoliberalism, and so on have contributed to the wearing away of simple claims to "pure experience," representationalism, and epistemic legitimacy. She notes that the variety of identities, naming practices, and descriptions of embodiment, experience, and self vary so widely among those people and communities usually considered within the framing of "trans" that such plurality and forms of difference "confound simplistic notions of material determinism, and mirror-style representational practices, in relation to questions of gender" (9). In this sense, as an interdisciplinary field, transgender studies takes as one of its foci the epistemic, ontological, and hermeneutical relationships between articulations of identity, positionality, and difference. Moreover, as Stryker and others propose, trans studies develops a rich method by which to contest the representational tropes inherent within discussions of gender, identity, and embodiment.

Consistent with Stryker's articulation of transgender studies, Dean Spade has elaborated a term called "critical trans politics" that deeply resonates with the account of multiplicitous agency developed throughout this book. Contextualizing the term, Spade writes that increased visibility for trans resistance arose in the 1990s, but that despite this heightened public attention, "there's been resistance to gender norms by various kinds of gender rule breakers wherever and whenever there have been gender norms" (Spade 2012, 42). Spade also remarks that trans political resistance is "often expected to follow in the footsteps of the gay and lesbian rights framework and make some of the same demands" (42). As such, for Spade and for our interests in this chapter, "critical trans politics" is naming a difference between mainstream LGBT+ inclusive-style politics, and, in Spade's words, is instead interested in "finding a way to talk about a trans

politics that isn't interested in military service, marriage, hate crime
legislation, or other elements of today's nightmarishly conservative
gay and lesbian rights agenda" (42). These functions of state recognition and security are thereby rejected within this specific approach
to trans politics. Rather than seeking to reify a nation-state's administrative apparatuses through legal protections or the enhancement of
policing and surveillance, critical trans politics seeks to demonstrate
the coimbrication of legal, security, and administrative systems and
their impact on the lives of trans and gender variant people. Such
institutions (legal, municipal, educational, medical, punitive, and so
forth) control the distribution of resources and services and make
trans people and other historically oppressed groups vulnerable to
the state's refusal. In response, Spade states that critical trans politics "centres transformative resistance to systems that are the most
harmful to trans people. It is part of critical political resistance that
raises demands like an end to wealth and poverty, an end to immigration enforcement, and the abolition of all forms of imprisonment
(immigration, criminal punishment, medical, and psychiatric). What
critical trans politics has to offer left social movements more broadly
is a particular frame for understanding how processes of gendered
racialization are congealed in violent institutions" (42–43). In this,
the term "critical" within "critical trans politics" points to a deep-
founded skepticism of individualizing notions of gender expression
and identity when they are used as a method to normalize, isolate, or
protect trans individuals through individual liberties, state surveillance
and control, or commercial commodification. The concern is that
such a focus on individual rights and patterns of inclusion misses the
very crucial structural conditions that perpetuate antitrans violence
and erasure. Against these approaches, critical trans politics takes a
transnational, sociopolitical, and historical scope, and seeks methods
to resist the material means by which trans and gender variant people, as a heterogeneous collective, face marginalization and violence,
including patterned racism, poverty, and sexual violence.

Building from Spade's conception of critical trans politics, I
consider one of the significant implications of this approach to be
that trans studies, as a field, must grapple with varying means by
which systems of exploitation and domination impact multiplicitous
ways of being gender variant and/or trans, while also, simultaneously,
finding ways to affirm the varied cultural, historical, embodied, and

politicized ways in which people have crafted meaning through confrontations with gender norms and patterned violence. In this sense, as I discuss later in this chapter, reading Anzaldúa through the lens of multiplicitous agency can build coalitional resources that respond to the material impacts of colonization, and the relationships between Chicanx and Indigenous communities who have forged practices of survival and collective meaning-making in distinct ways.

Turning to Anzaldúa's work directly, it is fairly clear that she does not identify as transgender, although there are a number of instances in which she mentions what we might consider trans framings of identity and embodiment. For example, in her 1993 piece titled "Border Arte" and in her introduction to what we could consider an expanded sequel to *This Bridge Called My Back* published in 2002, Anzaldúa appears to locate trans existence alongside other forms of liminal, border-crossing forms of experience and political significance.[1] At other times, Anzaldúa discusses her own experiences of "sexual/spiritual fantasies" and experiences of gendered embodiment that harken to trans experiences or trans desires.[2] Anzaldúa also offers some relevant distinctions regarding the "reality of raced-ness" in comparison to gender, which could be expanded to include a more careful discussion of the historical, cultural, and existential differences between processes of racialization and gendering (Anzaldúa 2015, 65).

Yet despite these particular mentions of transgender and gender variant themes, I will not be analyzing what Anzaldúa says directly about transgender identities or experiences. Rather, I would like to turn to what her trans and gender variant readers, including myself, may find in her work that is helpful for expanding a critical trans politics. That is, with Stryker's call for framings of positionality and epistemic authority in mind, we can ask whether Anzaldúa's work offers important contributions to a critical trans politics. Also, from a brief genealogy, we can see the relevance of Anzaldúa's work within the field of trans studies. This is important because trans studies and trans rights discourses have often tended to prioritize the experiences of white trans and gender variant peoples, while trans of color and Two Spirit communities are then required to define ourselves in relation to the experiences of dominant white narrations of trans experience. Rather than centering relations to racialized and gendered experience simultaneously, trans rights discourses, for example, may consider transphobia as a phenomenon distinct from that of racism.

Against such approaches, trans of color activists and scholars have attempted to redefine the relations between race and transness, for example, and in this sense, tracing the Anzaldúan insights within early white trans scholarship demonstrates the presence and importance of queer and trans of color theorizing and experience, even when such contributions and insights have been largely overlooked within mainstream depictions of trans life and history.

One pertinent example of this early influence in trans studies is Sandy Stone's now well-known critique of trans-exclusionary radical feminism titled "The Empire Strikes Back: A Posttranssexual Manifesto." Written in 1987, the piece includes a footnote citing Anzaldúa. In this note, which closes her manifesto, Stone urges trans people to "write [ourselves] into the discourses by which [we have] been written": "I also call attention to Gloria Anzaldúa's theory of the Mestiza, an illegible subject living in the borderlands between cultures, capable of partial speech in each but always only partially intelligible to each. Working against the grain of this position, Anzaldúa's 'new Mestiza' attempts to overcome illegibility partly by seizing control of speech and inscription and by writing herself into the discourse. The stunning 'Borderlands' is a case in point" (Stone 1987, 25). Anzaldúa's "new mestiza," what Anzaldúa would later refer to as a nepantlera, becomes, in the same year as the publication of *Borderlands/La frontera* (1987), utilized within transfeminist critique through Stone's work.

Talia Mae Bettcher has extended an analysis of Stone's citation in her work in the 2010s, including a 2016 chapter for the *Oxford Handbook of Feminist Theory*. In that piece, Bettcher identifies Stone as proposing a "beyond the binary" model of trans oppression that draws significantly from both Anzaldúa and Donna Haraway. Bettcher notes how Stone "celebrated the mixture of incongruent parts" and that such a mixture indicated a manner in which trans people could defy the prescribed narratives attributed to them, which included articulating specific sexual and gender narratives regarding both pre- and posttransition life (Bettcher 2016, 413). Turning to a model of integration, Bettcher describes Stone's interpretation of Anzaldúa as offering a model for mixture that would allow trans people to "own transsexual pasts and integrate that into their current self-identities" (Bettcher 2016, 413). Referring specifically to "male-to-female transsexuals," Bettcher writes that "such an embrace involves accepting one's male past, and by implication, accepting both one's history as oppressor and as oppressed, in much the way that Anzaldúa's mestiza is a mixture" (413). Here, Bettcher's reading of Stone draws a comparison between the racial, sexual, and gender liminality of *the new mestiza* of *Borderlands/La Frontera* to Stone's figuration of experience and identities of trans people as having contested, complicated, and conflicting conditions of oppression and possibilities for resistance.

Bettcher, too, discusses this conception of mestizaje and mixture from Anzaldúa in her work. She writes in her *Stanford Encyclopedia* entry on "Feminist Perspectives on Trans Issues," revised in 2014, that the "notion of mixture is . . . central in the work of Anzaldúa, who speaks against an emphasis on purity and in favor of the notion of mixed race (una raza mestiza) (1987, 99)" (Bettcher 2014a, citing Anzaldúa 1999, 102). Bettcher reads mestiza consciousness as "the capacity to see oneself in accordance with the dominant ways in which one is oppressively represented and constrained in different, and often conflicting ways" (Bettcher 2014a). Harkening to a "capacity to be conscious of this plurality of the self," Bettcher concludes that such an epistemic perspective "allows for resistance, since there is an awareness which outstrips the multiple forms of oppression by viewing them together, as well as in conflict" (Bettcher 2014a). In this sense, Bettcher, like Stone, highlights how Anzaldúa's notions of mestizaje, liminality, and multiplicity bear relevance for trans understandings of the self. Notably, some trans and Two Spirit authors have approached Anzaldúa's work as well. For example, readers have focused on her poetry (Mock 2014), the concept of "theories in the flesh" that she developed with Cherríe Moraga (Driskill 2016), her notion of "mita' y mita' " ("half and half") (Prosser 1998; Cuevas 2018), her framing of erotic desire (cárdenas 2016), and her relevance for trans studies in theology (Strassfeld and Henderson-Espinoza 2019). In these ways, we find Anzaldúa's work bearing continued relevance for trans theorizing for over thirty years. This reframing of the history of trans studies, including white trans authors, demonstrates the vital influence of contributions from Anzaldúa. The question I address below, however, will be whether such uses or appropriations of Anzaldúa from white theorists like Stone and Bettcher offer a framing of gender that is rich enough to support multiplicitous forms of trans and gender variant life among Indigenous people and communities of color. In this vein, we turn in the next section to

critiques of Anzaldúa's conception of mestizaje and the relevance of
such critiques for developing a critical trans politics that works in
the service of political projects like honoring Indigenous land and
bodily sovereignty.

Critique of Anzaldúan Mestizaje

Although mixture and mestizaje has provided an important component of Anzaldúa's writings, by the 1990s and 2000s, Anzaldúa
began grappling with some significant critiques of her theorization
of mestizaje. Importantly for our framings of the relevance of her
work for trans studies, some of these criticisms came directly from
theorists within Indigenous studies who addressed a range of issues
regarding core concepts and methods within her writings, and their
implications for questions of settler colonial violence. To address
the range of criticisms of her work, in this section I have grouped
her critics into three overlapping general areas of emphasis. Note,
however, that such groupings are not meant to mark disagreements
or lack of continuity between the authors' claims, but rather to help
clarify the range of issues that scholars of her work have pointed to
regarding Anzaldúa's relations to questions of settler colonialism and
the field of Indigenous studies. The three primary areas of critique
are (1) the primitivization of Indigeneity and lack of dialogue with
contemporary Indigenous writers, activists, and movements; (2) the
romanticization and appropriation of Indigenous histories and cultures, practices that ignore the violent existence of the settler state;
and (3) the risk of "subjectless" framings of agency/identity for
Indigenous communities and the threats such framings may pose to
Indigenous relations to land.

     Within the first critical approach, authors like Andrea Smith,
María Josefina Saldaña-Portillo, and Domino Renee Pérez have each
examined Anzaldúa's work for the problematic ways in which she
romanticizes Mexica/Aztec culture and history to the exclusion of
present-day Indigenous communities and political projects. Smith, for
example, writes that Anzaldúa's optimism and heralding of mixture
problematically locates Indigenous peoples in a historical past, specifically, the past of a more thoroughgoing mestiza feminist future. On
this point, Smith critiques queer of color theorists like Anzaldúa and

José Esteban Muñoz for rendering Indigenous peoples as a theoretical or historical precursor, or both, to a more "mature mestizaje" (Smith 2010, 52). Such queer discourses of hybridity or the "valorization of mixedness," she argues, can undermine positionalities of Indigenous communities who remain identified along oppositional lines to the continued occupation and colonization of Native lands (57).

Against such forms of erasure, Two Spirit critiques that engage settler colonial gender and sexual matrices of relations, for example, offer methods to shift out of scripts of Native disappearance and the occupation of Indigenous lands while also developing critiques of gender norms and oppression. Notably, as Michi Saagig Nishnaabeg author and activist Leanne Betasamosake Simpson states regarding Two Spirit and queer Nishnaabeg peoples:

> 2SQ [Two Spirit and queer] bodies and the knowledge and practices those bodies house as Indigenous political orders were seen as an extreme threat to settler society, sovereignty, dispossession, and the project of colonization, colonialism, and assimilation. The powerful relationships queer bodies house—consent, diversity, variance, spiritual power, community, respect, reciprocity, love, attachment— were the very first thing colonizers sought to eliminate, and they began celebrating what they thought was the genocide of 2SQ people in [the Nishnaabeg] nation long before colonization reached nations on the West Coast or in the north. (Simpson 2017, 126)

Simpson's work here calls attention to the importance of Two Spirit and queer Native presence and grounded normative practices from within Nishnaabeg demands for decolonization in what is currently the settler province of Ontario. In this vein, we could raise questions regarding whether the nonnative trans analyses offered above that turn to Anzaldúa's conceptions of mixture and border-crossing are coalitionally working toward Native sovereignty and the dismantling of settler colonization, facets of Two Spirit critique that are crucial to Indigenous self-determination.

Within this same area of critique and demonstrating concerns regarding the romanticization and appropriation of Indigenous communities, María Josefina Saldaña-Portillo (2001) has argued that

Anzaldúa's uses of Mexica/Aztec imagery and worldviews potentially support contemporary forms of Indigenous erasure in settler states like Mexico and the United States. Saldaña-Portillo writes that Anzaldúa did not appear aware of the Mexican national efforts "to resuscitate, through state-funded documentation, this particular, defunct Mexican Indian culture and history, to the exclusion of dozens of living indigenous cultures" (Saldaña-Portillo 2001, 416). The purpose then and now of such forms of resuscitation, Saldaña-Portillo avers, is to exclude and erase "contemporary indigenous subjectivity and practices on both sides of the border" (Saldaña-Portillo 2001, 416). As such, the use of mestizaje and the romanticization of Mexica/Aztec cosmologies by the Mexican settler state function as nationalist means to erase and primitivize Indigenous communities and their demands for land repatriation in Mexico. From this perspective, Anzaldúa's work remains precariously positioned in relation to contemporary efforts to repatriate Indigenous lands and to affirm Native and nonbinary modalities of kinship, desire, and embodiment among Indigenous communities.

Additionally, along these same critical veins, Domino Renee Pérez (2018) challenges Anzaldúa's account of mestizaje and another term the author used in her later work, "new tribalism," which refers to a conception of forming kinship and relational communities. Anzaldúa's use of the phrase "new tribalism" arose as a response to one of her critics, David Rieff (1991), who accused Anzaldúa of focusing too much on race and culture and of developing utopian visions for collectivities without examining socioeconomic class dynamics that placed her work within the academy. Anzaldúa and other Chicanxs have become, Rieff argued, "professional Aztecs" who profit as academics by exploiting Aztec mythology. Pérez's concern, however, considers Anzaldúa's framings of mestizaje, her use of the Mexica/ Aztec pantheon, and her articulation of "new tribalism" as a form of essentialism and primitivization that negatively impacts Indigenous peoples and cultures. Specifically, Anzaldúa, Pérez argues, became reliant on a form of intentional choice in her later writings, which participates within a kind of appropriative settler logic of "borrowing" Indigenous meanings, histories, and epistemologies.

Pérez focuses some of her critique on an interview response by Anzaldúa published in 2008 (four years after her death). In that interview, Anzaldúa states: "New tribalism is a kind of mestizaje.

Instead of somebody making you a hybrid without your control, you can choose. You can choose a little Buddhism, a little assertiveness, individuality, some Mexican views of the spirit world, something from blacks, something from Asians . . . you graft them together" (Lara 2008, 42, quoted in Pérez 2018, 247). Pérez notes that the conception of intentionality proposed is ambiguous in this passage. Notably, Anzaldúa appears to support both a form of voluntarism about identity—for example, "choose a little [of this and] a little [of that]"—and also a form of biological determinism, in terms of "grafting." For our purposes here, it is important to note that the term "grafting" was common in late nineteenth and early twentieth century discourses of evolutionary development, nation-building, and mestizaje (Novoa 2009, 32–34). Specifically, José Vasconcelos, the twentieth-century Mexican philosopher who Anzaldúa cites in her own framing of mestiza consciousness in *Borderlands/La frontera* (1987), uses the term "grafting" or *injertando* to describe processes of race mixture in Mexico (Vasconcelos 1979 [1925], 9, 32, 49, 72). Like such nineteenth- and early twentieth-century social theorists, Anzaldúa continues to grapple with tensions between the relationships between pregiven forms of natural change and willful efforts toward social transformation. Yet, as Pérez notes, such a framing of agency can be "at once superficial, a la carte spiritualism (either inclusive or independent of organized religious practices), culture, and personality[, and] also biological, like the creation of a hearty orange tree, its strength and quality of its yield attained by crossbreeding" (Pérez 2018, 248). Pérez considers the latter metaphor of the tree to be flawed because trees lack agency and therefore do not "choose to have [their] strength or productivity altered" (Pérez 2018, 248). In this sense, Pérez points to an assumed voluntarism within Anzaldúa's notion of new tribalism.

Pérez also examines how Anzaldúa uses the term "tribe" to describe forms of Chicanx identification that recognize and centralize Indigeneity and that shift away from settler colonial nationalisms, including Mexican nationalisms. In this sense, Pérez recognizes Anzaldúa's effort to undermine hegemonic forms of settler identification and categorization. Linking this notion of new tribalism with Anzaldúa's notion of nos/otras, Pérez states that this offers another attempt to disrupt neat categories of biology, kinship, heteronormativity, and so on. Pérez continues, however, that for a number of "historical, social, cultural, and political reasons" sovereign Indigenous nations are not likely to take up this form of identification (Pérez 2018, 250). Specifically, as we discussed in chapter 3 regarding "drawbridge" explanations for action, "blurring boundaries" or "constantly making and remaking Indigenous definitions of identity" is a risky strategy for communities who are fighting for a historicized connection to land, place, and collective stability (250). Moreover, Pérez notes that while there is value in the kind of dynamism that Anzaldúa offers, her view cannot account for the specific forms of appropriation and acquisition of Indigenous historical and cultural resources by those from dominant groups (250). Her work, on this reading, then, "does not promote the interrogation of the inherent subject position assumed by members of dominative groups . . . [and] it ostensibly sanctions cultural tourism and the fetishizing of difference and does not address the power relationship in this kind of taking" (250). Ultimately, Pérez concludes that Anzaldúa's attempts to forge coalition via these challenges to borders and linguistic categorizations that juxtapose novelty with history are "incomplete" and "boutique" in that she fails to attend to the specificities among Indigenous nations and authors who choose to emphasize and define Indigenous national borders as forms of Indigenous sovereignty (251, 252). Lastly, Pérez argues that Anzaldúa's approach is "an individualistic process rather than a relational one," and this view of agency leaves Anzaldúa's work with little resources for supporting community-based forms of sovereignty among Indigenous communities (251).

I return to this question of voluntarism raised by Pérez below, but for now, as a brief response, it may already appear difficult to position the strong form of individualism Pérez highlights within Anzaldúa's own commitments to self-description as a communal process and her own admission of the flawed and provisional character of her use of terms like "new tribalism" and "nos/otras." In this sense, shortly following the statement referencing "grafting" in her interview, Anzaldúa concedes:

> We need a new tribalism. We need a different way of shuffling the categories. As long as we rely on language, we'll have categories even though they're very limiting and imprisoning. Every few years we should blur the boundaries, make them porous. If we reshuffle all the categories, can we come up with new identity markers, new ways of

composing members of different groups into new groups? I've come up with "new tribalism" y allí estoy. I'm stuck [laughs]. Every so many years I add a little bit, extend the categories, pero I don't think the problem will ever be solved because life transforms all the time, so of course categories only work for so long. (Lara 2008, 42)

Likewise, years before, in an interview in 1994, Anzaldúa makes a similar statement that her conception of "nos/otras" and "the New Tribalism" are attempting to disrupt conventional category configurations (Anzaldúa 2000, 215). She notes that "categories contain, imprison, limit, and keep us from growing" (215). As such, identity categories must be disrupted and new conceptions of self must be invented. Perpetually marking the provisional and collective features of this process, she states, "The new [categories] will only be good for a few years and then somebody else will come along and say, 'These categories don't work, you didn't take into account this other part of reality.' Someone will come up with their own concepts" (215). Accordingly, she describes any identity category configurations as "very much in transition," "impermanent, fluid, not fixed," and she extends this to a broader view of "race and gender and sexual orientation," concluding that such identities are "not something that's forever and ever true" (215). Unfortunately, Pérez does not address this apparent fallibilism and temporal dynamism in Anzaldúa's discussion of these terms, and thus we turn below to whether such statements place her conception of agency within a collective meaning-making project, rather than an individualist framing. A response to these concerns about individualism also brings us back to whether Anzaldúa's work requires an interiorized, representational perspective on agency—a view that I am challenging in this book.

Yet such forms of temporal dynamism do not address Pérez's additional claim that constant "making and remaking" may be a risky strategy for Indigenous communities, whose claims to land and futurity are already threatened by settler forms of precarity and displacement. Addressing such issues further and pointing to the third critical strand mentioned above, authors within contemporary Native and Indigenous studies have examined what they describe as "a subjectless critique" circulating within queer theory and ethnic studies. For example, Smith (2011) argues that queer theory's rejection of individual subjecthood can provide a useful framework to critique the reliance of much of queer theory itself on settler colonial erasures and displacements of Indigenous peoples. In this sense, a "subjectless critique" within queer theory is a pattern of analysis, stemming from authors like Judith Butler (1990) and José Esteban Muñoz (1999), who offer lenses through which to purvey broad forms of normalization, patterned violence, and historiographical erasure (Smith 2010). Smith argues that there is no "proper subject *of* or object *for* the field" of queer studies (44, quoting Eng, Halberstam, and Muñoz 2005, 5). As such, queer theory, in this sense, rejects individualizing and insularizing tendencies. However, Smith points out that much queer theory presumes the continued existence of the settler state even while articulating a critique of its subject-driven discourses.

The resulting forms of relationality are those of conflict, shift, stabilization, and destabilization. Such imbrications within Indigenous studies, as Scott Lauria Morgensen opens his introduction to *Spaces between Us* (2011), are relational framings of the spaces between and among Native and non-Native peoples. Morgensen writes that "we are caught up in one another, we who live in settler societies, and our interrelationships inform all that these societies touch" (1). Noting the political valences of these relations, he continues that "Native people live in relation to all non-Natives in the context of the power relations of settler colonialism, though they never lose inherent claims to sovereignty as Indigenous peoples" (1). His critique throughout the book is that queer narratives of "inclusion" within an existing settler state, and queer of color critiques of LGBTQ racism that draw on the existence of "Native roots for queer culture and history," relied on a "non-Native relationship to imagining indigeneity" (13). This imagined relationship to Indigeneity further erases and displaces Indigenous peoples, both as scholars and activists of decolonization and anti-heteropatriarchy. As such, Morgensen urges non-Native queer theorists and activists to attend to their relations with Native scholars, organizers, and Indigenous methodologies to unsettle the colonial matrices of domination, exploitation, and elimination.

Regarding such a potential shift within queer studies toward decolonial relationalities, Jodi Byrd (Chickasaw) argues for "undoing the subject" of queer Indigenous studies. Namely, Byrd develops a conception of transitive relationality to account for the potential loss

of location, situatedness, and accountability that can occur through
the unmooring of subjectivity or identarian logics. Byrd writes that
a conceptual framing of Indigeneity requires "a political referent tied
to land, relation, and community, even if such referents are fluid and
mutable" (Byrd 2017, 216). Yet she continues that "as an ideolog-
ical referent that is always up for grabs, indigeneity remains elusive,
ontologically ephemeral, temporally challenged, and captured within
the discourses of discovery, enlightenment, and sovereignty" (216).
Such an interplay leads to "Indigenous subjectlessness at the site of
the queer" that moves "between colonialist practices of replacing the
Indigenous, on the one hand, and emptying the Indigenous of any
prior significance, on the other" (Byrd 2017, 216). Responding to this
tension, Byrd offers the notion of transitivity as a means to show the
fraught relations between Indigeneity and settler colonialism. Modern subjectivity, ontologies of substance, and the reification of place,
identity, and selfhood rely on the colonization and the displacement
of Indigenous peoples, lifeways, and cosmologies. Indigeneity as that
which "must have been" is an enabling condition of the stability of
settler subjectivity. She continues in this vein, "Within the structuring elements of settler colonialism, subjectivity, claiming to be, and
speaking for have gone hand in hand with the theft of lands, the
politics of replacement, and the forced normativities of compulsory
heterosexuality and lineal descent" (217). Here, Byrd marks several
important tenets of traditional framings of agency that transitivity
challenges as a response to settler colonialism. For example, "claiming
to be," as in an individualist, insularist, and isolationist statement,
requires the displacement of Indigenous peoples from territories,
governance, and even from theoretical framings of identity.

Regarding all three critical strands—primitivization, appropriation,
and subjectlessness—Sheila Marie Contreras (2008) likewise critiques
Anzaldúa's work, wherein Anzaldúa's "reconstructed pre-Columbian
mythology reproduces rhetorical strategies of self-fashioning" that are
deeply appropriationist, similar to what Chicano men have performed
through mythologizing Indigeneity, and have their roots in European
colonialist endeavors that uproot the specificity of Indigenous history
and meaning from place and context (Contreras 2008, 113–114).
Contreras writes that "although Anzaldúa strives to give expression
to the indigenous elements of Chicana identity in the present, her
persistent appeal to an Aztec pantheon represented by Coatlicue/

Serpent Skirt, Tlazolteotl, the snake, and smoking mirror effectively
dehistoricizes the relations between Chicanas/os and Natives" (117).
For Contreras, Indigenous mythology, although reappropriated for
feminist ends that respond to the violence of conquest, effectively
displaces "material history [and] the immediate moment" between
Indigenous and Chicanx communities (120). Alongside this critique,
Contreras also closely follows Anzaldúa's citations of Mexica/Aztec
mythology, storytelling, and history to show that the author is doing
something innovative within Mexica/Aztec historiography, and she
acknowledges that Anzaldúa herself criticizes Western primitivist
traditions that appropriate and "borrow" elements of Indigenous
spirituality, history, and culture. Yet, Contreras argues, even her own
challenges to these discourses end up re-creating them again through
the mythologization and periodization of the Indigenous peoples of
Mesoamerica (130). The latter of these, for example, resonate well
with Morgensen's criticisms of non-Native queer theorist's elisions
or romanticizations of Indigenous desires, embodiments, and lifeways. The reification of the settler colonial state and the assumed
permanence of colonization of Indigenous lands, even within queer
theory, Morgensen describes as "settler homonationalism" (Morgensen
2011, 120–121). As Morgensen's work demonstrates, erasing the
means whereby settler colonialism functions through understandings
of queer positionalities and relationalities is crucial.

Accordingly, the Anzaldúan multiplicitous approach to agency
that we have developed through this book that seeks to erode the
individualizing, imperialist, isolationist, and insularist tendencies of
the paradigm must also grapple with colonial expectations for the
permanence of the settler state and the naturalization of Indigenous
erasure.[3] Thus, the three strands of critique explored here point to
serious challenges to Anzaldúa's coalitional work with Indigenous
scholars and activists. This tension is important, and the authors
described above demonstrate the dangers of using conceptions of
mixture, queerness, or subjectlessness as tools that have the potential
to reify or naturalize settler colonialism and the inevitability of Indigenous erasure. These are careful concerns both for Anzaldúa scholars
and for trans theorists who rely on her work to interpret framings
of identity and gender. As noted above, for a critical trans politics
to work in the service of dismantling structural harms impacting
gender variant peoples, developing a sustained and careful critique of

settler colonialism and an affirmation of Indigenous land and bodily sovereignty are imperative.

On this latter point, regarding the relationship between bodily and land sovereignty, Alex Wilson (Opaskwayak Cree Nation) writes that recognition among Two Spirit peoples as Indigenous and resistant to colonial histories of "aggressive assimilation policies [that] have attempted to displace [their] understandings, practices, and teachings arounds sexuality, gender and positive relationships" is a form of "connection" to one's own peoples and to the land (2015, 1). Wilson notes that the "recognition and acceptance of gender and sexual diversity is reflected in the language, spirituality, and culture" of their community, the Swampy Cree Nation, including that their Cree dialect "does not include gender-distinct pronouns" (2). Yet forms of settler colonial gender and sexual violence, and the enforcement of assimilative practices impacting Indigenous communities like the Swampy Cree, have led to Two Spirit peoples being "subject to interconnected homophobia, transphobia and misogyny," both within their own communities and within mainstream contexts in which, Wilson writes, "structural and individual racism and classism" continue to harm them as well (3). Such forms of harm include elevated rates of HIV and risk of suicide among trans and gender variant Indigenous peoples, and that many live within conditions of poverty (3). Further, as Wilson also underscores, "Indigenous sovereignty over our lands is inseparable from sovereignty over our bodies, sexuality and gender self-expression" (4). As such, for both an Anzaldúan and a critical trans political project to resist state-based, individualist, isolationist, and imperialist forms of agency, dismantling the settler state must also be a central goal.

Resisting the Coloniality of Reality Enforcement

To engage the critiques outlined and their implications for both Anzaldúa's work and a critical trans politics, we can seek out resources that attempt to retain the pluralism among differing identity positions, while also retaining differential relations to power. In this, the hope is to avoid the seeming lack of accountability and relationality with approaches to "subjectlessness" as outlined by Byrd, Smith, and others. Likewise, to cleave room for responding to multiplicitous differences means that we must allow, as Byrd's conception of transitivity does, for the possibility that acting comes with something akin to the forms of relational ambivalence that we explored in chapter 3. Specifically, even in our efforts to resist, we exercise multiplicitous and ambivalent acts that must be continually situated with respect to their relations to others, places, and varied temporalities including differing trajectories of pasts, presents, and futures. While this opens space for a nontotalizing conception of multidimensional relations to power, it also reopens the possibilities for harming, reducing, or erasing agential relations with others. Here, the threats of insularism, isolationism, individualization, and imperialism reemerge as tropes of such a homogenized version of agency.

Cautious of many of these moves, Anzaldúa's critics point to relations to the settler colonial state and the erasure of Indigenous presence within her framings of mestizaje. In this sense, her work, while seeking to resist one form of oppression, potentially supports the continued oppression of Indigenous peoples. Such a tension, as I point out above regarding the normative aims of a critical trans politics, also likely places Anzaldúa's work in tension with affirming Two Spirit demands for Indigenous land and bodily sovereignty.

Following Levins Morales's call from the previous chapter to "remap" relations of power through our bodies, I would also like to turn to resources within trans philosophy to potentially find ways to augment the critical insights raised by Anzaldúa that seek to dismantle the settler state. Perhaps surprisingly, we find resources in Bettcher's work, written from the positionality of a white Canadian trans feminist, to help build a bridging framework for mapping possibilities for coalition building between non-Native trans communities and Two Spirit and queer Native communities. Notably, Bettcher offers a model of trans feminism that attempts a "transformative approach" to respond to concerns that she sees remaining despite the critical moves made by the "beyond the binary" and queer theoretical interventions within authors like Stone and perhaps also Anzaldúa. Moreover, due in part to the prominent influence of María Lugones within Bettcher's work, Bettcher's account seeks to preserve the multidimensionality of identity practices and embodied experiences, as well as the pluralisms of resistance to transphobia and gender violence. As such, her work becomes an attempt to bridge Anzaldúa's work with a critical trans politics that seeks a critique of

settler colonialism. Such a model, as I argue below, resists individualizing tropes that divide and distance non-Native trans and gender
variant peoples from the political projects of Indigenous communities.
Rather, her work, enacting a multiplicitous agential framing, places
non-Native trans people, including Latinx peoples, in relations of
accountability and responsibility for affirming Indigenous claims to
land and bodily sovereignty.

To clarify, Bettcher underscores how some versions of the
"beyond the binary" model of trans identity and oppression "inval-
idates trans people who identify within the binary," and this has
been pointed out in the theoretical work done by Bettcher herself
(2014b), as well as by other white trans theorists such as Viviane
Namaste (2005) and Jay Prosser (1998). In this vein, some "beyond
the binary" models propose that the *only* resistant positionalities
for trans people come from people who do not identify as men or
women. In response to this stance, which may, in effect, construct
trans existence as the "constitutive outside of the gender binary," she
argues that "beyond the binary" models may overlook the plurality
and existential descriptions of trans life from trans people themselves
(Bettcher 2016, 417, quoting Salamon 2010).

In this vein, we also see resonances between Bettcher's concerns
and Smith's critique above regarding the use of mestizaje as a valorization of mixedness, futurity, and a complicated conception of agency.
Smith writes that Anzaldúa's conception of mestizaje, which heralds
the new mestiza as developing a "tolerance" for ambiguity and which
becomes a generative source of agency, relegates the experiences of
Indigenous women as static and agentially uncomplicated. "Indigenous women are implicitly posited as non-'whole'—as subjects who
supposedly do not live and work though contradiction and ambiguity
as well" (Smith 2011, 62). Juxtaposing this to Bettcher's concern
outlined above, we see a parallel worry that people who do not identify as "trans" or as somehow "beyond" or against the gender binary
are viewed as static, complicit, or as duped by hegemonic forms of
gender organization. However, the resonances of staticness that Smith
points to that impact Indigenous peoples are part of a patterned
form of racialization, colonization, and genocidal logic that interprets
Indigeneity as primitive and "barbarous." Importantly, this is a form
of violence that is directed at Native peoples, and that non-Native
trans peoples are not forced to reckon with. As Wilson makes clear

above, the stakes of Indigenous claims to sovereign relations to the
land thus remain intimately connected to land in ways significantly
different from non-Native trans people. Yet, with this crucial difference to relations in mind, we can see that the rejection of colonial
binaries (such as Indigenous/European and man/woman) is the
implicit operative notion within both framings of agency and futurity.
Such an approach harkens to that of Lugones and Byrd, who both
consider the relationships between colonial binaries, their tensions,
and resonances as part of a politics of coalition, meaning-making,
and interdependence. In this, the rejection of the gender binary for
non-Native trans peoples could likewise note not simply a rejection
of a narrow colonial lens of the gender binary, but rather endorse
a critical positionality that contends that settler colonialism itself is
responsible for the enforcement of gender norms that pathologize
and structurally harm trans and gender variant peoples.

Building toward such a critique, regarding agency and futurity,
Bettcher proposes a framing of trans oppression that she considers
a pathway toward building coalitional ties among trans communities and beyond them. Rather than asking the question regarding
whether trans women are oppressed "like" cisgender women, for
example, she describes trans oppression along different lines. She
argues that trans and gender variant people experience what she calls
"reality enforcement," which is a "type of transphobia [in which] the
identity invalidation of [trans people] is situated in discourses about
appearance, reality, exposure, discovery, and deception" (Bettcher
2014b). Specifically, Bettcher identifies several features of this type
of oppression: identity invalidation, the deceiver/pretender double
bind, and genital verification:

1. identity invalidation—"the erasure of a trans person's
   gender identity through an opposing categorization
   (e.g., a trans person sees herself as a woman, but she
   is categorized as a man)."

2. the deceiver/pretender double bind—"[an appearance-
   reality] contrast is manifested in one of two ways that
   constitute a double-bind for trans people—namely,
   passing as nontrans (and hence running the risk of
   exposure as a deceiver) or else being openly trans (and
   consequently being relegated to a mere pretender)."

3. genital verification—"Genital verification can be a literal
    exposure . . . or else a discursive reveal through euphe-
    mistic comments like 'was discovered to be anatomically
    male.' These disclosures anchor identity invalidation in
    the notion of genitalia as a kind of concealed reality."
    (Bettcher 2014b)

Reality enforcement, thereby, implicitly contains a homogenizing
tendency to erase multiplicity and the heterogeneous forms of identification that arise from embodied experiences and desires. Genital
verification, identity invalidation, and the pretender/deceiver double
bind all mark ways in which identity must be linked to individualized,
interior framings of selfhood and gender presentation that somehow
cohere with a prescriptive account of genital status. In her work, Bettcher has called this assumed form of genital status "moral genitalia,"
an assumed bodily morphology that operates through framings of
"the genitalia that nature intended" (Bettcher 2014b, 393).[4]

Bettcher's analysis of reality enforcement explicitly focuses on
the coalitional links between reality enforcement and racial oppression. Pointing to the associations of sexual violence, aggression, and
rape made by people like Janice Raymond and other critics who
allege that trans women are deceptive and damaging participants
within feminist projects, Bettcher argues that her readers ought to
analyze reality enforcement as a facet of the very racial oppressions
that impact people of color, including trans people of color. Some
examples include the perpetuation of the myth that Black men are
sexually predatory and dangerous, and the erasure of the continued
sexual violence and degradation done to Black women, both of which
are ways in which reality enforcement functions within the systemic
violence enacted on Black communities.

Bettcher proposes conceptual resources such as identity invalidation, pretender/deceiver tropes, and genital verification as ways to
form coalitional ties among trans, intersex, and nontrans and nonin-
tersex people who are impacted in varying ways by these dynamics,
and which help shape "a coalition grounded in resistance against
multiple modalities of sexual violence" (Bettcher 2016, 424). Lastly,
Bettcher argues that among the resistant positionalities of trans communities, regardless of whether one identifies with the gender binary
or not, is that within many trans subcultures "gender presentation

simply provides no information at all about genital status" (421). In effect, she argues, this is a significant form of trans resistance to reality enforcement.

In these veins, I would like to further explore Bettcher's notions of identity invalidation, the deceiver/pretender double bind, and genital verification as resources to build coalitional strategies that seek the dismantling of settler colonization alongside queer/trans communities of color and Two Spirit and queer Native scholars/ activists. First, as Wilson, Simpson, and other Indigenous scholars argue, a number of Native communities have historical, cultural, and linguistic forms of existence that likewise do not enforce relations between gender presentation and genital status. While, as Native scholars like Wilson note above, Two Spirit, queer, and trans Native peoples still experience colonial enactments of reality enforcement in their home communities, for many, such enactments constitute the perpetuation of colonial violence within their communities, as it is the gender variance and bodily sovereignty of such communities that has been threatened and diminished by settler logics of assimilation. For example, Deborah Miranda (Ohlone–Costanoan Esselen Nation of California) describes a process of "gendercide" in which Spanish colonial missionaries attempted to destroy *las joyas*—a name given to gender variant Chumash peoples of Southern California—due to the threat that their perceived gender/sexuality presented to Spanish colonial conceptions of order (2013). Miranda argues that acts of murder, renaming, forced regendering through dress and bodily adornment, and the erasure and replacement of relations to communal labor and care among the Chumash Nation attempted to carry out the gendercide against *las joyas* (352–359). Yet Miranda also notes that "*joya* identity did not disappear entirely" and that contemporary Two Spirit peoples of California are reconstructing and reclaiming their relations to their joya ancestors, the land, and their current communities (360). In this sense, Chumash Two Spirit communities constitute resistant communities—both beyond non-Native metrics of gender and in the sense that Bettcher describes—in that they do not enact forms of reality enforcement that seek to diminish forms of trans and gender variant life.

Second, we can also locate an expanded conception of the deceiver trope extending throughout settler colonial logics. Consider, in this vein, Saldaña-Portillo's most recent research (2016) on Mexico-U.S. border territories and ongoing processes of settler colonization from both nation-states. She titles her most recent book *Indian Given* in an effort to demonstrate the dual settler logics within the U.S. and Mexican nation-states. While distinct, both states attempt to erase and exploit Indigenous populations for a settler futurity that seeks to ensure the dispossession of lands from Native communities. That is, in the United States, the trope of "Indian giver" "is someone who takes back something they have willingly given or sold, and the slur derives its meaning from another popular myth of U.S. history, that the Indians gifted colonists their land, fair and square, and now they unjustly demand its return" (Saldaña-Portillo 2016, 12). Within the Mexican model, she notes that

> Mexican historiography openly recognizes the violence and injustice of indigenous dispossession at the hands of Spanish conquistadors. . . . [Yet] the violence and suffering of indigenous people in the conquest is constantly, reiteratively affirmed and projected onto [the] landscape. . . . The generalization of indigenous injury to the entire Mexican population by the popular phrase "hijo de la chingada" (indeed as source of the population) paradoxically renders contemporary indigenous grievance impossible, just as the slur "Indian giver" renders contemporary indigenous redress unnecessary (because U.S. Indians presumably gave up their land voluntarily). (Saldaña-Portillo 2016, 12–14)

From this framing, she argues that the "dispersal of injury" within the Mexican settler state effectively denies the land sovereignty of Indigenous peoples. Accordingly, demands for distinct claims to land from present-day Indigenous peoples bordered within the Mexican settler state face a prominent mestizo nationalism that denies any relevant political distinctions or relations to place among its populations. As such, these two "myths" of relations to Indigeneity, as "fair and square" land acquisition by U.S. settlers and the erasure and dispersal of equal Indigenous injury and affectedness within the Mexican settler state, perpetuate a belief that Indigenous peoples today are merely attempting to "deceive," defraud, or deny settlers their assumed access to land, or as communities simply "pretending" to be Indigenous within a national context for the sake of access to resources that, according to this settler logic, should be available to all citizens given their shared relations to an Indigenous past.

Read in this way, Bettcher's framing of the pretender/deceiver trope can be read as a gender-focused critique of colonialism that would support the critical work of Indigenous scholars such as Gerald Vizenor's (Minnesota Chippewa Tribe) analysis of concepts such as "Indian simulation" and "postindian warriors" (1999). Specifically, Vizenor uses these terms to critique the conceptual and aesthetic framings of "Indianness" that have been demanded of Native peoples, creating double binds that assume a possible meaning for the term "Indian" that bears "no referent in tribal languages or cultures" (Vizenor 1999, 11). Accordingly, what Bettcher names as a double bind for trans communities is a much more multilayered problem within Two Spirit, queer, trans, and gender variant Native communities. The demand to confront claims of authenticity within Indigenous communities exists in relation to demands to confront colonial gender binarism and assumptions regarding the assumed naturalness of gender/sex positionalities. Combining this insight with the settler homonationalism of Morgensen, it is also the case that queer Native and Two Spirit people must confront the romanticized and exoticized expectations of queer and trans settlers who romanticize Indigenous communities as holding all the answers to forms of gender and sexual oppression.

For example, Joshua Whitehead's (Peguis First Nation) *Jonny Appleseed* (2018) is a story about the life of Jonny, a young Oji-Cree "urban NDN, Two-Spirit, femmeboy" who supports himself as a webcam performer for mostly queer settler men (Whitehead 2018, 45). Jonny notes early in the novel that he is often pursued on gay dating/hook-up apps like Grindr by "treaty chasers," who "fetishize the hell out of [him]" if he describes himself as Native (18). "Treaty chasers," Whitehead's nod to "chasers" as a term for cisgender people who fetishize trans people,[5] is a term the author uses to reference the manner in which gay white settler men seek out Native authenticity and sexualized conceptions of spiritualism and mysticism from Indigenous peoples. Morgensen's work demonstrates such patterned expectations for Native authenticity when analyzing "back-to-the-land forms of counterculturalism" by non-Native gay and lesbian communities like the Radical Faeries (Morgensen 2011, 67). Moreover, Whitehead's term "treaty chaser" also calls to mind an erotized form of domination circulating within an assumed right to access to the lands and bodies of Native peoples by settlers, that is, "chasing" a myth of legitimacy for contractual rights to Native bodies and lands. While Bettcher's conception of reality enforcement does not, in itself, do the work of such intricate theorizing of settler colonial relations, reality enforcement, in an extended sense, could be used to describe patterned gender and sexual demands within forms of settler colonial violence that impact Native and non-Native peoples in distinct ways, including the demands that non-Native queer and trans peoples place on Native peoples through exoticization and romanticization.

Relatedly, another way in which Bettcher's framing of reality enforcement may support forms of Two Spirit critique is through the anthropological exoticization and fascination of Indigenous sexuality and gender practices. Such objectifying forms of curiosity add further layers of academic participation with genital verificationism, demonstrating its use as a tool of gender oppression inflicted on Indigenous communities in specific ways. That is, as Qwo-Li Driskill, Chris Finley, Brian Joseph Gilley, and Morgensen suggest in their discussion of the development of Two Spirit theorizing and critique in the 1990s, the use of the term "Two-spirit" as a broad identification of forms of Indigenous framings of gender and sexual diversity arose as a response to a form of identity invalidation from anthropological and non-Native queer communities (Driskill et al. 2011, 11). Notably, the term "berdache" had circulated throughout the 20th century within gay and lesbian anthropological studies (Morgensen 2011, 67). In response to this anthropological naming, Morgensen notes "by the late 1980s, Native queer activists . . . called berdache an erroneous colonial term that represented Native peoples in primordial and generalizing terms, while projecting masculinism and sexualization onto them" (81). This latter point, about the masculinization and sexualization of Indigenous peoples, stemmed from anthropologists who, through the promotion of berdache discourses, "naturalized specifically masculinist colonial discourses and generic or specific references to male embodiment and desire as focal points of the sexual nature and rights defined in sexology and homosexual emancipationism by white men" (47). Later, in the 1980s, feminist anthropologists like Harriet Whitehead would critique berdache roles as appropriating women's spheres within Native societies, a critique that Morgensen aptly connects to other "radical feminist suspicions that male-to female transsexuals [are enacting] a conspiratorial agenda of male appropriation of women's power" (61). Thus, here, as with the anti-trans work of Janice Raymond, we have another instance of a deceiver trope being enacted by a feminist critic, yet, in this case, the feminist critic utilizes the epistemic authority of the anthropological sciences to further invalidate Indigenous peoples' perspectives about their own bodies, communities, and relationalities.

In response to this, the international meetings of American Indian and First Nations Gays and Lesbians taking place during the late 1980s and early 1990s declared the need for a "a new term for Native sexualities and gender diversity" (81). The term served different ends for different Native activists and scholars, for example, by rejecting the masculinism of the term berdache, as Beverly Little Thunder (Standing Rock Lakota) states, or by resolving "a separation from tribal identity, language, or society caused by racism and assim-ilation" as Wilson (Cree) and Michael Red Earth (Sisseton Dakota) state (81). Morgensen writes: "Two-spirit announced a Native identity that refused to be identical to or to be absorbed by berdache or any other gender or sexual identity defined on non-Native terms" (82). In this vein, the critical discourses of Two Spirit identification and meaning reject the harms of identity invalidation from both non-Native queer/trans and cis/heteronormative communities, and serve to undermine settler colonial deceiver tropes in ways that exemplify acts of bodily self-determination. As such, Bettcher's work, when put in the service of considering colonial dimensions of the gender binary, may function as a bridging framework to demonstrate resis-tant positionalities against colonialism among both non-Native trans communities and Two Spirit/LGBTQ Native communities. That is, one of Bettcher's primary concerns is to show that binary-identifying trans and gender variant people can create community norms whereby "gender presentation simply provides no information at all about genital status" (Bettcher 2016, 421). In effect, she argues, this is a significant form of resistance to reality enforcement. As such, reconfiguring embodied norms and community relations through the lens of relations to land and community becomes a means through which to resist violence across Indigenous, Black, brown, and white settler communities. Importantly, this entails that however non-Native trans peoples identify ourselves and the forms of oppression that we face, that we do so with an explicit understanding that when our deepest senses of belonging and futurity rely on our "right" or need to be recognized, affirmed, or included within the settler state, we are situating Two Spirit and all Indigenous peoples in relations of further displacement, marginalization, and erasure.

Multiplicitous Coalition Building

Thus, to build a critical trans political project that affirms Indigenous sovereignty means that we can shift to an account of gender violence that is dynamic enough to interpret the multiplicitous ways in which trans, Two Spirit, queer Native, and other gender variant peoples confront harms, including the very different valences in which differing communities will be impacted by framings of colonial violence, racialized violence, systemic poverty, the medical industrial complex, and so on. However, as Byrd cautions, such dynamism cannot become so unstructured that it leads to the forms of "emptying" of Indigenous claims to relations to land or other politicized positionalities that assert bodily self-determination. Regarding Anzaldúa's work we should attend to how differing practices of naming and meaning-making may invalidate projects of Indigenous sovereignty, including her reenvisioning of terms such as "mestizaje" and "tribalism." Rather than a dismissal of Anzaldúa's work (which some Two Spirit and Native feminist scholars have also chosen not to do),[6] I propose that her conception of nos/otras, when read as a form of multiplicitous agency, may support an interpretation of the stakes of inclusion and exclusion within resistant projects like those described in the previous sections from Anzaldúa's critics and Bettcher. Accordingly, we can now revisit Anzaldúa's later writings to develop a multiplicitous framing for relational agency that aids in coalition efforts between such resistant communities. This account of relational agency will hopefully, through an analysis of historical and material conditions impacting Chicanxs in the U.S. Southwest, address some of the concerns regarding mythologization and primitivization that critics like Smith, Contreras, and Pérez raise in their critiques. Also, as her critics have noted, Anzaldúa's work potentially obfuscates contemporary Indigenous demands for sovereignty and land repatriation, and, in this vein, we could explore whether, as

Morgensen and Saldaña-Portillo do, what shifts within Anzaldúa's own work would more carefully connect her writings to dismantling settler colonization and would better engage contemporary Indigenous theory, activism, and calls for Native sovereignty (Morgensen 2011, 181–185; Saldaña-Portillo 2001, 414–415). In this vein, Anzaldúa's work demonstrates a deep tension within the agential framings of Chicanx relations to mestizaje and Indigenous sovereignty and land repatriation movements, all issues that non-Native trans theorists who draw from her work must also consider.

Perhaps one of her most prominent critics, Saldaña-Portillo, points out that Anzaldúa's critiques of borders and her desires for theorizing border experiences bears potential for a decolonial turn. She writes that if Anzaldúa's conception of new mestiza consciousness is able to deconstruct "us" and "them" framings of people, cultures, and politics from the "artificial duality of the [Mexico-U.S.] border," then her work would "unsettle" how mestizaje has functioned for the Mexican nation-state and the Chicano rights movement as well. This would require an examination of how Chicanx communities, Mexican communities, and Indigenous communities, in their complex pluralities, are situated vis-à-vis relations of power to one another. Specifically, she asks whether Anzaldúa's work can "place each of these positionalities in that uneasy and 'constant state of transition' within a capitalist world-system that depends on our difference for its own reproduction" (Saldaña-Portillo 2001, 414). Saldaña-Portillo appears to take note here of the economic, colonial, and political stakes whereby state borders shore up, distribute, and deny resources based on settler colonial fantasies of national identity and futurity, themes that we touched upon in the previous section and chapter within the context of ablenationalism. Saldaña-Portillo then concludes, however, that Anzaldúa fails in *Borderlands/La frontera* to break from a 1970s iteration of mestizaje and thus falls back into a romanticized Indigenous past that does not examine the extant power relations between Chicanx and Native communities.

In response to Saldaña-Portillo's critique, in a 2003 interview with *SAIL: Studies in American Indian Literatures*, Anzaldúa stated that she believed that Saldaña-Portillo had misread her work and that she had not read enough of her work published after *Borderlands/La frontera*. She agrees with the author that "a lot of us Chicanas/os have Eurocentric assumptions about indigenous traditions" (Anzaldúa 2009, 289). She also notes that Chicanxs (and we could add, Latinxs) "do to Indian cultures what museums do—impose western attitudes, categories, and terms by decontextualizing objects and symbols, by isolating them, disconnecting them from their cultural meanings or intentions, and then reclassifying them within western terms and contexts" (289). Conceding that she belongs to a group that has not been critical enough about Native-Chicanx relations, she suggests that her later writings offer responses to her critics. In this same interview, Anzaldúa distinguishes between appropriation by settlers that seek to perpetuate Indigenous erasure and genocide, and a form of appropriation by Chicanx communities who are seeking forms of collective life and struggle against the harms of colonization, work in which she sees herself participating. As such, to examine whether Anzaldúa's work can address the political aims proposed by Saldaña-Portillo and other Indigenous studies scholars, including those whose work bears relevance for critical trans politics, I propose that we can follow her suggestion and examine whether her later work, including her account of nos/otras, does, in fact, offer resources to examine some of the concerns that Saldaña-Portillo and her other critics name.

Before we shift to Anzaldúa, however, we can add a layer of complexity regarding Saldaña-Portillo's critique. It is important to note that Saldaña-Portillo continues to address relations between Chicanx and Native communities in her own research, and has returned to the issue that Anzaldúa raised regarding how Chicanx communities "borrow" from Indigenous cultures in a later work. That is, in a 2015 article, María Eugenia Cotera and Saldaña-Portillo examine what they refer to as "Chicano indigeneity," which are claims by politicized Mexican-descended peoples to recognize and honor their Indigenous ancestry and relations to such peoples and places. Cotera and Saldaña-Portillo trace the shifting forms of settler logics impacting what is currently the U.S. Southwest, and mark the differences that impact Indigenous and mestizo communities within those regions.[7] Likewise, Saldaña-Portillo and Cotera shift away from an individualizing focus on a single author, like Anzaldúa, and instead explore the historical conditions that may help readers make sense of collective relationships among Chicanx and Indigenous communities. They write that the 1848 Treaty of Guadalupe Hidalgo required mestizos living on the newly defined U.S. side of the border to disavow their

Indigenous heritage in order to maintain private property rights. Specifically, in places like California, "Mexican landowners had to prove they were no more than 1/32 indigenous or afromestizo in order to have their land titles recognized as legitimate by the state government" (Cotera and Saldaña-Portillo 2015, 562). This form of disavowal was in sharp contrast to the prevailing Mexican mestizo racial logic in which citizenship rights and national belonging were tied to descendancy from Indigenous ancestry. As such, they write, "In state and federal legislatures, and before the Courts, Mexicans could not be Indians and Indians could not be Mexicans" (Cotera and Saldaña-Portillo 2015, 562). These differing colonial logics thereby created specific relations to Indigeneity among those U.S. communities who were formerly recognized as being granted relations to land and place within the Mexican nation-state.

Accordingly, Cotera and Saldaña-Portillo call this loss of relations after 1848 "mestizo mourning." They describe this as "mourning for the loss of a historically *filial* relationship with indigenous peoples forged over centuries of interaction, intermarriage, collaboration, and alliance" (558). These filial relations were severed, they argue, not by biology, but by a U.S. racial logic that demanded a strong disidentification with Indigeneity in order to remain in relations of place. They conclude that Chicanx claims to Indigenous heritage, then, are a form of mourning of those lost filial relations, rather than simply an appropriative attempt to include themselves within Native tribal identities (558).

We could then read this form of mourning as functioning within Anzaldúa's discussions of Chicanidad and Indigeneity. For example, she states "I don't call myself an india, but I do claim an indigenous ancestry, one of mestizaje" (Anzaldúa 2009, 282). We can then read her discussion of mestizaje and her relational claims to Indigeneity as functioning through this form of mestizo mourning. At first glance, we might consider such Chicanx claims of indigeneity as practices of settler appropriations of Indigeneity, a common strategy that Eve Tuck (Unangax) and K. Wayne Yang call "settler nativism" (Tuck and Yang 2012). Settler nativism occurs when settlers "locate or invent a long-lost ancestor who is rumored to have had 'Indian blood,' and they use this claim to mark themselves as blameless in the attempted eradications of Indigenous peoples" (10). Tuck and Yang consider this move a "settler move to innocence," whereby settlers avoid confronting their responsibility and accountability for colonialism and the continued occupation of Indigenous lands without "giving up land or power or privilege, without having to change much at all" (10). These concerns outlined by Tuck and Yang also point us to the criticisms regarding romanticization and lack of engagement with contemporary Indigenous writers leveled by Contreras, Saldaña-Portillo, and Pérez mentioned above.

However, we might also consider whether Chicanxs are "settlers" within such a framing of "settler nativism." Cotera and Saldaña-Portillo note that a number of Indigenous, mestizo, and afromestizo peoples participated in the northern expansion of Mexico, and as such they may be more aptly considered "arrivants," to use the phrase Byrd adapts from Kamau Brathwaite to describe the diasporic movements of nonwhite peoples in relation to Native communities and their relations to land (Byrd 2011, xix).[8] Namely, Spanish and *criollo* administrators encouraged, and sometimes required through force, the participation of mestizos, afromestizos, and Indigenous peoples in the northern expansion of the Spanish settler state in the late eighteenth and early nineteenth centuries. In response, differing bands and members of mestizo, afromestizo, and Indigenous communities participated with (and resisted) the settler state in various ways in Mexico (Cotera and Saldaña-Portillo 2015, 557). For example, under Spanish and later Mexican state policies, arrivants to the regions that are now the U.S. Southwest were granted enfranchisement and often offered land in exchange for their participation in the military exploits of the Spanish and Mexican governments. However, after the annexation of northern Mexico by the United States following the 1848 Treaty of Guadalupe Hidalgo, much of the qualifications for citizenship were determined by state governments. As Cotera and Saldaña-Portillo note, U.S. state legislatures often chose not to honor the political status that arrivants once held under the Mexican state. In California, New Mexico, Arizona, and Texas, they write that Anglo-American legislators found numerous ways to deny land rights to Mexican Indigenous peoples, mestizos, and afromestizos. They point out that "the second article of California's 1849 state constitution, for example, explicitly restricted suffrage to 'Every white male citizen of the United States, and every white male citizen of Mexico, who shall have elected to become a citizen of the United States' " (559–560). With these framings of differing settler states

in mind, Cotera and Saldaña-Portillo argue that Chicanx claims of
Indigenous identity are ways for many descendants of these generations of Indigenous, mestizx, and afromestizx peoples to mourn a
lost relationship to Indigeneity that was once able to coexist with
their political participation with the settler state and able to remain
in relation to other Indigenous nations and the land. Saldaña-Portillo
and Cotera then conclude, unlike a settler move to innocence, that
"Chicana/o indigenism cannot be reduced to a settler fantasy" (560).
The reason is that such an interpretative "would be to recapitulate
the 'colonizing trick' that exiled U.S. *mestizos* from their familial,
cultural, and epistemological links to indigeneity; links that, under
Spanish colonialism and Mexican independence, had contributed
to the survival of indigenous cultural expression amongst *mestizos*"
(560). From this framing, they acknowledge the deep multiplicity
of meanings of Indigeneity, including the forced displacement and
colonial demands placed on Indigenous, mestizx, and afromestizx
communities across settler states in the Americas. Returning to
such a collective set of relationalities among Indigenous communities, including mixed-status and displaced communities, Cotera and
Saldaña-Portillo suggest that we read Anzaldúa's commentary on
Indigeneity from within this multidimensional lens.

    With this in mind, we can examine whether Anzaldúa's discus-
sions of Indigeneity (in which she responds to Saldaña-Portillo) and
the resources in her later writings potentially open some possibilities
for interpreting her as taking on this form of mourning. Namely,
she states in the 2003 *SAIL* interview:

> To have an Indian ancestry means to fear that la india
> in me that has been killed for centuries continues being
> killed. It means to suffer psychic fragmentation. It means
> to mourn the losses—loss of land, loss of language, loss
> of heritage, loss of trust that all indigenous people in this
> country, in Mexico, in the entire planet suffer on a daily
> basis. La gente indigena suffer a loss that's cumulative
> and unrecognized by the masses in this country, a loss
> generations old, centuries old. To have Indian ancestry
> means to bear a relentless grief. (Anzaldúa 2009, 283)

Anzaldúa also invokes concepts from her framings of agency and
identity in this interview, noting that, at present, the form of mes-

tizaje that she envisions may indeed serve to erase the specific claims to Indigeneity among "mixed-blood" peoples (283). However, she encourages dreaming of a futurity in which Indigeneity is secured as a continued presence alongside mixed-blood and mestizo/a status, without the threat of tropes of perpetual Native disappearance. In this, she appears to respond to concerns about how her critique of identarian forms of identification still preserve place for the deep-seated relations to land and history that Indigenous communities hold.

As noted in previous chapters, Anzaldúa's framing of multiplicitous agency is neither an erasure of differences nor the unification of all seemingly disparate political efforts. Rather, as Anzaldúa states in an earlier work, "La Prieta" published in *This Bridge Called My Back*, "el mundo zurdo" is a "path of two-way movement—a going deep into the self and an expanding out into the world, a simultaneous recreation of the self and a reconstruction of society" (Anzaldúa 1981, 208). This movement between self and social change does not require unification of identities or common oppressions. She writes a few lines later, "Not all of us have the same oppression, but we empathize and identify with each other's oppressions" (209). This is an acknowledgment of differing relations of power, and she notes that "we do not have the same ideology, nor do we derive similar solutions. . . . But these different affinities are not opposed to each other" (209). Regarding shared coalitional space, she concludes that "in El Mundo Zurdo I with my own affinities and my people with theirs can live together and transform the planet" (209). Following these threads, readers of Anzaldúa such as AnaLouise Keating and Mariana Alessandri have noted that El Mundo Zurdo is a vision of spaces of coalition for oppressed peoples (Keating 2009, 322; Alessandri 2019). Rather than assuming common causes of oppression or common identities, Anzaldúa understood such coalitional spaces as retaining differences in position, histories, and experiences. Among the unifying features of such coalitional spaces were shared visions of ending multiple oppressions and the coexistence of shared concerns. Similarly, we could interpret the coalitional links between Indigenous feminists and Chicanx feminists within Anzaldúa's editorial projects as efforts to form such shared visions for resisting multiple forms of oppression and relational forms of coexistence and affirmations of difference.

To elaborate one such interpretation of Anzaldúa's work, Two Spirit author Deborah A. Miranda (Ohlone–Costanoan Esselen

Nation of California) (Miranda and Keating 2002), discusses some
significant issues that divide Indigenous and Chicanx communities.
In particular, Miranda's articulation of the relationship between
Anzaldúa's work and Indigenous self-determination returns to the
question of whether Anzaldúa's writings on mestizaje or nos/otras
can contribute to critiques of settler colonialism that affirm forms of
Native sovereignty. Miranda writes that there are significant differences in how Indigenous peoples are impacted by the settler state
of the United States and how Chicanx communities are impacted by
the United States. Miranda writes that in the settler United States,
the reservation system, treaties, and paternalism impact Indigenous
communities in ways that are specific to these communities:

> Chicana/os never had a reservation system. While this
> means they have not been legally restrained to certain
> patches of land, it also means Chicana/os do not "own"
> even a portion of their homeland as token recognition of
> indigenous rights. Being Indian means growing up on,
> or with the idea of, "the Rez." Even urban, non- or off-
> reservation Indians, like it or not, have this construction
> of being internally boundaried, or interned within our own
> homeland. The idea of the Rez has both restrained and
> connected U.S. Indians to the idea of homeland. (Miranda
> and Keating 2002, 205)

Such relations of containment and control impact Indigenous communities in ways distinct from mestizxs in the United States. The
forced disavowal of Indigenous ancestry by mestizxs is not equivalent
to the forcing of a reservation system and carceral control of Native
movement and community associations to one another and to the land.

Additionally, Miranda argues that "blood quantum," "ID
cards," and the administrative violence that many Indigenous people
suffer at the hands of the settler state for access to health care and
educational resources do not impact Chicanx communities in the
same manner. Lastly, she writes that there are deep differences in
how Chicanx and Indigenous communities have been impacted by
the anthropological sciences. That is, "Indians are a separate race
to be studied, used, documented, and filed away. I have not seen
many dissertations on the ceremonial uses of Chicana/o artifacts,

or the differences between contemporary and traditional Chicana/os" (206). The result of this, she writes, is that "U.S. Indians learn to essentialize our Indianness because to do otherwise is to vanish completely, legally erased" (206). From this, she proposes that Native communities impacted by a U.S. settler logic fight against any denials of "Indianness" because the United States does not tolerate any " 'official' category for mixedbloods" (206). Such denials within the settler United States would amount to "a heresy that would ensure the futility of any fight for justice or repatriation or reparation; and that, we will not allow" (206). Accordingly, Miranda points here to forms of state intervention that impact Indigenous communities in ways that are distinct from the mestizx populations of the U.S. Southwest, and, as Anzaldúa's other critics note, she highlights that any proposal to embrace mestizaje risks erasing Indigenous solidarity and survival.

Yet it is important to note that Miranda then shifts her analysis to the terms that divide Chicanx and Indigenous communities. Bringing in the question of Chicanx-Indigenous solidarity, she offers a framing of potential coalition building that appears to support the reading offered by Tamez in the previous chapter:

> By using the word Mestiza, I suddenly realize that it is much larger than simply blood or genetics: "Mestiza" is even larger than gender, despite its gendered origins. Mestiza means that which does not obey or even see boundaries; that which blurs sharp distinctions in favor of what is best or most appropriate; that which thrives in ambiguity because ambiguity means survival, creation, movement. Mestiza is all that is transgressive to "the norm," all that breaks the rules of male/female, white/not-white, normal/abnormal. Mestiza is richly fluid, deeply strong. (206)

This passage echoes Anzaldúa's conception of nos/otras, as an analysis that forces us to examine the conditions that divide communities, like those of the settler U.S. and Mexican nation-states and the terms by which communities must identify in their effort to gain recognition and distinction. These include different demands for relations to place, as Saldaña-Portillo and Cotera discuss, including how identification with Indigeneity becomes a means for survival and community stability. Moreover, changing norms that attempt to erase and destabilize community futures, including those of Indigenous peoples, is antithetical to both Miranda's and Anzaldúa's shared projects. Harkening to an account of such multiplicitous agential positionings, Miranda states:

> Thus, all people who engage in breaking boundaries are engaged in what I would call "mestiza acts." Mestiza may have originated as a racial term to indicate mixed-race, but the ways that I am seeing that word and that way of being now are much more about self-directed identities, a personal, historically, psychically informed and aware construction of self that resists static definitions, craves the joy found in constant, organic, positive change. After all this time! I am finally beginning to understand what Gloria meant by the term "mestiza consciousness." We are just beginning to form the Mestiza Nation that she saw twenty years ago. That's got to be the ultimate in heresies. (206–207)

Here, Miranda marks a conception of mestizaje and agency that is neither the harmonized vision of Mexican nationalism nor an erasure of Indigenous subjectivity under a U.S. settler racial logic. Rather, Anzaldúan "mestizaje" becomes more like an attentive, contextual, and historically informed way of transgressing norms, a view much more akin to the account of multiplicitous relational agency that we have explored in this book.

Anzaldúa too appears to share this reading of her own work, and, in fact, concedes the very points that Miranda raises. In a 2003 interview, just a year before her death, she states: "[Chicanxs] don't have tribal affiliations but neither do we have to carry I.D. cards establishing tribal affiliation" (Anzaldúa 2009, 289). She also notes differences in layers of colonial erasure: "Indians suffer from a much more intense colonization, one that is even more insidious because it is covered up, and white and colored Americans remain ignorant of it" (289). She concludes, then, that "Natives are really invisible; they are not even put on the map unless the U.S. government wants to rip them off," which demonstrates the differential legal and historiographical logics that Chicanxs and Indigenous peoples experience (289). Agreeing again with Miranda's reading, she rejects the biologized conception of mestizaje when she states, "Maybe identity depends more on which community you identify with, how you are reared, and less on the drops of blood in your veins. But roots are important; who was here on this continent first does matter" (287). Anzaldúa thus resituates mestizaje as more than a biologized conception of ancestry and indicates something much more politicized and normative regarding inclusion/exclusion within communities resisting structural oppression. This additional "something" is the kind of critically situated ambivalence that we underscored in chapter 3. It is the result of retaining multiplicity within our agential framings of action and identification. Such a reliance on ambivalence and the possibility of continuing to locate further sites of oppression, including, for example, the competing racial logics of settler states, are part of this resistant coalitional work.

Lastly, following from this analysis and returning to our original question of resources within Anzaldúa's work for critical trans politics, if, as Bettcher suggests, one way in which trans and gender variant communities have resisted reality enforcement is to delink genital status from gender presentation, then understanding mestizaje as engaging in a historically, culturally, and personally attentive form of "boundary breaking" may be to consider agential positions as necessarily responsive to multiplicitous oppressive norms, including those of the settler state as we discussed above (Miranda and Keating 2002, 207). Moreover, such a framing of agency and resistance creates interpretive space to underscore the patterned self-definition of Two Spirit and Indigenous communities as distinct from non-Native LGBTQ forms of identification and experience. Accordingly, Anzaldúa writes that "Raza feminism and mainstream feminism [and critical trans politics we could add] must include among their issues the erasure of the cultural practices of Native people, land rights, sovereignty, and self-determination" (Anzaldúa 2009, 290). She appears here to be seeking resources for doing coalitional work, and she describes "needing to dialogue about identity, community, culture, language, activism, representation, and continuance" (290). Finally, she suggests that "we need to do collaborative work that reveals how connected our past histories and present situations are" (290). Through this quote, Anzaldúa calls for a new kind of work, and new framings of resistance and coalitional strategies, perhaps responding to what

Saldaña-Portillo describes above as settler capitalism's "difference(s) [that are necessary] for its own reproduction" (Saldaña-Portillo 2001, 214). Thus, we can consider nos/otras as a critical relational politics that seeks to interrogate the many economic, political, and otherwise normatively laden sites of separation and constructions of difference among Chicanx and Indigenous communities. In this sense, Miranda's interpretation of Anzaldúa returns us to El Mundo Zurdo and the task of building coalitions that thrive on difference and shared visions for ending oppressions, sometimes irrespective of how those oppressions directly coincide with our specific existential selves or identities. In this manner, the shared strategies are based on relational differences and shared concerns that impact distinct yet connected communities in struggle.

Conclusion

From *Nos/otras to Nos/otrxs*

To return to our opening discussion, we can see now how, as Stuart Hall notes, that "identities are a matter of 'becoming' as well as of 'being'" (Hall 1994, 225). Throughout this book, we have sought to interpret actions, dialogues, and embodied movements in a multiplicitous register, and we have done so in an effort to avoid reifying an interiorized, individualized, and imperialist framing of agency. As Anzaldúa writes: "Identity grows out of our interactions, and we strategically reinvent ourselves to accommodate our exchanges. . . . We must push against any boundaries that have outlived their usefulness" (Anzaldúa 2015, 75). Using this approach toward reorienting and restructuring our notions of agency, I offer this reading within Latinx feminist theory and from the critical race, disability, trans, and Indigenous resources engaged in this book, to foreground the multiplicitous, contextual, and relational aspects of negotiating identities and actions.

Such a framing has brought us to tensions and entwinements that cleave open ambiguity and create normative demands for further inquiry and movement. Acting from within such a "pluralistic mode [where] nothing is thrust out, the good, the bad, and the ugly" means that we grapple with the politics of reconfiguration, re-membering, and the reorientation of our words, our bodies, and our histories (Anzaldúa 1999, 101). Accordingly, this means that our academic production, as multidimensional and including many demands for uptake, inevitably leads to ambivalence. However, such ambivalence, as we have seen, can move us to explore and remap the material arrangements in which we find ourselves and the printed words, enfleshed presence, and archival traces of others. To hold Anzaldúa, or any author at all, in a multiplicitous way, we can thereby resist closure, finality, and the elimination of such generative ambivalence.[1]

As I have explored throughout the book, Anzaldúa's conception of mestizaje, unlike simplistic theories of mixture or nationalistic framings of mixed-status identity, becomes, by her later work, transformed into a conception more akin to the notion of nos/otras, an approach to agency that requires us to understand the political, normative, and historical conditions that divide and separate communities in struggle. She remains critical of settling on identity terms that fix or demarcate forms of identification, and notes that linguistic labels will always be insufficient to the task of accounting for embodied relational existence. Yet her work is illustrative of the many ways in which we experiment with identities and with the differing forms of agential relations that we can adopt. She proposed in 2002, in the introduction to *This Bridge We Call Home: Radical Visions for Transformation*, that this edited work was an extension and revision of the ideas and goals of *This Bridge Called My Back* (1981). She invites her readers to "move beyond separate and easy identifications, creating bridges that cross race and other classifications among different groups via intergenerational dialogue" (2). Seeking such pliancy and "impassioned and conflicted engagements in resistance," Anzaldúa's corpus urges readers to resist simply attributing agential bridgework to the categories that we have at the moment (2). She calls instead for "more expansive configurations of identities—some of which will soon become cages and have to be dismantled" (4). In this, Anzaldúa's work always calls beyond itself and beyond her own words, and thus her work seeks continual transformation.

As her terms like nos/otras and nepantleras mark a politicized configuration of a femme or feminine border crosser, I hope to have offered some pathways for extending her work beyond a dualistic gender binary. In the last chapter, we explored solidarity work with Indigenous communities and the coalitional spaces of resistance that work against reality enforcement and settler colonial fantasies of place. In this, I offer the term *nos/otrxs* as a nonbinary and embodied formulation for multiplicitous agential framings. Given that the pronunciation within spoken Spanish and English requires embodied phonemic adjustments,[2] I encourage us to continue to move with

Anzaldúa and to carry her critical insights into forms of political negotiation and contextualizing projects that seek to interpret the multiplicitous ways in which agency, oppression, and resistance take shape.

Nos/otrxs takes its direction and normative force from the many queer, trans, and Two-spirit authors who have found affirmation and resistant coalition with Anzaldúa's body of work. For example, in *Asegi Stories: Cherokee Queer and Two-Spirit Memory* (2016), Qwo-Li Driskill (Cherokee) describes both Anzaldúa and Cherríe Moraga as "queer Indigenous feminist writers" alongside authors such as Paula Gunn Allen (Laguna Pueblo), Beth Brant (Bay of Quinte Mohawk), and Chrystos (Menominee). Driskill turns to Anzaldúa and Moraga's notion of "theory in the flesh" to describe the author's own embodied orientation and response to settler colonial gender histories of the southeastern U.S, including the radical potential of Cherokee basket-weaving traditions. Anzaldúa's work is thus called in as supportive of and aligned with Driskill's project. Likewise, trans Latina feminist theorist and artist micha cárdenas turns in several places to Anzaldúa's work, including a piece on algorithmic poetics (2016a) and an article on trans Latina reproductive futures (2016b). cárdenas plays with the erotic poetry of Anzaldúa, referring to being "an alien in new territory" and when "the heart in [her] cunt starts to beat" as arising from cárdenas's own explorations with "hormonal chemistry" and the process of cryogenic tissue banking (cárdenas 2016b, quoting Anzaldúa 1999, 70 and 73). Noting that "I don't think [Anzaldúa] imagined this particular mystery," cárdenas nevertheless describes affinities with Anzaldúa "as a mixed race mujer/a woman pregnant with life" (cárdenas 2016b, 52). Shifting the terms of pregnancy from a cisheteronormative experiential frame, cárdenas calls upon the erotic queer of color experiences of bodily transformation and pleasure that both she and Anzaldúa share. In this, both cárdenas and Driskill extend the embodied relational insights that we have explored in this book to sites of critique and desire that move us beyond binary framings of nos/otras and in productive tension with nos/otrxs.

Along related lines, T. Jackie Cuevas's book *Post-Borderlandia: Chicana Literature and Gender Variant Critique* (2018) brings Anzaldúa's "tolerance for ambiguity" into engagement with Chicanx genderqueerness and other forms of gender multiplicity. Akin to

our multiplicitous agential framing here, Cuevas cites the work of
Macarena Gómez-Barris and Licia Fiol-Matta, who use the term
"Latinx" to signify a shift away from gender binary framings among
Latin American-descended communities (2018, 20). Cuevas cites
from their work: "From the South and in the borderlands, the 'x'
turns away from the dichotomous, toward a void, an unknown, a
wrestling with plurality, vectors of multi-intentionality, and the transitional meanings of what has yet to be seen" (Gómez-Barris and
Fiol-Matta 2014, 504; quoted in Cuevas 2018, 20). Akin to the
movement of language and mathematics, "x" is a call for multiplicity
and relatedness among variables, among specific contexts of meaning
and norms (Castro 2018). Within such a relational framing, Cuevas
examines Anzaldúa's "Heche" story, an unpublished manuscript in
the LLILAS Benson Latin American Collection at the University of
Texas at Austin. While "Heche" contains problematic accounts of
intersex and gendered existence, such as the title's play on "he/she,"
Cuevas nonetheless finds in this work a "desire to think beyond a
fixed gender dichotomy" (Cuevas 2018, 124–125). Cuevas describes
themes of drug-induced hallucinations, shapeshifting between human
to animal form, and orgiastic scenes that frame a fluid relationship
between gendered embodiment and desire. Elsewhere, in unpublished
poems like "Intersex—Breast with Penis," Cuevas points out, Anzaldúa
also explored embodied gender variance as well. Adding to Cuevas's
reading, I propose that we continue to explore Anzaldúa's work and
its relevance for trans, Two-Spirit, and gender variant readers. One
example is Anzaldúa's description of the figure of Julio Cortázar,
who she described as a presence in her life in Austin, Texas. This
figure, she notes, appeared at times as "a spirit I clothed in male
garb but could have been female," which appeared as a muse and
as a familial presence. In such ways, Anzaldúa's work, including her
explicit mentioning of the importance of trans authors in *This Bridge
We Call Home* and her use of language such as "mitad y mitad,"
which, while derogatory for trans and gender variant communities
today, at the very least speaks to an awareness of and dedication to
multiplicitous gendered experiences (Anzaldúa 2009, 141; Anzaldúa
2002, 3).

From this, I extend nos/otras to nos/otrxs as an approach to
help approximate the range of political and normative movements
that circulate across our communities and bodies. As Dotson's work

on ambivalence and Lugones's writings on liberatory syllogisms proposes, we need new ways to epistemically and affectively hail one another within the complex networks of meaning and material engagement in which we are connected. In this way, nos/otrxs is a call for further investigation, further movement, and new ways of interpreting one another in struggle and in resistance to structural oppressions. As I have attempted to show through Anzaldúa's work and her readership, we can turn to new liberatory accounts that seek to frame our agential connections to one another. As bridging work, or work that requires opacity, separation, or withdrawal, our capacity to reconfigure meaning remains an ambivalent process of becoming. This can be both a terrifying experience and one of vulnerability, as well as a wellspring for transformation and new modes of coalition. Whatever the case, it leaves us perpetually seeking to further situate one another, our seemingly bounded existential selves, within the living ecologies in which we share collective forms of accountability and interdependence.

Lastly, a further reason to consider Anzaldúa's work relevant is that it allows us to reinterpret the material conditions and connections in which she was embedded during her own lifetime. This requires a contextual and historicized account of her work, as well as the readership that she has impacted after her life. For example, we can attempt to move with the words of Lee Maracle (Stó:lō Nation) when she describes "lik[ing] the feel of hearing Gloria listen" and that "Gloria affirms that the place we take is our own" (Maracle 2008, 211). As in El Mundo Zurdo, through affirmation of our own and others' relational differences and agential communities, Anzaldúa's multiplicitous agency requires politicized, but not ontologically stagnant, boundaries among selves. In this, Maracle's commentary on Anzaldúa moves us away from the interiority, the individualism, and the boundary-determinations of identity to create a model for "place, position, and power" among communities who are forging collective struggles together (211). This is not a beatification of Anzaldúa. Rather, we are seeking to understand her work in its complexity and generative ambivalence, the good, the bad, and the ugly. As Driskill notes in an epistolary piece dedicated to Anzaldúa on the topic of disability justice, "As influential as your work is, it is not perfect. Nor should we expect it to be. Taking your work seriously means grappling and arguing with it. I doubt you would disagree" (Driskill, Morales, and Piepzna-Samarasinha 2012, 89). Echoing Driskill's words here, I hope to have grappled with Anzaldúa's body of work and to show how her theoretical contributions affirm that agential framings, including how we interpret, engage, and resist together, do not constitute a perfect process. Nor is any coalitional process guaranteed to succeed, as Harris's insurrectionist ethics reminds us in chapter 3. Rather, multiplicitous agency requires holding one another, at least provisionally, as situated within "a pluralistic mode," which means leaving room for others to interpret and to challenge, yet knowing that they, too, do not fully encompass our relational complexities. While there is much further interpretive work to continue through the notion of multiplicitous agency, and many political and philosophical discourses that can be revisited in light of this approach, I leave it to you now, reader, to continue working through our implications. What I hope to have offered is a way to continue to hold, to complicate, and to create nos/otrxs.

Notes

Introduction

1. See, for example, Immanuel Kant, *Critique of Pure Reason*, ed. Paul Guyer and Allen W. Wood (New York: Cambridge University Press, 1998), A235–236/B294–295; Ilona Katzew, *Casta Painting: Images of Race in Eighteenth-Century Mexico* (New Haven: Yale University Press, 2004).

2. See, for example, Daniel Brewer, "The *Encyclopédie*: Innovation and Legacy," in *New Essays on Diderot*, ed. James Fowler (New York: Cambridge University Press, 2011); Seth Rudy, *Literature and Encyclopedism in Enlightenment Britain: The Pursuit of Complete Knowledge* (New York: Palgrave, 2014).

3. Regarding multiplicitous identities, Edwina Barvosa (2008) has charted a genealogy of pluralistic selfhood within Western philosophy, beginning with David Hume and including theorists such as William James, Max Horkheimer, Theodor Adorno, and Sigmund Freud.

4. See, for example, Charles Darwin, *On the Origin of Species*, ed. Joseph Carroll (New York: Broadview Press, 2003); Earl Lewis and Nancy Cantor, *Our Compelling Interests: The Value of Diversity for Democracy and a Prosperous Society* (Princeton: Princeton University Press, 2016).

5. See, for example, Sara Ahmed, *On Being Included: Racism and Diversity in Institutional Life* (Durham: Duke University Press, 2012); Edward Telles, *Pigmentocracies: Ethnicity, Race, and Color in Latin America* (Chapel Hill: University of North Carolina Press, 2014).

6. The term "diverse practitioners" is drawn from Dotson (2012). As I address in the concluding chapter in further detail, my choice to use the term "Latinx" throughout this chapter reflects a recent linguistic effort that has sought to add a novel gender-neutral term to gender binary terms like "Latina" and "Latino." Namely, the term "Latinx" has been in circulation since roughly the mid-2000s across social media outlets, online

popular press articles, academic journals, and various other venues (Salinas and Lozano 2017; M. de Onís 2017). The term "Latinx" has been used by many people as an inclusive term that reflects transgender, nonbinary, and gender variant people of Latin American descent. As such, the term aims to offer a gender-neutral descriptor that can be used across a variety of gender identities. Within some Spanish-speaking contexts, the -e ending has been used ("Latine" instead of "Latino," or "todes" instead of "todos") to signal a gender neutral or gender inclusive variation within the phonetic conventions of the Spanish language (see, for example, Mantilla 2019; Clarín. com 2020; and López 2019).

7. See North Carolina General Assembly, "HB 2/SL 2016-3: Public Facilities Privacy and Security Act," www.NCLEG.gov. Accessed February 26, 2020. https://www.ncleg.gov/BillLookup/2015E2/h2.

8. Lugones cites Pérez 1999 (79), who draws from the work of Hall and Gilroy regarding the notion of "diaspora" (79).

Chapter 1

1. See, for example, Solomon 2001 and Dreyfus and Wrathall 2009.

2. See, for example, Al-Saji 2009; Fanon 2008; Guenther 2013; Lee 2014; Ortega 2016; Salamon 2010; Weiss 2015; Yancy 2008; Young 2005.

3. Paccacerqua (2016) also offers a rich analysis of the relationship between unification and multiplicity in Anzaldúa's work.

4. Many thanks to Mariana Allesandri for raising this point.

5. For more on this poem in Anzaldúa's work, see Bost 2010 and Lioi 2008.

6. I would also add that her view harkens to the spiritist and theosophy traditions of the late nineteenth and early twentieth century, the latter traditions having an impact on one of the main architects of a philosophical conception of mestizaje, José Vasconcelos, who influences her early writings on mestizaje (see, for example, Novoa 2018).

7. For more on Anzaldúa's conception of spirituality, see Delgadillo 2011.

8. For more on Frances E. W. Harper and nineteenth-century Black women's freedom narratives, see Bowman Lewis 2017.

9. Sandoval's reference to "*amor en Aztlán*" harkens back to Laura Pérez's work in Chicana/o aesthetics (Sandoval 2000, 205n15). Also, for theoretical work on both Anzaldúa and Barthes, see Ortega 2008.

Chapter 2

1. Note also that a number of classical philosophical issues are also implicated through these features. For example, ontological dualism, liberal individualism, the subjective-objective distinction, correspondence versus coherence conceptions of truth, free will and determinism, the a priori and a posteriori distinction, and transcendental versus empirical argumentation are all, in various ways, characterized by features of these facets of agency. As such, multiplicitous agency, as I develop in this book, cuts across a number of philosophical paradigms in the Global North, including areas of classical epistemology and metaphysics, social/political philosophy, ethics, aesthetics, and philosophy of history. Similarly, developing a multiplicitous account of agency thereby allows us to frame anew these classical areas of analysis. However, such tasks will be left to other scholars more versed in these respective areas than myself, but I do hope this book can invite others to undertake such further research.

2. See, for example, Varela, Thompson, and Rosch 2016.

3. See, for example, Lugones 1992.

4. I have more carefully examined the relationship between Anzaldúa and Vasconcelos in Pitts 2014.

5. For a critique of such "bootstrapping," see Bassichis, Lee, and Spade 2011.

6. For contemporary enactivist accounts of cognition, see Gallagher 2017; Hutto and Myin 2013; and Hutto and Myin 2017.

7. From Anzaldúa's unpublished paper "Self-Representation and Identity in Contemporary Ethnic/Other Autobiography," we know that Anzaldúa was familiar with Molloy's writings on Latin American autobiography (Gloria Evangelina Anzaldúa Papers, Benson Latin American Collection, University of Texas at Austin, Box 95, Folder 9, August 22, 1990).

8. The capitalization of "Deaf" as a modifier refers to "people who use sign language and consider themselves members of a cultural community" (Bauman and Murray 2014, xiii) The lowercase term, "deaf," describes a broader category of people who do not primarily use auditory sensory modalities as a perceptual register.

9. It is important to note that Maffie does read some tensions between Anzaldúa's framing of nepantla and Nahua metaphysics, and he describes Anzaldúa as "expand[ing] nepantla to include unresolvable ambiguity; perpetual instability; anomie; psychic restlessness and woundedness; psychic, gender, racial, and cultural disorientation; intellectual crisis; and *tierra desconocida*" (Maffie 2017). However, Maffie also notes that Anzaldúa reclaims a "positive, transformative, and creative component of nepantla"

that was lacking from previous interpreters of the term such as Durán and León-Portilla (1974, 1990).

Chapter 3

1. For more on the term "Latinx," see M. de Onís 2017.
2. We could read her dissertation as an early iteration of care ethics, published before Carol Gilligan's *In a Different Voice* (1982), a text that is often cited as the origin of feminist care ethics in Anglophone philosophy.

Chapter 4

1. See, for examine, Garland-Thomson 2011; Siebers 2008; Tremain 2017.
2. See, for example, Rydström 2020; Frank and Delleria 2020.
3. Such lectures include "Nos/Otras: Making Multi-Cultures and Alliances," in Gloria Evangelina Anzaldúa Papers, Benson Latin American Collection, University of Texas at Austin, Box 156, Folder 36, February 1, 1994; and "Reimagining Identities: The Geography of Our Many Selves," in Gloria Evangelina Anzaldúa Papers, Benson Latin American Collection, University of Texas at Austin, Box 96, Folder 8, May 9, 1996.
4. For more on the organizational complexity of Casa Amiga, see Wright 2002.

Chapter 5

1. See, for example, Anzaldúa 2009, 180, and Anzaldúa 2009, 245.
2. See, for example, Anzaldúa 2009, 83 and 92, and Anzaldúa 1987, 19.
3. For more on the assumed permanence of the settler state in "Truth and Reconciliation" processes and in settler-state language revitalization projects, see Million 2013 and Meissner 2018.
4. Bettcher (2012) and Bettcher's forthcoming book also elaborate framings of the moral order of dichotomously sexed bodies that are regulated through politicized and colonial notions of publicness and privacy.
5. Amy Marvin has recently been developing a historical and cultural account of "chasers" in "The Chaser Continuum" (2018).
6. See, for example, Driskill 2012; Miranda and Keating 2002; and Maracle 2008.

7. This issue of shifting racial and colonial logics of the U.S. Southwest is one that Saldaña-Portillo also addresses in *Indian Given: Racial Geographies across Mexico and the United States* (2016).

8. For a reading critiquing Jodi Byrd's framing of the term "arrivants," and a resituating of the term within Brathwaite's work, see De Line and O'Shaughnessy 2018.

Conclusion

1. Many thanks to Carla O. Alvarez, the archivist of the Gloria Evangelina Anzaldúa Papers at the Benson Latin American Collection at the University of Texas at Austin, for their emphasis of this point regarding Anzaldúa's writings.

2. For pronunciation possibilities of this term, see López 2019.

Bibliography

Adamson, Joni. 2012. "¡Todos somos indios! Revolutionary Imagination, Alternative Modernity, and Transnational Organizing in the Work of Silko, Tamez, and Anzaldúa." *Transnational American Studies* 4, no. 1: 1–26.

Adell, Hilary. 1999. "Endangering Women's Health for Profit: Health and Safety in Mexico's Maquiladoras." *Development in Practice* 9, no. 5: 595–600.

Ahmed, Sara. 2006. *Queer Phenomenology: Orientations, Objects, Others*. Durham: Duke University Press.

Ahmed, Sara. 2012. *On Being Included: Racism and Diversity in Institutional Life*. Durham: Duke University Press.

Alarcón, Norma. 1993–94. "Anzaldúa's Frontera: Inscribing Gynetics." *Anuario de Letras Modernas* 6: 143–159.

Alcoff, Linda Martín. 1991–92. "The Problem of Speaking for Others." *Cultural Critique* 20: 5–32.

Alcoff, Linda Martín. 2000. "Is Latina/o a Racial Identity?" In *Hispanics/ Latinos in the United States: Ethnicity, Race, and Rights*, edited by Jorge J. E. Gracia and Pablo De Greiff. New York: Routledge.

Alcoff, Linda Martín. 2006. *Visible Identities: Race, Gender, and the Self*. New York: Oxford University Press.

Alcoff, Linda Martín. 2019. "Multiplicitous Selves." *Symposium on Gender, Race, and Philosophy* 13, no. 1: 1–5.

Alessandri, Mariana. 2019. "El Mundo Zurdo." Unpublished manuscript.

Al-Saji, Alia. 2009. "A Phenomenology of Critical-Ethical Vision: Merleau-Ponty, Bergson, and the Question of Seeing Differently." *Chiasmi International* 11: 375–398.

Althusser, Louis. 1970. *For Marx*. Translated by Ben Brewster. New York: Random House.

Alvarado, Lisa. 2007. "Conspiring with Margo Tamez." *LaBloga.com*. April 19. Accessed July 22, 2019. https://labloga.blogspot.com/2007/04/conspiring-with-margo-tamez.html.

Anzaldúa, Gloria. 1981. "La Prieta." In *This Bridge Called My Back: Writings by Radical Women of Color*. Watertown, Mass.: Persephone Press.

Anzaldúa, Gloria. 1983. *This Bridge Called My Back: Writings by Radical Women of Color*. New York: Kitchen Table Press.

Anzaldúa, Gloria. 1990a. "*Mujeres que cuentan vidas*: Writing the Personal and Collective Histories of the Subject and Problematizing Assumptions about Autorepresentation in Contemporary Racial Ethnic/Other *Autohistorias-teorías*." Gloria Evangelina Anzaldúa Papers, Benson Latin American Collection, University of Texas at Austin, Box 94, Folders 2–3, 1990.

Anzaldúa, Gloria. 1990b. "Self-Representation and Identity in Contemporary Ethnic/Other Autobiography." Gloria Evangelina Anzaldúa Papers, Benson Latin American Collection, University of Texas at Austin, Box 95, Folder 9, August 22, 1990.

Anzaldúa, Gloria. 1994. "Nos/Otras: Making Multi-cultures and Alliances." Gloria Evangelina Anzaldúa Papers, Benson Latin American Collection, University of Texas at Austin, Box 156, Folder 36, February 1, 1994.

Anzaldúa, Gloria. 1996. "Reimagining Identities: The Geography of Our Many Selves." Gloria Evangelina Anzaldúa Papers, Benson Latin American Collection, University of Texas at Austin, Box 96, Folder 8, May 9, 1996.

Anzaldúa, Gloria. 1999. *Borderlands/La Frontera: The New Mestiza, 2nd edition*. San Francisco: Aunt Lute Books.

Anzaldúa, Gloria. 2000. *Interviews/Entrevistas*. Edited by AnaLouise Keating. New York: Routledge.

Anzaldúa, Gloria. 2009. *The Gloria Anzaldúa Reader*. Edited by AnaLouise Keating. Durham: Duke University Press.

Anzaldúa, Gloria. 2015. *Light in the Dark: Luz en lo Oscuro: Rewriting Identity, Spirituality, Reality*. Edited by AnaLouise Keating. Durham: Duke University Press.

Anzaldúa, Gloria, and AnaLouise Keating. 2002. *This Bridge We Call Home: Radical Visions for Transformation*. New York: Routledge.

Armstrong, Elizabeth A., and Suzanna M. Crage. 2006. "Movement and Memory: The Making of the Stonewall Myth." *American Sociological Review* 71, no. 5: 724–751.

Arrizón, Alicia. 2006. *Queering Mestizaje: Transculturation and Performance*. Ann Arbor: University of Michigan Press.

Barvosa, Edwina. 2008. *Wealth of Selves: Multiple Identities, Mestiza Consciousness, and the Subject of Politics*. College Station: Texas A&M Press.

Bassichis, Morgan, Alexander Lee, and Dean Spade. 2011. "Building an Abolitionist Trans and Queer Movement with Everything We've Got." In *Captive Genders: Trans Embodiment and the Prison Industrial Complex*, edited by Eric A. Stanley and Nat Smith. Edinburgh: AK Press.

Bauman, H-Dirksen L. 2004. "Audism: Exploring the Metaphysics of Oppression." *Journal of Deaf Studies and Deaf Education* 9: 239–246.

Bauman, H-Dirksen, and Joseph J. Murray. 2014. *Deaf Gain: Raising the Stakes for Human Diversity*. Minneapolis: University of Minnesota Press.

Beauvoir, Simone de. 2011. *The Second Sex*. Translated by Constance Borde and Sheila Malovany-Chevallier. New York: Vintage Books.

Bettcher, Talia Mae. 2012. "Full-Frontal Morality: The Naked Truth about Gender." *Hypatia* 27, no. 2: 319–337.

Bettcher, Talia Mae. 2014a. "Feminist Perspectives on Trans Issues." In *The Stanford Encyclopedia of Philosophy*, edited by Edward N. Zalta. Spring. Accessed July 23, 2019. https://plato.stanford.edu/archives/spr2014/entries/feminism-trans.

Bettcher, Talia Mae. 2014b. "Trapped in the Wrong Theory: Rethinking Trans Oppression and Resistance." *Signs: Journal of Women in Culture and Society* 39, no. 2: 383–406.

Bettcher, Talia Mae. 2016. "Intersexuality, Transgender, and Transsexuality." In *The Oxford Handbook of Feminist Theory*, edited by Lisa Disch and Mary Hawkesworth, 413. New York: Oxford University Press.

Bost, Suzanne. 2010. *Encarnación: Illness and Body Politics in Chicana Feminist Literature*. New York: Fordham University Press.

Bowman Lewis, Janaka. 2017. *Freedom Narratives of African American Women: A Study of 19th Century Writings*. Jefferson, N.C.: McFarland & Company.

Brewer, Daniel. 2011. "The *Encyclopédie*: Innovation and Legacy." In *New Essays on Diderot*, edited by James Fowler. New York: Cambridge University Press.

Butler, Judith. 1990. *Gender Trouble: Feminism and the Subversion of Identity*. New York: Routledge.

Byrd, Jodi A. 2011. *Transit of Empire: Indigenous Critiques of Colonialism*. Minneapolis: University of Minnesota Press.

Byrd, Jodi. A. 2017. "Loving Unbecoming: The Queer Politics of the Transitive Native." *Critically Sovereign: Indigenous Gender, Sexuality, and Feminist Studies*. Durham: Duke University Press.

Campbell, R. Joe. 1985. *A Morphological Dictionary of Classical Nahuatl: A Morpheme Index to the* Vocabulario en lengua mexicana y castellana *of Fray Alonso de Molina*. Madison, Wis.: Hispanic Seminary of Medieval Studies.

Caputi, Jane. 2010. "Goddess Murder and Gynocide in Ciudad Juárez." In *Making a Killing: Femicide, Free Trade, and* La Frontera. Edited by Alicia Gaspar de Alba and Georgina Guzmán. Austin: University of Texas Press.

cárdenas, micha. 2016a. "Pregnancy: Reproductive Futures in Trans of Color Feminism." *TSQ: Transgender Studies Quarterly* 3, nos. 1–2: 48–57.

cárdenas, micha. 2016b. "Trans of Color Poetics: Stitching Bodies, Concepts, and Algorithms." *Scholar & Feminist Online* 13, no. 3: n.p. Accessed February 22, 2020. http://sfonline.barnard.edu/traversing-technologies/micha-cardenas-trans-of-color-poetics-stitching-bodies-concepts-and-algorithms/2/.

Carel, Havi. 2008. *Illness: The Cry of the Flesh*. Stocksfield, UK: Acumen.

Carel, Havi. 2011. "Phenomenology and Its Application in Medicine." *Theoretical Medicine and Bioethics* 32, no. 1: 33–46.

Carel, Havi. 2012. "Phenomenology as a Resource for Patients." *Journal of Medicine and Philosophy* 37, no. 2: 96–113.

Carrasco, David. 2012. *The Aztecs: A Very Short Introduction*. New York: Oxford University Press.

Carter, Jacoby Adeshei. 2012. "Alain Leroy Locke." In *The Stanford Encyclopedia of Philosophy*, edited by E. N. Zalta. Summer. http://plato.stanford.edu/archives/sum2012/entries/alain-locke/.

Carter, Jacoby Adeshei, and Leonard Harris. 2010. *Philosophic Values and World Citizenship: Locke to Obama and Beyond*. Lanham, Md.: Lexington Books.

Castro, Julian. 2018. "What It Means to Be 'Latinx,' and What That Means for America." *New York Times*, November 14. Accessed February 22, 2020. https://www.nytimes.com/2018/11/14/books/review/latinx-ed-morales.html.

Clare, Eli. 2009. *Exile and Pride: Disability, Queerness, and Liberation*. Boston: South End Press.

Clare, Eli. 2013. "Body Shame, Body Pride: Lessons from the Disability Rights Movement." In *The Transgender Studies Reader 2*, edited by Susan Stryker and Aren Aizura. New York: Routledge.

Clarín.com. 2020. "Una lucha del feminismo y el colectivo LGBTQI: Qué es el lenguaje inclusivo y cómo utilizarlo." *Clarín.com*, February 22. Accessed March 1, 2020. https://www.clarin.com/sociedad/lenguaje-inclusivo-utilizarlo_0_8ryGzM3v.html.

Code, Lorraine. 1991. *What Can She Know? Feminist Theory and the Construction of Knowledge*. Ithaca: Cornell University Press.

Collins, Patricia Hill. 2000. *Black Feminist Thought: Knowledge, Consciousness, and the Politics of Empowerment*. 2nd ed. New York: Routledge.

Contreras, Sheila Marie. 2008. *Blood Lines: Myth, Indigenism, and Chicana/o Literature*. Austin: University of Texas Press.

Cotera, María Eugenia, and María Josefina Saldaña-Portillo. 2015. "Indigenous but Not Indian? Chicanas/os and the Politics of Indigeneity." In *The World of Indigenous North America*, edited by Robert Warrior. New York: Routledge.

Cuevas, T. Jackie. 2018. *Post-Borderlandia: Chicana Literature and Gender Variant Critique*. New Brunswick: Rutgers University Press.

Darwin, Charles. 2003. *On the Origin of Species*. Edited by Joseph Carroll. New York: Broadview Press.

Delgadillo, Theresa. 2011. *Spiritual Mestizaje: Religion, Gender, Race, and Nation in Contemporary Chicana Narrative*. Durham: Duke University Press.

De Line, Sebastian, and Frances H. O'Shaughnessy. 2018. "Waves of Arrivance." *Junctures* 19: 138–145.

Dotson, Kristie. 2012. "How Is This Paper Philosophy?" *Comparative Philosophy* 3, no. 1: 3–29.

Dotson, Kristie. 2013. "Querying Leonard Harris' Insurrectionist Standards." *Transactions of the Charles S. Peirce Society: A Quarterly Journal in American Philosophy* 49, no. 2: 74–92.

Dreyfus, Hubert L., and Mark A. Wrathall. 2009. *A Companion to Phenomenology and Existentialism*. Malden, Mass.: Blackwell.

Driskill, Qwo-Li. 2016. *Asegi Stories: Cherokee Queer and Two-Spirit Memory*. Tucson: University of Arizona Press.

Driskill, Qwo-Li, Chris Finley, Brian Joseph Gilley, and Scott Lauria Morgensen. 2011. *Queer Indigenous Studies: Critical Interventions in Theory, Politics, and Literature*. Tucson: University of Arizona Press.

Driskill, Qwo-Li, Aurora Levins Morales, and Leah-Lakshmi Piepzna-Samarasinha. 2012. "Sweet Dark Places: Letters to Gloria Anzaldúa on Disability, Creativity, and the Coatlicue State." In *El Mundo Zurdo 2: Selected Works from the 2010 Meeting of the Society for the Study of Gloria Anzaldúa*, edited by Sonia Saldívar-Hull, Norma Alarcón, and Rita E. Urquijo-Ruiz. San Francisco: Aunt Lute Books.

Eng, David L. J. Halberstam, and José Esteban Muñoz. 2005. "Introduction." *Social Text* 23, nos. 3–4/84–85: 1–17.

Fanon, Frantz. 2008. *Black Skin, White Masks*. Translated by Richard Philcox. New York: Grove Press.

Frank, S. E., and Jac Delleria. 2020. "Navigating the Binary: A Visual Narrative of Trans and Genderqueer Menstruation." In *Palgrave Handbook of Critical Menstruation Studies*, edited by Chris Bobel, Inga T. Winkler, Breanne Fahs, Katie Ann Hasson, and Elizabeth Arveda Kissling. Singapore: Palgrave Macmillan.

Gallagher, Shaun. 2017. *Enactivist Interventions: Rethinking the Mind*. New York: Oxford University Press.

Garland-Thomson, Rosemarie. 2009. *Staring: How We Look*. New York: Oxford University Press.

Garland-Thomson, Rosemarie. 2011. "Misfits: A Feminist Materialist Disability Concept." *Hypatia* 26, no. 3: 591–609.

Gaspar de Alba, Alicia. 2010. "*Feminicidio*: The 'Black Legend' of the Border." In *Making a Killing: Femicide, Free Trade, and* La Frontera, edited by Alicia Gaspar de Alba and Georgina Guzmán. Austin: University of Texas Press.

Gómez-Barris, Macarena, and Licia Fiol-Matta. 2014. "Introduction: Las Américas Quarterly." *American Quarterly* 66, no. 3: 493–504.

Guenther, Lisa. 2013. *Solitary Confinement: Social Death and Its Afterlives*. Minneapolis: University of Minnesota Press.

Gunn Allen, Paula. 1992. *The Sacred Hoop: Recovering the Feminine in American Indian Traditions*. Boston: Beacon Press.

Hall, Stuart. 1994. "Culture Identity and Diaspora." In *Colonial Discourse and Post-Colonial Theory*, edited by Patrick Williams and Laura Chrisman. New York: Columbia University Press.

Harris, Leonard. 1989. *The Philosophy of Alain Locke: Harlem Renaissance and Beyond*. Philadelphia: Temple University Press.

Harris, Leonard. 1992–93. "The Horror of Tradition or How to Burn Babylon and Build Benin While Reading a Preface to a Twenty-Volume Suicide Note." *Philosophical Forum* 24 (1–3): 94–118.

Harris, Leonard. 1997. "Alain Locke and Community." *Journal of Ethics* 1, no. 3: 239–247.

Harris, Leonard. 1999. *The Critical Pragmatism of Alain Locke: A Reader on Value Theory, Aesthetics, Community, Culture, Race, and Education*. Lanham, Md.: Rowman and Littlefield.

Harris, Leonard. 2002. "Insurrectionist Ethics: Advocacy, Moral Psychology, and Pragmatism." In *Ethical Issues for a New Millennium*, edited by J. Howie. Carbondale: Southern Illinois University Press.

Harris, Leonard. 2014. "Telos and Tradition: Making the Future—Bridges to Future Traditions." *Philosophia Africana* 16, no. 2: 59–71.

Harris, Leonard, and Charles Molesworth. 2008. *Alain Locke: Biography of a Philosopher*. Chicago: University of Chicago Press.

Henderson-Espinoza, Robyn. 2016. "The Entanglement of Anzaldúan Materiality as Bodily Knowing: Matter, Meaning, and Interrelatedness." *Electronic Theses and Dissertations* 1168. https://digitalcommons.du.edu/etd/1168.

Hutto, Daniel D., and Erik Myin. 2013. *Radicalizing Enactivism: Basic Minds without Content*. Cambridge: MIT Press.

Hutto, Daniel D., and Erik Myin. 2017. *Evolving Enactivism: Basic Minds Meet Content*. Cambridge: MIT Press.

Jameson, Fredric. 1984. "Postmodernism, or the Cultural Logic of Late Capitalism." *New Left Review* 146: 53–92.

Johnson, Harriet McBryde. 2003. "The Disability Gulag: As the Author Fiercely Resists the World of State-Sponsored Institutionalization, She Argues That for Herself and Others with Severe Disabilities, Having Needs Shouldn't Mean Losing All Freedom." *New York Times*, November 23. Accessed March 24, 2021. https://www.nytimes.com/2003/11/23/magazine/the-disability-gulag.html.

Kant, Immanuel. 1998. *Critique of Pure Reason.* Edited by Paul Guyer and Allen W. Wood. New York: Cambridge University Press.

Karttunen, Frances. 1983. *An Analytical Dictionary of Nahuatl.* Norman: University of Oklahoma Press.

Katzew, Ilona. 2004. *Casta Painting: Images of Race in Eighteenth-Century Mexico.* New Haven: Yale University Press.

Keating, AnaLouise. 2008. " 'I'm a Citizen of the Universe': Gloria Anzaldúa's Spiritual Activism as Catalyst for Social Change." *Feminist Studies* 34, nos. 1–2: 53–69.

Keating, AnaLouise. 2009. "Appendix 1: Glossary." In *The Gloria Anzaldúa Reader*, edited by AnaLouise Keating. Durham: Duke University Press.

Keating, AnaLouise. 2015. "Re-envisioning Coyolxauhqui, Decolonizing Reality: Anzaldúa's Twenty-First-Century Imperative." In *Light in the Dark: Luz en lo Oscuro: Rewriting Identity, Spirituality, Reality,* edited by AnaLouise Keating. Durham: Duke University Press.

Keating, AnaLouise, Kelli Zaytoun, and Betsy Dahms. 2016. "Working with Anzaldúa's Writing Notes: An Archival Experiment in Three Parts." In *El Mundo Zurdo 5: Selected Works from the 2015 Meeting for the Society for the Study of Gloria Anzaldúa.* San Francisco: Aunt Lute.

Lapiak, Jolanta. 2007. "Unleashed from Phonocentrism." Paper presented at Interakcje: IX Miedzynarodowy Festiwal Sztuki. Bielsko-Biala, Poland, May 15.

Lapiak, Jolanta. 2010. "Deconstruct W.O.R.D." Edmonton Poetry Festival, Edmonton, Canada, April 23.

Lara, Irene. 2008. "Daughter of Coatlicue: An Interview with Gloria Anzaldúa." In *EntreMundos/AmongWorlds: New Perspectives on Gloria Anzaldúa,* edited by AnaLouise Keating. New York: Palgrave.

Lee, Emily S. 2014. *Living Alterities: Phenomenology, Embodiment, and Race.* Albany: State University of New York Press.

León-Portilla, Miguel. 1974. "Testimonios Nahuas sobre la conquista espiritual." *Estudios de cultura náhuatl* 11: 11–36.

León-Portilla, Miguel. 1990. *Endangered Cultures.* Translated by Julie Goodson-Lawes. Dallas: Southern Methodist University Press.

Levine, Amala. 2008. "Champion of The Spirit: Anzaldúa's Critique of Rationalist Epistemology." In *EntreMundos/AmongWorlds: New Perspectives on Gloria Anzaldúa*, edited by AnaLouise Keating. New York: Palgrave Macmillan.

Levins Morales, Aurora. 2013. *Kindling: Writings on the Body*. Cambridge, Mass.: Palabrera Press.

Lewis, Earl, and Nancy Cantor. 2016. *Our Compelling Interests: The Value of Diversity for Democracy and a Prosperous Society*. Princeton: Princeton University Press.

Lioi, Anthony. 2008. "The Best Loved Bones: Spirit and History in Anzaldúa's 'Entering into the Serpent.'" *Feminist Studies* 34, nos. 1–2: 73–98.

Livingston, Julie. 2006. "Insights from an African History of Disability." *Radical History Review* 94: 111–126.

López, Alma. 2003. *La Llorona Desperately Seeking Coyolxauhqui*. Screen print. University of Texas at San Antonio, Special Collections. https://digital.utsa.edu/digital/collection/p15125coll11/id/140/.

López, Ártemis. 2019. "Tú, yo, elle y el lenguaje no binario." *La Linterna del Traductor: La revista multilingüe de Asetrad* 19.

Lorde, Audre. 1984. "The Uses of the Erotic: The Erotic as Power." In *Sister Outsider: Essays and Speeches*. Berkeley: Crossing Press.

Lorde, Audre. 1996. *Sister Outsider: Essays and Speeches*. Berkeley: Crossing Press.

Lovell, Terry. 2003. "Resisting with Authority: Historical Specificity, Agency, and the Performative Self." *Theory, Culture & Society* 20, no. 1: 1–17.

Lugones, María C. 1978. "Morality and Personal Relations." PhD diss., University of Wisconsin.

Lugones, María C. 1990. "Structure/Antistructure and Agency under Oppression." *Journal of Philosophy* 87, no. 10: 500–507.

Lugones, María C. 1991. "On the Logic of Pluralist Feminism." In *Feminist Ethics*, edited by Claudia Card. Lawrence: University Press of Kansas.

Lugones, María. 1992. "On Borderlands/La Frontera: An Interpretive Essay." *Hypatia* 7, no. 4: 31–37.

Lugones, María. 2003. *Pilgrimages/Peregrinajes: Theorizing Coalition against Multiple Oppressions*. Lanham, Md.: Rowman and Littlefield.

Lugones, María. 2007. "Heterosexualism and the Colonial/Modern Gender System." *Hypatia* 22, no. 1: 186–209.

Lugones, María. 2014. "Reading the Nondiasporic from within Diasporas." *Hypatia* 29, no. 1: 18–22.

Lugones, María C., and Elizabeth V. Spelman. 1983. "Have We Got a Theory for You! Feminist Theory, Cultural Imperialism, and the Demand for the 'Woman's Voice.'" *Women's Studies International Forum* 6, no. 6: 573–581.

Luna, Jennie, and Martha Galeana. 2016. "Remembering Coyolxauhqui as a Birthing Text." *Regeneración Tlacuilolli: UCLA Raza Studies Journal* 2, no. 1: 7–32.

MacIntyre, Alasdair. 1984. *After Virtue*. Notre Dame, Ind.: University of Notre Dame Press.

Maffie, James. 2008. "Consciousness and Reality in Nahua Thought in the Era of Conquest." In *Ontology of Consciousness: Percipient Action*, edited by Helmut Wautischer. Cambridge: MIT Press.

Maffie, James. 2014. *Aztec Philosophy: Understanding a World in Motion*. Boulder: University Press of Colorado.

Maffie, James. 2017. "Nepantla." Unpublished manuscript. June 1.

Maldonado-Torres, Nelson. 2006. "The Time of History, the Times of Gods, and the Damnés de la terre." *Worlds and Knowledges Otherwise* 1, no. 3: 1–12.

Mantilla, Jesús Ruiz. 2019. "El lenguaje inclusivo tensa a 'todes' en Argentina." *El País*, March 30. Accessed March 1, 2020. https://elpais.com/cultura/2019/03/30/actualidad/1553959465_205850.html.

Maracle, Lee. 2008. "This Is Personal: Revisiting Gloria Anzaldúa from within the Borderlands." In *EntreMundos/AmongWorlds: New Perspectives on Gloria Anzaldúa*, edited by AnaLouise Keating. New York: Palgrave.

Martinez, Jacqueline. 2000. *Phenomenology of Chicana Experience and Identity: Communication and Transformation in Praxis*. Lanham, Md.: Rowman and Littlefield.

Marvin, Amy. 2018. "The Chaser Continuum." Paper presented at "Thinking Trans/Trans Thinking" Conference, Washington, D.C.

McBryde Johnson, Harriet. 2003. "Unspeakable Conversations." *New York Times*, February 16.

McRuer, Robert. 2006. *Crip Theory: Cultural Signs of Queerness and Disability*. New York: NYU Press.

M. de Onís, Catalina. 2017. "What's in an 'x'? An Exchange about the Politics of 'Latinx.'" *Chiricú Journal: Latina/o Literatures, Arts, and Cultures* 1, no. 2: 78–91.

Medina, José. 2012. *The Epistemology of Resistance: Gender and Racial Oppression, Epistemic Injustice, and the Social Imagination*. New York: Oxford University Press.

Meissner, Shelbi Nahwilet. 2018. "The Moral Fabric of Linguicide: Unweaving Trauma Narratives and Dependency Relationships in Indigenous Language Reclamation." *Journal of Global Ethics* 14, no. 2: 266–276.

Mignolo, Walter. 2000. "Local Histories and Global Designs: An Interview with Walter Mignolo," by Elena Delgado and Rolando J. Romero. *Discourse* 22, no. 3: 7–33.

Mignolo, Walter. 2012. *Local Histories/Global Designs: Coloniality, Subaltern Knowledges, and Border Thinking (with new preface)*. Princeton: Princeton University Press.

Mignolo, Walter D., and Catherine E. Walsh. 2018. *On Decoloniality: Concepts, Analytics, Praxis*. Durham: Duke University Press.

Million, Dian. 2013. *Therapeutic Nations: Healing in an Age of Indigenous Human Rights*. Tucson: University of Arizona Press.

Minich, Julie Avril. 2014. *Accessible Citizenships: Disability, Nation, and the Cultural Politics of Greater Mexico*. Philadelphia: Temple University Press.

Miranda, Deborah. 2013. "Extermination of the *Joyas*: Gendercide in Spanish California." In *The Transgender Studies Reader 2*, edited by Susan Stryker and Are Z. Aizura. New York: Routledge.

Miranda, Deborah A., and AnaLouise Keating. 2002. "Footnoting Heresy: Email Dialogues." In *This Bridge We Call Home: Radical Visions for Transformation*, edited by Gloria E. Anzaldúa and AnaLouise Keating. New York: Routledge.

Mitchell, David T., and Sharon L. Snyder. 2015. *The Biopolitics of Disability: Neoliberalism, Ablenationalism, and Peripheral Embodiment*. Ann Arbor: University of Michigan Press.

Mock, Janet. 2014. *Redefining Realness: My Path to Womanhood, Identity, Love & So Much More*. New York: Atria Books.

Molloy, Sylvia. 1991. *At Face Value: Autobiographical Writing in Spanish America*. Cambridge: Cambridge University Press.

Moraga, Cherríe. 1993. *The Last Generation*. Boston: South End Press.

Moraga, Cherríe, and Gloria Anzaldúa. 1983. *This Bridge Called My Back: Writings by Radical Women of Color, 2nd edition*. Latham, N.Y.: Kitchen Table Press.

Morgensen, Scott Lauria. 2011. *Spaces between Us: Queer Settler Colonialism and Indigenous Decolonization*. Minneapolis: University of Minnesota Press.

Muñoz, José Esteban. 1999. *Disidentifications: Queers of Color and the Performance of Politics*. Minneapolis: University of Minnesota Press.

Namaste, Viviane. 2005. *Sex Change, Social Change: Reflections on Identity, Institutions, and Imperialism*. Toronto: Women's Press.

North Carolina General Assembly. 2016. "HB 2/SL 2016-3: Public Facilities Privacy and Security Act." www.NCLEG.gov. Accessed February 26, 2020. https://www.ncleg.gov/BillLookup/2015E2/h2.

Novoa, Adriana. 2009. "José Martí and Evolution: An Analysis on Nation and Race." In *Interdisciplinary Essays on Darwinism in Hispanic Literature and Film: The Intersection of Science and the Humanities*, edited by Jerry Hoeg and Kevin S. Larsen. Lewiston, N.Y.: Edwin Mellon Press.

Novoa, Adriana. 2018. "The Indian Veil: The Metaphysics of Racial Origins in the Americas." In *Comparative Studies in Asian and Latin American Philosophies: Cross-cultural Theories and Methodologies*, edited by Stephanie Rivera Berruz and Leah Kalmanson. New York: Bloomsbury.

Ortega, Mariana. 2008. "Wounds of Self: Experience, Word, Image, and Identity." *Journal of Speculative Philosophy* 22, no. 4: 235–247.

Ortega, Mariana. 2016. *In-Between: Latina Feminist Phenomenology, Multiplicity, and the Self*. Albany: State University of New York Press.

Ortega, Mariana. 2017. "Decolonial Woes and Practices of Un-knowing." *Journal of Speculative Philosophy* 31, no. 3: 504–516.

Ortega y Gasset, José. 1961. *Meditations on Quixote* (*Meditaciones del Quijote*). Translated by Evelyn Rugg and Diego Marin. New York: W.W. Norton.

Oyěwùmí, Oyéronké. 1997. *The Invention of Women: Making an African Sense of Western Gender Discourses*. Minneapolis: University of Minnesota Press.

Paccacerqua, Cynthia M. 2016. "Gloria Anzaldúa's Affective Logic of Volverse Una." *Hypatia: A Journal of Feminist Philosophy* 31, no. 2: 334–351.

Pérez, Domino Renee. 2018. "New Tribalism and Chicana/o Indigeneity in the Work of Gloria Anzaldúa." In *Routledge Handbook of Chicana/o Studies*, edited by Francisco A. Lomelí, Denise A. Segura, and Elyette Benjamin-Labarthe. New York: Routledge.

Pérez, Emma. 1999. *The Decolonial Imaginary: Writing Chicanas into History*. Bloomington: Indiana University Press.

Pérez, Laura E. 2019. *Eros Ideologies: Writings on Art, Spirituality, and the Decolonial*. Durham: Duke University Press.

Piepzna-Samarasinha, Leah Lakshmi. 2018. *Care Work: Dreaming Disability Justice*. Vancouver: Arsenal Pulp Press.

Pitts, Andrea. 2014. "Toward an Aesthetics of Race: Bridging the Writings of Gloria Anzaldúa and José Vasconcelos." *Inter-American Journal of Philosophy* 5, no. 1: 80–100.

Pitts-Taylor, Victoria. 2016. *The Brain's Body: Neuroscience and Corporeal Politics*. Durham: Duke University Press.

Pohlhaus, Gaile, Jr. 2012. "Relational Knowing and Epistemic Injustice: Toward a Theory of Willful Hermeneutical Ignorance." *Hypatia* 27, no. 4: 715–735.

Prosser, Jay. 1998. *Second Skins: The Body Narratives of Transsexuality*. New York: Columbia University Press.

Puar, Jasbir. 2007. *Terrorist Assemblages: Homonationalism in Queer Times*. Durham: Duke University Press.

Puar, Jasbir. 2017. *The Right to Maim: Debility, Capacity, Disability*. Durham: Duke University Press.

Quijano, Aníbal. 2000. "Coloniality of Power, Eurocentrism, and Latin America." *Nepantla: View from the South* 1, no. 3: 533–580.

Rieff, David. 1991. "Professional Aztecs and Popular Culture. *New Perspectives Quarterly* 8, no. 1: 42–46.

Rivera Berruz, Stephanie. 2014. "Extending into Space: The Materiality of Language and the Arrival of Latina/o Bodies." *Inter-American Journal of Philosophy* 5, no. 1: 24–43.

Roelofs, Monique. 2014. *The Cultural Promise of the Aesthetic*. New York: Bloomsbury.

Roelofs, Monique. 2016. "Navigating Frames of Address: María Lugones on Language, Bodies, Things, and Places." *Hypatia* 31, no. 2: 370–387.

Román-Odio, Clara. 2013. *Sacred Iconographies in Chicana Cultural Productions*. New York: Palgrave Macmillan.

Ross, Loretta J. 2006. "The Color of Choice: White Supremacy and Reproductive Justice." In *Color of Violence: The INCITE! Anthology*, edited by INCITE! Women of Color Against Violence. Durham: Duke University Press.

Rudy, Seth. 2014. *Literature and Encyclopedism in Enlightenment Britain: The Pursuit of Complete Knowledge*. New York: Palgrave.

Ruíz, Elena. 2011. "Feminist Border Thought." In *Routledge International Handbook of Contemporary Social and Political Theory*, edited by Gerard Delanty and Stephen P. Turner. New York: Routledge.

Ruíz, Elena Flores. 2016. "Linguistic Alterity and the Multiplicitous Self: Critical Phenomenologies in Latin Feminist Thought." *Hypatia: A Journal of Feminist Philosophy* 31, no. 2: 421–436.

Rydström Klara. 2020. "Degendering Menstruation: Making Trans Menstruators Matter." In *Palgrave Handbook of Critical Menstruation Studies*, edited by Chris Bobel, Inga T. Winkler, Breanne Fahs, Katie Ann Hasson, and Elizabeth Arveda Kissling. Singapore: Palgrave Macmillan.

Salamon, Gayle. 2010. *Assuming a Body: Transgender and Rhetorics of Materiality*. New York: Columbia University Press.

Salamon, Gayle. 2012. "The Phenomenology of Rheumatology: Disability, Merleau-Ponty, and the Fallacy of Maximal Grip." *Hypatia* 27, no. 2: 243–260.

Saldaña-Portillo, María Josefina. 2001. "Who Is the Indian in Aztlán? Re-Writing Mestizaje, Indianism, and Chicanismo from Lacandón." In *The Latin American Subaltern Studies Reader*, edited by Ileana Rodríguez. Durham: Duke University Press.

Saldaña-Portillo, María Josefina. 2016. *Indian Given: Racial Geographies across Mexico and the United States*. Durham: Duke University Press.

Salinas, Cristobal, Jr., and Adele Lozano. 2017. "Mapping and Recontextualizing the Evolution of the Term Latinx: An Environmental Scanning in Higher Education." *Journal of Latinos and Education* 18, no. 4: 1–14.

Sandoval, Chela. 2000. *Methodology of the Oppressed*. Minneapolis: University of Minnesota Press.

Scolieri, Paul. 2004. "Coyolxauhqui's Impact: Aztec Historiography and the Falling Body." *Women and Performance: A Journal of Feminist Theory* 14, no. 1: 91–106.

Scott, David. 1999. *Refashioning Futures: Criticism after Postcoloniality*. Princeton: Princeton University Press.

Scully, Jackie Leach. 2012. "Disability and the Thinking Body." In *Embodied Selves*, edited by Stelle Gonzalez-Arnal, Gill Jagger, and Kathleen Lennon. New York: Palgrave Macmillan.

Siebers, Tobin. 2006. "Disability Studies and the Future of Identity Politics." In *Identity Politics Reconsidered*, edited by Linda Martín Alcoff, Michael Hames-Garcia, Satya Mohanty, and Paula M. L. Moya. New York: Palgrave.

Siebers, Tobin. 2008. *Disability Theory*. Ann Arbor: University of Michigan Press.

Simpson, Leanne Betasamosake. 2017. *As We Have Always Done: Indigenous Freedom through Radical Resistance*. Minneapolis: University of Minnesota Press.

SisterSong. 2019. "Reproductive Justice." SisterSong.net. Accessed June 29, 2019. https://www.sistersong.net/reproductive-justice.

Smith, Andrea. 2010. "Queer Theory and Native Studies: The Heteronormativity of Settler Colonialism." *GLQ* 16, nos. 1–2: 41–68.

Smith, Andrea. 2011. "Against the Law: Indigenous Feminism and the Nation-State." *Affinities: A Journal of Radical Theory, Culture, and Action* 5, no. 1: n.p.

Solomon, Robert C. 2001. *Phenomenology and Existentialism*. Lanham, Md.: Rowman and Littlefield.

Sommer, Doris. 1999. *Proceed with Caution, When Engaged by Minority Writing in the Americas*. Cambridge: Harvard University Press.

Spade, Dean. 2012. "Toward a Critical Trans Politics," interview by Rob Nichols. *Upping the Anti: A Journal of Theory and Action* 14: 37–51.

Stewart, Jeffrey C. 1992. "Introduction." In *Race Contacts and Interracial Relations: Lectures on the Theory and Practice of Race*, by Alain LeRoy Locke. Washington, D.C.: Howard University Press.

Stone, Sandy. 1987. "The Empire Strikes Back: A Posttransexual Manifesto." SandyStone.com. http://sandystone.com/empire-strikes-back.pdf.

Strassfeld, Max, and Robyn Henderson-Espinoza. 2019. "Mapping Trans Studies in Religion." *TSQ: Transgender Studies Quarterly* 6 (3): 283–296.

Stryker, Susan. 2006. "(De)Subjugated Knowledges: An Introduction to Transgender Studies." In *The Transgender Studies Reader*, edited by Susan Stryker and Stephen Whittle. New York: Routledge.

Sullivan, Nikki. 2014. "'BIID'? Queer (Dis)Orientations and the Phenomenology of 'Home.'" In *Feminist Phenomenology and Medicine*, edited by Kristin Zeiler and Lisa Folkmarson Käll, 119–40. Albany: State University of New York Press.

Svenaeus, Fredrik. 2000a. "Das Unheimliche—Towards a Phenomenology of Illness." *Medicine, Health Care, and Philosophy* 3, no. 1: 3–16.

Svenaeus, Fredrik. 2000b. *The Hermeneutics of Medicine and the Phenomenology of Health: Steps toward a Philosophy of Medical Practice*. Dordrecht: Kluwer Academic.

Tamez, Margo. 2012. "The Texas-Mexico Border Wall and Ndé Memory: Confronting Genocide and State Criminality, beyond the Guise of 'Impunity.'" In *Beyond Walls and Cages: Prisons, Borders, and Global Crisis*, edited by Jenna M. Loyd, Matt Mitchelson, and Andrew Burridge. Athens: University of Georgia Press.

Tatonetti, Lisa. 2014. *The Queerness of Native American Literature*. Minneapolis: University of Minnesota Press.

Taylor, Charles. 1989. *Sources of the Self: The Making of Modern Identity*. Cambridge: Harvard University Press.

Telles, Edward. 2014. *Pigmentocracies: Ethnicity, Race, and Color in Latin America*. Chapel Hill: University of North Carolina Press.

Toombs, S. Kay. 1987. "The Meaning of Illness: A Phenomenological Approach to the Patient-Physician Relationship." *Journal of Medicine and Philosophy* 12, no. 3: 219–40.

Toombs, S. Kay. 1988. "Illness and the Paradigm of Lived Body." *Theoretical Medicine* 9, no. 2: 201–226.

Toombs, S. Kay. 1995. "The Lived Experience of Disability." *Human Studies* 18, no. 1: 9–23.

Tremain, Shelley L. 2001. "On the Government of Disability." *Social Theory and Practice* 27, no. 4: 617–636.

Tremain, Shelley L. 2005. *Foucault and the Government of Disability*. Ann Arbor: University of Michigan Press.

Tremain, Shelley L. 2017. *Foucault and Feminist Philosophy of Disability*. Ann Arbor: University of Michigan Press.

Tuck, Eve, and K. Wayne Yang. 2012. "Decolonization Is Not a Metaphor." *Decolonization: Indigeneity, Education & Society* 1, no. 1: 1–40.

Varela, Francisco, Evan Thompson, and Eleanor Rosch. 2016. *The Embodied Mind: Cognitive Science and Human Experience, Revised Edition*. Cambridge: MIT Press.

Vasconcelos, José. 1979. *The Cosmic Race/La raza cósmica*. Baltimore: Johns Hopkins University Press.

Vizenor, Gerald. 1999. *Manifest Manners: Narratives of Postindian Survivance*. Lincoln: University of Nebraska Press.

Weiss, Gail. 2015. "The Normal, the Natural, and the Normative: A Merleau-Pontian Legacy to Feminist Theory, Critical Race Theory, and Disability Studies." *Continental Philosophy Review* 48, no. 1: 77–93.

Wendell, Susan. 2013. *The Rejected Body: Feminist Philosophical Reflection on Disability.* New York: Routledge.

Whitehead, Joshua. 2018. *Jonny Appleseed.* Vancouver: Arsenal Pulp Press.

Wieseler, Christine. 2018. "Missing Phenomenological Accounts: Disability Theory, Body Integrity Identity Disorder, and Being an Amputee." *IJFAB: International Journal of Feminist Approaches to Bioethics* 11, no. 2: 83–111.

Wilson, Alex. 2015. "Our Coming In Stories, Cree Identity, Body Sovereignty and Gender Self-Determination." *Journal of Global Indigeneity* 1, no. 1: 1–5.

Wright, Melissa W. 1998. "Maquiladora Mestizos and a Feminist Border Politics: Revisiting Anzaldúa." *Hypatia* 13, no. 3: 114–131.

Wright, Melissa W. 2002. "A Manifesto against Femicide." *Antipode* 33, no. 3: 550–566.

Yancy, George. 2008. *Black Bodies, White Gazes: The Continuing Significance of Race.* Lanham, Md.: Rowman and Littlefield.

Ybarra, Priscilla Solis. 2009. "Borderlands as Bioregion: Jovita González, Gloria Anzaldúa, and the Twentieth-Century Ecological Revolution in the Rio Grande Valley." *MELUS: Multi-Ethnic Literature of the United States* 34, no. 2: 175–189.

Young, Iris Marion. 2005. *On Female Body Experience: "Throwing Like a Girl" and Other Essays.* Oxford: Oxford University Press.

Young, Iris Marion. 2006. "Responsibility and Global Justice: A Social Connection Model." *Social Philosophy and Policy* 23, no. 1: 102–130.

Young, Iris Marion. 2011. *Responsibility for Justice.* Oxford: Oxford University Press.

Young, Stella. 2015. "I'm Not Your Inspiration, Thank You Very Much." *TED.* Accessed February 10, 2015, http://www.ted.com/talks/stella_young_i_m_not_your_inspiration_thank_you_very_much?

Zaytoun, Kelli D. 2015. " 'Now Let Us Shift' the Subject: Tracing the Path and Posthumanist Implications of La Naguala/The Shapeshifter in the Works of Gloria Anzaldúa." *MELUS: Multi-Ethnic Literature of the United States* 40, no. 4: 1–20.

Index

ableism, 10, 96–97, 105
ablenationalism, 91, 109
academia, radical resistance in, 112–13
action: chained actions, 79; individuated forms of, 84; top-down and street-level views of, 78. *See also* agency; liberatory syllogisms
Adamson, Joni, 110–11
agency: erasure of disabled people's agency, 90; and Latinx feminist theory, 10; locus of, 33–34; positionality and meaning in, 16; relational agency, 57, 149, 165; retaining multiplicity in, 159; unification *versus* multiplicity in, 9–10. *See also* multiplicitous agency
agential ambivalence, 25–26, 26–27, 82–86
Ahmed, Sara, 58
Alarcón, Norma, 39
Alcoff, Linda Martín, 6, 10, 17, 46; "The Problem of Speaking for Others," 45; *Visible Identities*, 14
Alessandri, Mariana, 155
Allen, Paula Gunn, 79, 163
Althusser, Louis, 39

ambiguity: in concept of nepantla, 169n9; instability as, 81; and mestizaje, 157; in our actions, 24; tolerance for, 59, 141, 163; vulnerability to, 3
ambivalence: externally and internally generated, 69–72, 75; and resistance to generalizing, 75; resolution of inversion of, 59; scholarship on multidimensionality and, 161–62; in understanding of mestizaje, 159; uneasiness with the world, 81. *See also* agential ambivalence; insurrectionist ethics; maquiladoras; nepantla
American Indian and First Nations Gays and Lesbians, 148
amputees, experiences of, 105–6
animism and new animism, 17
anthropological fascination with Indigenous practices, 147–48, 156–57
Anzaldúa, Gloria E.: books and, 49–50; as a Chicana or lesbian writer, 54–55; coalitional politics of, 20–24; on cognition and the brain, 31–32; as crip theorist, 88, 92–95, 114; epistemic resistance in writing practices of,

coalition building *(continued)*
and, 9; multiplicitous agency
and, 3; nos/otras in, 26;
permeable boundaries in, 165;
process of, 166; and reality
enforcement, 143–44; between
resistant communities, 149;
through authohistoria-teoría,
44; ways of interacting in,
82–83. *See also* Coyolxauhqui;
disability justice; Indigenous
sovereignty; liberatory syllogisms;
maquiladoras
Coatlicue state, 55
Code, Lorraine, 57, 58
cognition and cognition studies,
31–32, 43, 77. *See also* epistemic
resistance
Collins, Patricia Hill, 54
Colvin, Claudette, 84
Combahee River Collective, 20–21
conocimiento, 36, 52, 55, 81. *See
also* Coyolxauhqui imperative
consciousness of kind, 64
Contreras, Sheila Marie, 137–38,
149
Cortázar, Julio, 164
Cotera, María Eugenia, 151–52,
153–54, 157
Coyolxauhqui: Anzaldúa's retelling
of story of, 26, 88, 97, 105,
110; dismemberment and
re-membering of, 100–101;
and gendered violence, 119;
monolith depicting, 99, 107;
queer Latinx reading of, 103,
104; relationship to wholeness,
109; story of, 98; as symbolic
of birth and menstruation, 99,
100, 102; as symbol of genocidal
violence, 116–17; women's
uteruses as, 104

Coyolxauhqui imperative, 52–53,
56, 57, 101, 102, 105–10
creativity and creative practices, 36,
50, 51
crip theory, 88, 92–95, 114
critical trans politics: affirmation of
Indigenous sovereignty within,
149; aims of, 126; Anzaldúa's
relevance to, 123, 127;
Bettcher's bridging of Anzaldúa's
work with, 140–41; boundary
breaking in, 159; and coalitional
politics, 124; critique of settler
colonialism in, 26, 138–39;
solidarity with Latinx feminisms,
87; use of term, 124, 125–26
Crummell, Alexander, 61
Cuevas, T. Jackie, 164; *Post-
Borderlandia*, 163
Cynthia (maquiladora mestiza),
119–20, 121

deafness and audism, 48–49, 169n8
debility, 117–18, 119
deceiver/pretender double bind,
142, 143, 144–46, 148
decolonial love, 23
diaspora as identity through
difference, 7
differential consciousness, 22–23
disability: Anzaldúa's identity with,
97; author's relationship to,
88–90; embodied affirmation
within, 114–15; exceptionalism
in, 91, 121; experience of living
with, 105–6; methodological
approaches to, 90–91; as
set of relations, 93. *See also*
environmental racism; identarian
politics
disability justice: Anzaldúa on,
165; Anzaldúa's relevance to,

26, 88, 121–22; movement for, 95–96, 97; solidarity with Latinx feminisms, 87
Disability Justice Collective, 95
disability studies and theorists, 48, 92
disabled populations: queer people of color and, 96–97; re-membering for meaning and affirmation, 106–7; tropes of tragedy and heroism and, 105, 106; uneven distribution of resources to, 117
Dotson, Kristie: on ambivalence, 69–70, 73, 75, 164–65; analysis of Garner murder case, 70–72; and bases for action, 60; connection of work to Anzaldúa, 73; criteria for an insurrectionist ethics, 25, 65–67, 72, 80; on transvaluation of social identities, 68
drawbridges, agential position of, 82, 83, 86, 120–21, 134
Driskill, Qwo-Li, 147, 165; *Asegi Stories,* 163
dualisms, 25, 29, 30, 142, 162. *See also* Latinx
Durán, Diego, *Historia de las Indias de Nueva España y Islas de Tierra Firme,* 41–42

Earth, Michael Red, 148
embodiment: Anzaldúa's approach to, 18; disability as framework for, 88, 90; as orientation to building multiplicitous relationships, 110; phenomenological concept of, 91; theory in the flesh, 163; trans framings of, 125, 127. *See also* identity; Indigenous peoples; transgender studies

environmental racism, 88, 110, 111, 115–16, 118, 119
epistemic resistance, 53–55
epistemic responsibility, 55–57, 58
exceptionalism, 91
existential phenomenology, 13–17, 23, 91

la facultad, concept of, 94
feminism and feminist theory: Anzaldúa and, 24; critiques of male-to-female transsexuals, 148; and Indigenous culture and sovereignty, 159; new materialism in, 19–20; nonethnocentric forms of, 76; trans feminism, 128, 140; women's solidarity in, 74–75, 78, 83, 87. *See also* Chicanxs; Latina and Latinx feminist philosophers; Latinx feminisms and solidarity
Finley, Chris, 147
Fiol-Matta, Licia, 164
Florentine Codex, 98, 99, 107
Foucault, Michel, Sandoval on, 38–39
friendship, 73–74

Gadamer, Hans-Georg, 14
Galeana, Martha, 98, 99–100, 101, 102, 104
Garner, Margaret, murder case, 70–72, 83
Gaspar de Alba, Alicia, 118
gay populations. *See* LGBTQ communities and spaces
gender binaries: constraints of, 123; and deceiver/pretender double bind, 146, 148; interpretations beyond, 79, 141; and Latinx terminology, 167n6; rejection of, 69, 142
gendercide, 144

29; and classic philosophical
issues, 169n1; and constraints of
gender binaries, 79; definition
of, 29, 30; Dotson's work
and, 73; identarian politics to
combat, 112; internalization of
neocolonial attitudes, 35; Latinx
resistance to, 85–86. *See also*
disability justice
in-betweenness, 9. *See also*
nepantla; nepantleras; Ortega,
Mariana
Indigenous art, 98, 101
Indigenous peoples: and
agricultural labor movements,
110–11; erasure of, 114, 132,
136, 140, 157; and framings
of gender, 129; harms to, 20;
interconnectedness for, 18;
mixture and purity in, 83, 119;
primitivization of, 130–32,
137–38, 141, 149; resistance
to reality enforcement, 162;
romanticized appropriation of
culture, 101, 130, 131–32, 134,
137, 138, 146; self-definitions
among, 159; subjectlessness of,
130, 135–37, 138, 139; U.S.
controls on, 156, 157; women as
statically non-whole, 141. *See also*
Chicanxs; Mexica/Aztec history
and worldview; Two Spirit
communities
Indigenous sovereignty: importance
of affirmations of, 139; mestizaje
and, 123–24, 140, 155;
remaking of identity as risk to,
131, 134, 135, 137; settler
states' rejection of land claims,
145; and shifts in Anzaldúa's
work, 150; solidarity with Latinx
feminisms, 87

Indigenous studies' critiques of
Anzaldúa. *See* Contreras, Sheila
Marie; Pérez, Domino Renee;
Saldaña-Portillo, María Josefina;
Simpson, Leanne Betasamosake;
Smith, Andrea; Wilson, Alex
individualism: in the academy, 114;
agency in, 37–38; and classic
philosophical issues, 169n1; in
conceptions of selfhood, 10;
definition of, 29, 30; Dotson's
work and, 73; and Indigenous
displacement, 137; in the new
tribalism, 134–35; and queer
theory, 136; representative
heuristics and, 66. *See also*
disability justice; nepantla;
subjectivity
instrumental reasoning, 66–67
insularity: and classic philosophical
issues, 169n1; definition of,
29–31; Dotson's work and, 73;
in framing decision making, 31;
and Indigenous displacement,
137; and queer theory, 136;
representative heuristics and,
66; and Sandoval's thought
on subjectivity, 38–39. *See also*
disability justice
insurrectionist ethics and acts: and
ambivalence, 25, 67–68, 69–72,
75; criteria for, 65–66, 71, 72;
instrumental reasoning in, 66–67;
as morally meritorious, 65, 66;
normative framings of, 60; and
representative heuristics, 63;
utilization of identity categories
in, 61
intention and intentionality: in
Anzaldúa's new tribalism, 132; in
individualized models of agency,
16; intersubjectivity and, 78,

metaphysics, relational approaches
to, 18–19
Mexica/Aztec history and
worldview, 107, 118–19,
130, 132, 137–38. *See also*
Coyolxauhqui
Mexico, Indigenous dispossession
in, 132, 145
Mignolo, Walter, 41, 43
Mingus, Mia, 95
Minich, Julie Avril, 91
Miranda, Deborah, 83, 144,
155–57, 160
Mitchell, David T., 91, 109, 121
Molesworth, Charles, 61–62
Molloy, Sylvia, 48
Moore, Leroy, Jr., 95
Moraga, Cherríe, 20, 92–93,
99–100, 129, 163
moral agency, 73, 74–75, 79
moral philosophy, 73–74
Morgensen, Scott Lauria, 101,
138, 146, 147, 148, 150; *Spaces
between Us,* 136
Mudimbe, V. Y., 62
multiplicitous agency: Anzaldúa's
framing of, 155; and criteria
for insurrectionist ethics,
66; and dependence on
interconnectedness, 37;
dimensions of, 23–24;
interpretation of meaning and
self-understanding through,
16, 26; mestizaje as, 158; as
model for understanding human
action, 2–3, 166; and modes of
address, 49; ontological framing
of, 19; and reframing of classical
philosophical paradigms, 169n1;
in support of political projects,
10; and women in border
areas, 120. *See also* agency;

ambivalence; coalitional politics;
environmental racism; existential
phenomenology; identity;
insurrectionist ethics and acts;
liberatory syllogisms; relational
ontology; resistance
multiplicity: challenge and
experience of, 1–4, 10; resistance
while maintaining, 9; sense-
making within, 2; in trans
understanding of the self, 129;
vulnerability in, 3
el mundo zurdo, 155, 160, 165
Muñoz, José Esteban, 131, 136
mysticism, 18
myth-making, 45, 52. *See also*
Coyolxauhqui

nagual/nahual (shapeshifter),
50–51, 69
Namaste, Viviane, 141
National Women's Studies
Association, 82
Native-Chicanx relations, 150–52,
154, 156
Native sexuality and gender
diversity, 144, 147, 148. *See also*
Two Spirit communities
Ndé Lipan Apaches, 110, 116, 119
nepantla: Anzaldúa's framing of,
43–44, 169n9; emergence and
use of term, 40–42; epistemic
friction and, 55; as existential
ambiguity, 81–82; as form of
transvaluation, 68; and Nahua
metaphysics, 169n9
nepantla brain, 31, 43
nepantleras: as agential
communities, 42; concept of,
41, 162; description of, 25; and
external forms of identity, 111;
interpretation of meaning and

www.ingramcontent.com/pod-product-compliance
Lightning Source LLC
Chambersburg PA
CBHW030330270326
41926CB00010B/1570